Please return/renew this item by the last date shown on this label, or on your self-service receipt.

To renew this item, visit **www.librarieswest.org.uk** or contact your library

Your borrower number and PIN are required.

LibrariesWest

Ellen Teresa Doherty
(16 April 1942–20 August 2014)

Patsy 'The Skelper' Doherty
(21 September 1939–30 January 1972)

The Skelper And Me

A MEMOIR OF MAKING HISTORY IN DERRY

TONY DOHERTY

MERCIER PRESS

For Paddy and Anna Walsh

MERCIER PRESS

Cork

www.mercierpress.ie

© Tony Doherty, 2019

ISBN: 978 1 78117 673 3

Printed and bound in the EU.

CONTENTS

ACKNOWLEDGEMENTS

People look at me strangely when I mention that Christmas 1982 in H2 ranks high as one of the best Christmases in my lifetime. But it was. In much the same way that the younger generation of the Doherty and Quigley family describe my mother's wake in August 2014 as the best wake ever. Had they been around for our Patrick's wake in November 1990, their opinion would be keenly tested. For me, it's the unplanned blend of people, place and circumstances that make such occasions memorable, whether about imprisonment or death.

My acknowledgements span two eras within the book; being inside and being outside. From the inside, my conversation with Figs in February 2018 proved both remarkable and invaluable. Figs is a shy and reserved man who won't take kindly to public praise, so I'll just say that this book would have been impossible for me to start if it wasn't for him. Others from Crumlin Road include the two knaves from the Short Strand, Glit Carlisle and Smurf Smyth, and Mickey and Jap, who provided the goods on the Sinn Féin doctor and Wee Hessie Phelan's 'escape'.

Conor and Declan Murphy and Peter Lynch from Camloch filled in many of the blanks relating to Christmas 1982, as did chance encounters with Kevin 'Two-stroke' Lynch from Donagh and Dermot Finucane from Belfast. Also Jacqui Maxwell, the Belfast punk.

On the outside, I am very lucky that both our Paul and Benny McLaughlin have the collective memory of a supergrass, as they were able to pick things out from the days after my release and help me join the dots. I couldn't have written about our Patrick at all had it not been for our Karen's painful recollections, backed up by those of Glenn, Colleen and my young aunt Lorraine.

My wife, Stephanie, deserves more than a mention, as the idea of someone, anyone, writing anything about her would otherwise be regarded as anathema. She too gave me great memories of our Patrick, the death of her brother Charles, and our life and times in Lower Nassau Street. On the campaign trail, I am deeply indebted to Robin Percival, Martin Finucane, Paul O'Connor, John Kelly, Gerry Duddy and John 'Baldy' McKinney for helping me piece together the chronology of events from the late 1980s to 2010.

In terms of the conceptual process, I would like to thank Freya McClements for her usual insightful critique of several early chapters; Dave Duggan, a good friend and the true architect of this trilogy of books; and Amanda Doherty and Mickey Dobbins for providing their periodic critiques and, more importantly, their unstinting encouragement.

Finally, I wish to acknowledge Paddy and Anna Walsh. Paddy was an immensely brave, kind and generous man, who provided solace to my father as he lay shot in the shadow of the Rossville Flats. Anna now rests in peace with Paddy. I am glad I knew them both.

Tony Doherty
September 2019

PART ONE

1

THRESHOLD

My story doesn't begin here. But here is where history put me. When I was a young boy I believed I was the sole subject of a secret but widespread experiment with the human form, and that everyone and everything around me was a part of it. Had I heard of and understood the words sociological or anthropological at that time, it would have been that type of study. I'd lie awake sometimes at night, convinced that, even then, at that moment, in the street-lit darkness of the bedroom that I shared with our Karen, Patrick and Paul, someone was observing me through the slate roof and making notes on a clipboard. Of course, for such a grand conspiracy, characters like our Paul, Dooter McKinney and Gutsy McGonagle would be part of it. Even the dogs in the street. And so would me granny and granda Quigley. And me ma and da. Everyone. I'd close my eyes, dearly hoping and wishing it wasn't true.

In the weeks after me da was suddenly taken from us, I believed even more that this whole life thing just had to be a weird experiment beyond my knowing or control, and that, someday soon, someone would bring him safely home, letting me in on the conspiracy. Those forlorn thoughts were in the darkest of February nights when I pined for him to come back. I'd close my eyes and, before eventually drifting off to sleep, hope against hope that the study of me was actually true, that his killing, his waxy face, the wake, the hollow, hungry feeling inside me were just elements of the experiment.

After growing up and getting sense, I still wondered why it was me, or us, that this thing happened to. Was there something special about the Dohertys from Hamilton Street? Were we cursed? Did someone put the blight on us? Growing up knowing you've been part of a hugely tragic event marks you. You become known for it. It makes you a part of history, no matter how terrible the story. Are we marked forever by our history? As I grew older I often asked myself whether history had made me who I was, and would I, in turn, make history with that?

In January 1972 a young British Army marksman executed my unarmed father. He died along the same stretch of Derry road where he was born in September 1939, and where he was reared until he left his native Derry for England in search of work twenty years later. He was picked off by the sniper, casually utilising his well-honed rifle skills from a range of fifty yards. A single, crack shot. A 'Texas Star shot', as it was later described in a courtroom in London. Some say he cried out that he didn't want to die on his own, but the medical evidence suggests death was much more rapid, the SLR bullet traversing the full length of his trunk, severing the muscles protecting his heart.

Paddy Walsh, roughly the same age, crawled out from the protective concrete pillars of Joseph Place, eyes glassy with terror, and whispered the Act of Contrition into my father's dead ear. A bullet from the same sniper sliced through the collar of Paddy's corduroy jacket as he spoke the hallowed words. Two Paddys: one dead and the other alive by a quarter inch because his head was low in almost silent prayer. Paddy Walsh was a fierce brave man. But he got no medals or commendations for his bravery. The sniper did, though, being cited in despatches, a huge accolade for the young soldier.

Hundreds of Irish heads stooped to the gutter as the bodies of men and boys slumped around them. In fear and panic the survivors dashed up the hill to Creggan, loud shots ringing in their ears, bounding the hard steps in twos and threes, and tramping the frozen ground to their homes in Malin Gardens, Dunmore Gardens and Iniscarn Road. All Donegal place names.

Doherty is a Donegal name too. It was originally Ó Dochartaigh but had been anglicised to Doherty centuries before I came into being in January 1963. I had just turned nine when news of my father's death filtered along the cold road, beginning in Rossville Street, passing the place of his birth on the Lecky Road, towards our house in Hamilton Street, that he had met his fate at the far end, over in the Bogside. A number of those who hurtled up the hill homewards, heads down, were soon to find out that their younger or older brothers had been killed too and were now piling up on the slabs in Altnagelvin Hospital in the Waterside. Thirteen of them: a butcher's dozen. A city in chaos, left to bury its thirteen sons, labelled by their killers, and then by the highest judicial office in Britain, as gunmen and bombers. What a day for the Empire.

During me da's wake I swore revenge many times against the British. However, vengeance was not my only thought as my tear-filled eyes scanned the row of coffins stretching the full width of the altar of St Mary's Chapel. *Can we not just have him back?* I also pleaded. I could almost see him stepping through the door with his curled-lip smile and his speckled coat with the black fur collar. It was all happening so suddenly it just couldn't be true. But no, this nightmare *was* actually true. There would be no waking up in a cold sweat, breathing relief that it was only a bad dream. He was gone. I felt his loss each morning for long afterwards, in the gap between blissful sleep and awakening to the new dawn, knowing that he was gone for ever.

Eight years later, I took my oath to the Irish Republican Army (IRA) in a house only a few yards from where my father was born. The long war had already created its probabilities and certainties for those volunteering to take part in it. As I faced the Irish tricolour I was duly warned that my prospects were imprisonment, life on the run, or death.

A few months later, the Royal Ulster Constabulary (RUC) arrested me – the same police force that didn't think my father's death was significant enough to merit a criminal investigation. I was interrogated and admitted my part in an attempted bombing raid on a furniture shop in Derry city centre.

***

The metal door of Cell 5 clanged heavily behind me. I instantly realised I was in someone else's space as I eyed the resident prisoner for the first time. In effect, I had just moved into his bedsit. It was 1 March 1981. Anto had not journeyed more than a few hundred yards since the summer of 1979, when he had been taken from his home in County Tyrone, interrogated by the RUC in Derry and transported to prison in Belfast.

'Aye, it's a brave while OK. A bad year for Strabane town, ye know!' grinned Anto through his bushy sandy moustache, his kind, smiling eyes making light of the sheer length of time he had spent in this cell. It was almost two years! But he seemed at perfect peace with himself as he sat in his turned-up flared jeans on a single bed with his back against the cell wall. I stood rooted to the floor with my brown paper bag of possessions in hand. Standing up was all I could do to stall or challenge what was happening to me. It was far too early to sit down and accept where I was.

'Jesus! August '79! That's more than a year and a half!' was all I could say. It was truly hard to take in. I felt as if I had entered an alternate reality.

The year 1979 was when we got served pints of beer at the Rock Bar across the border on a Sunday, that I started doing a steady line with Maire, and that our Patrick came out and headed off to London to live the gay life. That summer we thumbed up to Malin Head with the Shantallow boys to Dessie Doherty's ma's caravan, where we ran mad around Five Finger Strand as the golden sands lit up the blackest of moonless nights. And that was the year my best friend, Eddie O'Donnell, died so tragically young in an accident.

'Ye can sit down, ye know,' Anto gestured towards the bottom bunk. I sat down and contemplated my new surroundings. The cell was about 8 feet across and 16 feet long from the door to the high Perspex window that arched in tandem with the gentle curve of the brickwork ceiling, its mortared ruts blanketed and shadowed by more than a century of smoke and whitewash. A single bare bulb hung from a yard of flex. There were three black, high-gloss, metal-framed beds: Anto had the single bed, the pillow-end just next to the red metal door, and mine was one of the bunk beds, set at the back end of the cell, just below the window. Along the wall opposite Anto's bed stood a small table displaying an open brown bag of fruit, a stack of books, a bottle of Robinson's Orange Barley Water and two white plastic mugs. *Could I be here, in this one place, until 1983?* I thought. *Two whole years? Is that even possible?*

'Ye fancy a wee cordial?' he asked, getting up from the bed. He proceeded to pour water from a plastic water container, known as a 'water gallon', into the mugs, before pouring in a drop of the Barley Water.

'Ye want a wee custard cream?'

'Aye, surely. A wee custard cream would be grand.'

'What did they charge ye with?' he asked, handing me a brown bag of assorted biscuits, mostly custard creams and ginger nuts.

'Causing an explosion, possession of a gun and IRA membership.'

'Did ye sign a statement?'

'Aye, I did. And I'm a stupid fucker for doing so.'

Anto went quiet for a while as he sat sipping his drink. The custard creams tasted pleasantly sweet with the cordial. In our house, I'd eat a full packet of them with a mug of tea.

Voices, footsteps and the slide of buckets out in the wing echoed around our silence. This was C Wing swinging into action on the first day of the week. A key rattled in the door and Mr Kyle, a screw in his thirties with jet-black hair and a black moustache, said, 'You're to see the MO.' I looked over at Anto, who gave me a thumbs up and said, 'The MO is the Medical Officer; it's just a wee check. I'll see you in a minute.'

Mr Kyle led me out onto the bustling wing, past striped-shirted orderlies brushing and mopping the long, black-painted floor. The orderlies watched me as I passed but made no attempt to speak, nod or make eye contact.

The MO was a small Belfast man with a sharp, squeaky voice. He wore a white coat but had the pale blue screw's shirt on underneath.

'Anthony Doherty?' he asked as Mr Kyle presented me. He pronounced Doherty as Dockerty, as most Belfast people do.

'Dockerty; you must be another wee Londonderry lad with a name like that.'

'Aye, I'm from Derry OK.'

'Is that not Londonderry, Dockerty?' he posed from his wee twisted face. The dual effect of Londonderry and Dockerty was annoying. Deliberately annoying.

'Whatever ye want yourself. I call it Derry.'

'Well,' he squeaked, 'young Dockerty from Londonderry,

you'll not be seeing it for a long time anyway, I hear.' He paused. 'Have you any medical complaints?' he asked when I didn't respond.

'My gums were bleeding when I was in Castlereagh.'

'Castlereagh? You must've been a bad Londonderry boy for them to take you the whole way up to Castlereagh? Open up and let me see,' he said. 'They're a bit inflamed all right. That's pyorrhoea that you have, young Dockerty from Londonderry.' His voice rose to a helium-like pitch with the excitement of the telling. 'It looks like you're going to lose all your teeth now, doesn't it?'

I'm fuckin' sure I won't be losing me teeth! I thought to meself. I loved me white teeth and me ma always told me that I was toothed like me da and smiled like him sometimes with my top lip curled up like Elvis. *I'll brush the hell out of them six times a day, if only so as not to give this bitter wee hoor of an MO any pleasure!* I thought as I stared blankly back at him sitting down behind his desk and filling in his forms.

'That's you now, Dockerty from Londonderry. You can go. Get yourself ready to say goodbye to your teeth,' he said as Mr Kyle led me out.

'Fuck you, ye wee bitter fucker. You and yer Londonderry!' I said under my breath as we came out, and Mr Kyle looked at me as if he should say something but then smiled and turned his face away.

The orderlies, stripped down to their white vests by now, were puffing and blowing as they pushed and pulled huge, wooden, blanket-covered buffers to shine the long black floor of the wing as we passed by on the way back to Cell 5: my new home. While the buffing work looked really hard, they must've been glad all the same that there was only one floor to shine on the wing, the two floors above being restricted to long walkways of iron grids and steel grilles with a wide void in the centre. This void between the walkways was filled with metal mesh, presenting the eye with a confused tapestry of criss-crossing tracks, traps and tripwires.

When I returned to the cell, the screws had left me a white block of soap, a toothbrush and toothpaste, and a navy-blue bath towel. Anto was sitting up against his pillow reading a newspaper, and he smiled and nodded as I came in. He had his transistor on and 'In the Air Tonight' by Phil Collins was playing low.

'Well? Are ye livin' or dyin'?' he asked.

'That wee hoor of an MO said I'm goney lose me teeth; they were bleedin' when I was in Castlereagh. Is it OK to brush them in here?'

'Oh God, aye; just use that pot there. It's clean,' he said, pointing to one of two plastic chamber pots in the corner beside the door.

'So what's the craic the day, Anto? What do we do now?' I asked as I rinsed.

'The craic is, sir, that we stay in the cells all day the day until teatime, when we get out to the canteen. The loyalists are in the yard, so the marra we get out to the yard. We take turns at everything and never mix on the wing.'

'Where's the yard?'

'Out there,' he nodded, looking up to the high window set deep in the wall above.

'Is it OK to look out?'

'Aye. C'mon up for a jook,' and both of us knelt on the top bunk as he pulled the window from the top and it lay on the flat of the deep sill.

The view was of a triangular yard, hemmed in to the right by a high wall with rolls of barbed wire on top and kept in check by the three-storey sandstone walls of B Wing. The arched windows on each floor had sturdy vertical bars. The windows were all closed on account of the freezing cold. Despite the cold, though, there were around 100 loyalists walking around the yard in small groups, puffing smoke into the frosty winter air. Several of them looked up at our window as they passed but then continued on their triangular journey.

'P. T. Jones 121 for a visit; P. T. Jones!' came a harsh call from a loudspeaker.

'J. C. Dobson 122 for a visit; J. C. Dobson!'

'C. C. Campbell 127 for a visit; C. C. Campbell!'

'Ye see yer man there with the wee blue book under his arm?' pointed Anto.

'Aye, what about 'im?'

'He's in for beating a Catholic to death with a breeze block in Portadown. He's a born-again Christian now. He never lets the Bible out of his hands. Every time he's in the yard, he has it tucked under his arm.

'Ye see that big tall bucko there?' continued Anto, pointing to a barrel-chested man with dark, coppery hair and a red-white-and-blue checked coat with a white fur collar. He glided past our window, his eyes set straight ahead. 'That's

John Somerville from Moygashel outside Dungannon; he's a sergeant in the UDR [Ulster Defence Regiment] and he's charged with killing the Miami Showband. He's a bigwig in the UVF.'

Directly opposite our window there was a covered stand, like an open shed with a corrugated roof, where other men stood in clumps of threes and fours, smoking and chatting. They looked a bit on the miserable side, I thought. In saying that, the whole yard looked drab, grey and depressing. The only colour to be seen was on the four or five green-painted metal posts holding up the roof of the stand, and the array of blue jeans and coats worn by the loyalist prisoners. The leaden sky bore down heavily, placing a firm lid on the grey triangle.

It was a relief when Anto said, 'Here, we'll close this winda; it's buckin' freezin'!', and we retreated to the cell, which was warmed by two heating pipes running along the base of the back wall, directly underneath the bunk beds.

'I've never been this close to loyalists in my life,' I said.

'You'll get used to that, sir. When you're passin' them on the wing or on visits, just say nothin' and they'll say very little to you.'

'So, what do we do now?' It was a question I was to continue to ask for a few days until I got my bearings.

'We're in the cell all day till we get our tea later the night in the canteen.'

'Do they not give you dinner?' I asked, wondering about the gap in between.

'They do aye, but we're not takin' it on account of it being the first day of the second hunger strike. It was on the news there earlier: Bobby Sands refused his first meal this mornin'.'

'D'ye know him?' I asked.

'Naw, he was long gone to the Blocks way before I came in.'

'D'ye think the Brits'll give in this time?'

'Dunno; it doesn't look the best.'

'So, how did you end up in here?' I asked.

'It's simple; I opened me mouth when I should've kept it shut.'

'Did you sign a statement, like me?'

'I did. But I didn't do anything and I'm not in nothin'.'

'So what happened ye?'

'I was arrested out of the house out of the blue and took to Strand Road Barracks,' said Anto, turning his face away, remembering. 'I was never lifted before and by fuck, sir, they can fair pile the pressure on ye once they have ye in.'

'I know! Sure look at me!'

'On the second day next thing they were saying that such and such told us everything about me. I couldn't believe it, as I just told them ye know I had done fuck all and that I shouldn't even be in here. They were roarin' an' shoutin' into me face and I could hear others roarin', shoutin' and cryin' down the corridor. It was like a madhouse.'

'Did the other boys sign too?'

'Wait till ye hear. Next thing the cop said to me, "We know what you did, boy. Your friends have told us everything about you. You need to get this off your chest, pay your debt to society and get your life back."

'I just said back that I didn't know what they were talkin' about, but they kept at it, shoutin' and roarin' into me face. It gets to ye after a while, ye know. Next thing the head cop says, "Do you want us to bring your friend in to see you?" and I said, "Bring him in if ye want; I've got nothin' to hide."

'So next thing the door opens and in walks this fella I knew from school, but that was all, and he says, "I've told them everything, Anto. I've got it all off me chest. You should do the same. Tell them all ye know!"

'And I said, "I don't know what you're on about. I didn't do anything so ye have no business givin' my name for anything!" And then the head cop said, "Young man, do you want us to leave you alone with your friend?" and I said, "Do what ye want; it'll make no difference to me."

'So, out the cops go, closing the door behind them, and there's just me and yer man in the room. And I says to him, "What the fuck are ye at? What the fuck are ye givin' my name for? I hardly even know ye!" And he says, "But I'm gettin' out; I'm a youth leader and I've an alibi for everything that I told them."

'"Out my fuck! You're goin' nowhere, ye stupid hoor! D'ye not realise that? Jesus Christ, what did ye tell them ye done?"

'He says, "I told them I was in the IRA, that we talked about setting up a UDR man and that we carried out bombins in Strabane town centre. But I have alibis for all the times and dates, as I was at meetings in the youth club."

'And I says, "What the fuck did ye give them my name for?" and he says they just kept telling him that these other fellas were there, includin' me, and he just agreed. I signed a statement the next day. I just couldn't take any more. And now I'm charged with membership and conspiracy.'

'And yous had nothing to do with any of it?' I asked, remembering my own battles in Castlereagh; I knew how isolating and, at times, terrifying an experience it was.

'There were four of us charged. All innocent. The other three think they're goin' to get off. Not a chance in a no-jury court. We're goin' down; the only question is for how long.'

'Jesus, that's really unbelievable!' I said, feeling a strange relief that at least I had done what I'd signed for.

'Well, there ye go. We're not the only wans in here that are innocent, ye know; there's many more,' said Anto. Falling silent, he rested his head back on his neatly folded bed pack of brown blankets, white sheets and white pillow on top.

'Will ye be gettin' a visit the day?' he asked.

'I dunno; I'm not sure what's happenin'.'

'Is it your ma and da who'll be up, d'ye think?'

'Me da's dead; he was killed on Bloody Sunday,' I said, going red as I said it, as if me da's death was a stigma of some sort.

'What age were ye when he was killed?'

'Nine.'

Anto paused for a minute and then said, 'Have you brothers and sisters?'

'Aye, three brothers and two sisters.'

'I've a visit the day wi' me da and me brother. They get the PDF bus up from Strabane. We'll get a wee food parcel later. We're goney need it.'

Anto had turned his cell into his home. Everything was

neat and tidy, and there was a faint smell of disinfectant in the air. He even had his house-slippers placed neatly underneath the table, and smiling pictures of his family on the cork board beside his bed.

I had only a few fags left in my twenty box. I lit up and sat back on my bed pack on the bottom bunk, struggling to keep up with the thoughts buzzing in my head. It was hard to settle on one thing for more than a moment before something else squeezed its way past. The draw on the Embassy Regal brought some calming order to things as I blew the white smoke up into the springs and mattress above my head. I wondered what people would think of me for signing a statement in Castlereagh. I did feel myself that I had let people down; that I, the son of a man murdered by the British on Bloody Sunday, should admit my part in an IRA operation. I was in here for doing wrong according to the law, but what about the bigger wrong done to me and my family, my city? Did that not count? What will Maire do? Will she finish with me? Should I just finish with her? What about her ma and da? Would they encourage her to finish with me? Probably, I concluded, but she's her own girl at the same time, so you never know.

That Anto fella's a hairy brute, I thought. He had pulled off his white T-shirt to put on a denim shirt with white, pearly buttons for his visit, only to reveal a mass of black hair sprouting from his gut up to his neck, the dark forest continuing the whole way up his arms and even across his broad shoulders! My chest by comparison was more like a desert oasis, a small pitiful growth in the middle of a sea of white skin.

A key turned loudly in the door-lock.

'A. C. Doherty, you have a visit. Come with me,' said the screw, a younger man than Mr Kyle.

'Stand down there at the grille until they're ready,' he said, pointing to the metal bars at the end of the wing. A few other prisoners made their way towards me before being let through with a screw as an escort, passing across the highly polished circle area linking the four wings of the prison.

I was directed to a room with a series of cubicles on either side of a central corridor. The prisoners sat on the inside against the wall while their visitors – wives, mothers, fathers, children and friends – sat with their backs to the corridor. Screws patrolled up and down, speaking at times in hushed tones to those in the cubicles. I had no idea who was coming to see me. I sat for a few minutes on my own until me ma and Maire were ushered in. I was delighted to see them. We hugged and then sat down facing each other across the powder-blue table.

'How are ye, son?' asked me ma.

'I'm all right, Ma. I'll be all right,' checking their eyes to see if they believed me but feeling very aware of the huge uncertainty of my new status.

'Everybody's asking for you,' said Maire. 'You're a wile popular fella, hi,' she smiled. 'Our phone hasn't stopped since last week.'

'Our phone's the same and the house hasn't emptied since ye were lifted,' said me ma.

'What's it like in here, Tony?' asked Maire.

'I dunno, I'm only in the door!'

'What's the food like?' asked me ma.

'Well, it's not the Steakhouse!' I smiled.

'Are ye in a cell wi' anybody?' asked me ma.

'Aye, I'm in wi' a fella from Strabane called Anto; he's been in since 1979.'

'1979!' said Maire, shock and trepidation on her face. Her brown hair was cut short at the back and sides but swept long across her forehead with a single cerise-coloured wisp cupping her face. She had a number of earrings in each ear, not just in the lobe but further up the edge of the ear as well.

The visiting room, fogged in smoke, hummed with awkward conversations and controlled emotions. It was a microcosm of the prison wing itself, where even the good or troubled news from home was restricted to cubicles and invigilated by screws. Crying children, laughing children, dressed for the occasion of seeing their daddies. Wives and girlfriends clinging to their husbands and boyfriends. Friends visiting friends with tales of the bar, the dance hall and the disco, and who was doing a line with who.

'Aye, 1979,' I repeated back to her. 'Hard to believe, isn't it?' and she nodded back with tearful eyes.

'Do think you'll get bail?' asked me ma.

'I don't know, Ma. It'll take a few weeks, I'd say, before I'm up for it. We'll just have to see.'

'We're goney go and see a few people this week to see if they'll do bail for ye. Me and Maire. With a bit of luck, you'll be right as rain for Karen's wedding in August.'

'That's grand. Sure we'll see what happens,' I said, preferring not to talk in certainties or get people's hopes up too much. It was a constrained conversation, speaking about the unknown, keeping a brave face despite the possibility that this was as good as it was going to get for a long time to come. Behind me ma and Maire, visitors and prisoners came and left as their visits started and ended. In a quiet moment, as I lit an Embassy Regal, I heard a female voice in the next cubicle weeping in despair and then a male one whispering solace and reassurance.

'What's your cell friend like?' asked Maire.

'Cellmate,' I said.

'Cellmate,' repeated Maire.

'He's dead on. He gave me orange dilute and custard creams. The luxuries ye get in Cell 5!' I laughed.

'God, there ye go; number 5,' said me ma. 'That's a good sign; we're No. 15 Brookdale and we came from 15 Hamilton Street.'

'What's that got to do wi' anything?' I laughed, as Maire looked on, bemused to see what the logic was with the number five.

'Ach, ye know what I mean; it's a good sign. All the fives.'

'It's not effin' bingo, ye know, Ma!' I laughed.

'Shut you up! I know what I'm on about! Yer not too big for a skelp around the ear!'

'So, how're ye keeping, Maire?' I asked, and could tell by her face what the answer was.

'Ach, ye know the craic. I'm out hunting for another boy-friend,' she smiled through tear-filled eyes.

'He'd need to be better than the last cowboy ye had now, wouldn't he?' I joked.

'We left ye a parcel,' said me ma. 'Tony Hassan told us

what we could bring and I left ye up some clean clothes too.'

'That's grand. We'll have a wee party the night wi' all the custard creams and cordial.'

'Stop you taking the hand out of yer mammy!' chided Maire.

'I know; I'm only joking. I really appreciate it, Ma.'

'I know ye do, son. Here, gimme a kiss now and I'll let ye's have a wee minute to yerselves.'

'Can ye do that?' asked Maire.

'I dunno. This is only my first visit too, ye know!'

The big screw came down to us and said that me ma could stand at the far end of the room near the exit. Maire sat forward on her chair leaning across the table and so did I, to spend the last few minutes closer together.

***

I could still smell Maire's perfume in the cell later, as the door opened for us to go and collect our daily rations, dispensed across a counter onto steel trays to be carried back to the cell. I followed Anto, who refused everything, only filling his white plastic mug with tea. It was with heavy heart that I sat quiet at the table in the cell to eat the alternative of cheese and crackers, while Anto sat sideways on his bed with one leg up and the other on the floor, mug in hand.

'Ye know, me da knew yer da,' he said.

'Aye?'

'Aye, he knew him from working in Du Pont. He said his nickname was The Skelper.'

'Aye, that's him OK.'

'He said he couldn't believe yer da was among the dead that day. Nobody knew until the following morning when word got round the workplace.'

It was then I remembered me ma telling us once that a man by the name of Maxi Gallagher from Bishop Street had called in his car to our house in Hamilton Street to collect me da for work at six o'clock the morning after he was killed.

I always found myself feeling embarrassed when someone mentioned me da, especially when they had just found out about him being killed. Even though Anto was clearly a nice fella and meant no harm, I found myself not wanting to talk any further about the subject. It felt really odd that both me ma and Maire were now on the road back to Derry and that I was here with nowhere to go. I was also worried that I was indeed going to lose my teeth, so I continued to brush them vigorously every hour or so, spitting the cerise-pink foam into the pisspot in the corner beside the door.

We spent the rest of my first day chatting and listening to the radio. Every time Joe Dolce's 'Shaddap You Face' came on, though, Anto would turn the radio off, complaining, 'It does my buckin' head in.' Anto was a reader, and he offered me a selection of paperback novels, but my head was too busy to sit long enough to read. He, on the other hand, sat upright on his bed, book in hand, as if he hadn't a bother in the world.

The door opened and the screw said, 'Ye's have a parcel', and both me and Anto walked up the corridor to the parcels office and were each handed two brown bags across the counter, one with clothes and the other food. When we got back to the cell it was like we'd just got back from Wellworths with the messages. There was fruit, biscuits, cheese and meat wrapped in tinfoil and, for me, forty Embassy Regal. A buzz of excitement hummed round the cell as we put things in their rightful place on the table, as if expecting guests for a party.

Letters fell to the ground through the flap in the cell door. There was one in a pink envelope for me and one in a white envelope for Anto. I recognised the writing as Maire's, and Anto giggled at me for getting a pink letter. I sat up in bed reading the four or five pages of Maire's letter written on pink pages and didn't lift my head for about twenty minutes.

'Well, does she love ye or what?' he smiled.

'None of your business!' I laughed back.

'Was she the girl with the big guide-dog for the blind?'

'Aye, you're good craic, hi!'

'It'll not be long now till we get out to the canteen at five. We'll bring some grub out wi' us as I don't think we're takin' the tea either.'

'What do we use to write back to people?'

'Ye have to get up in the morning to request a letter when they come round the doors. If you're not up wi' your clothes on, they don't take your requests.'

'What other requests are there?'

'Ye can ask for letters, or to see the doctor or the dentist or the governor. If I wanted to take the hand out of ye, I'd tell ye to order a beef curry.'

'A beef curry?'

'Aye, many's the man was put up to ordering a beef curry for dinner or a box of Milk Tray or two pints of milk to the door. Wan fella even stood ready by the door with his togs and towel rolled up under his arm for the swimming pool! By the way, when we go to the yard the marra, if someone asks you have you seen the Sinn Féin doctor yet, ye just tell them to piss off.'

'The Sinn Féin doctor? What's that?'

'There's no such thing, but it sounds the part for boys just landin' in. Just tell them to piss off.'

'OK, I'll take your word for it.'

Anto gave me his copy of the *Strabane Chronicle*, the first local paper I'd ever read or knew of apart from the *Derry Journal*. I half sat and half lay on the bed going through the paper page by page, though I was taking little of it in. I struggled to accept the reality of my new situation and wondered how Anto could be so at ease with himself, lying there on the bed reading as if he was on the sofa in his house in Strabane. I wondered would I be here in 1982, or even 1983? Never mind that, would I still be here this Friday or next Monday? How am I going to stick it in this wee cell with the fruit and the biscuits, the bare light, the pisspots and the screws looking in through the flap on the door every hour? How am I going to put my time in? Surely I'll get bail in a few weeks' time and bugger off across the border to Buncrana and not come back? Naw, Jesus, not Buncrana! I couldn't bear Buncrana in the rain! I'll head on down the country, to Galway or Kerry or somewhere. And what if I don't get bail? Our Karen is getting married in August; the first of our crowd to get married and the first of me granny and granda's grandwains to go up the aisle. That's in August – six months away. Could I still be here in the summer? Jesus, in this wee cell with nothing to do!

'Lock-up C Wing; C Wing lock-up!' called the screw's voice over the loudspeaker in the yard. Looking out the window I could see that the loyalists were ignoring the call and continued to walk round the yard. It was only when the screw repeated, 'Lock-up C Wing; C Wing lock-up!' that they began drifting in small groups towards the entry at the far end of C Wing to come in. Out on the wing there was a considerable rattling of keys, screws click-clacking or squeaky-booting, and metal doors being locked and bolted.

Sometime later, our door opened and the screw said, 'Canteen there.' I followed Anto up the wing as other cells were opened, allowing prisoners to make the short journey to the place of entertainment. This turned out to be much like a school canteen, with three long rows of tables, a pool table, board games, a small case filled with books, and a TV on a shelf near the door. High up on the TV wall a pair of eyes constantly scanned the area through a metal slit.

My cousin, Patsy Doherty, was in C Wing. His da, J.J., was in A Wing, as was his brother John, and his other brother Danny was in prison in Portlaoise. There were a lot of fellas my age and quite a few older. One was Seán Mack from Belfast's Ardoyne area, who heard Patsy call me 'Dutchie'.

'So, where did you get Dutchie from?' he asked.

'It's my childhood nickname,' I replied. 'My schoolteacher called out "Anthony 'Dutch' Doherty" one day during roll call and the name just stuck. Apparently, he got it from an IRA man who'd recently been arrested on the border.'

'He was right, Dutchie; Anthony "Dutch" Doherty lived around the corner from our house in Ardoyne!'

I was introduced to Liam Hamilton, a ruddy-faced man with a shock of greying black hair greased forward and cut straight across his forehead. He was the OC of republican prisoners in C Wing. I also met Pete Ryan, whose cell was just across from ours. Both were from Tyrone. Pete was stocky, red-cheeked and snub-nosed, and wore short cowboy boots. He was the Intelligence Officer, the IO, of the wing. He called me 'cub'. At six o'clock the eighty or so prisoners gathered in front of the TV to hear the newsreader announce that Bobby Sands had indeed refused all his food that day in the H-Blocks of Long Kesh, protesting that he was a political prisoner and that the British had no right to treat him, and all republican prisoners, as common criminals. Afterwards, the hum of previously excited chattering gave way to whispered gloom and foreboding.

We were back in the cell before 7.30 p.m., the prison falling quiet for the night. Suddenly, however, a huge eruption of door-banging resounded throughout the wing, causing me to spring to my feet, assuming that a riot had broken out. Anto just lay there on his bed grinning through the deafening din and, after it had abated, said, 'That's the Tyrone boys and Big T's Country Club coming on the radio. They're mad about their country music. Philomena Begley 'n' all.'

We lay on our bunks chatting until the lights went out

at 11 p.m. Anto told me his granny and granda were sold on the same day in 1930 to a Gortin farmer at the Strabane Hiring Fare. His granda was from Loughrea in Galway and his granny from Dungloe in Donegal. They eventually saved enough money to take the boat from Derry Quay and settled in New Jersey until his granny came back some years later to Strabane with her children, including Anto's father, who was a car mechanic and handy with anything with an engine.

I recalled for him the childhood stories of me granda Connor enlisting with the 'Suitcase Brigade' during the Second World War and working in the factories in Coventry. Northern Irish men could only be conscripted into the British services if they stayed in Britain 100 days or more in a row. So, on their ninety-eighth or ninety-ninth day, they took flight for the Belfast boat home for a short spell before returning for another ninety-nine-day stint. Famously, when a nephew asked him in the 1960s why he didn't just enlist in the British Army to fight, as many Derrymen did, Connor lowered the newspaper where he was studying the racing form, pushed his specs down his nose, glared at the nephew, and scowled, 'Sure what did the Germans ever do on me?'

***

It had been a long day that had dragged on. *How many more of these days will there be*, I wondered as I stared at the brickwork ceiling faintly visible in the light from the yard. My mind drifted here and there before settling on a memory of gathering praties on Scoot Doherty's farm in Ardmore, just outside Derry, with Kevin 'Boiler' Boyle and Conor McCloskey.

We were a squad of about fifteen teenagers, boys and girls, in five groups spaced out along the pratie drill. Scoot drove the digger in front of us, scooping spuds high into the air, which we gathered from the dirt, bagged and stacked to the side before he came round again to churn up the next drill.

'D'ye see now how Scoot got his name?' asked Conor between deep, laboured breaths.

'What d'ye mean?' I said.

'He's got a turbo charge in that fuckin' tractor o' his; he scoots up and down the drills like a farmer possessed,' laughed Conor, and we all laughed, but it was no joke either as pratie-gathering was nothing short of teenage slavery.

'Here the fucker comes; look at the speed of the hoor!' cried Conor in despair. And the morning had only just started! We had a whole day of this to put in, never mind the rest of the week!

Scoot's fields were on a slope, which meant it was difficult enough gathering uphill, but was sheer murder as we followed the tractor downhill, where we had to stoop further to gather the praties. As the morning progressed we became slower at the gathering, affronted before the sturdy Ardmore girls in front of and behind us. More often than not Scoot had to stop the digger at our backsides to give us more time. On a few occasions he even got off the tractor to help with the gathering, complaining that he'd have to bring us in a pair of specs each the next day as we weren't lifting half of the scattered praties. He walked in slow motion like John Wayne.

We prayed for rain, as only rain could stop the digger.

'Rain, ya bastard, rain!' screamed Boiler, his mucky hands held up to the grey-skied heavens.

'Aw fuck, please Lord, give us rain!' we pleaded, as we stacked the full spud bags to the side for collection later.

'Please, Lord, pish from the heavens on us!' as Scoot broke land-speed records on his way up the drills, with the objects of our slave labour, Kerr's Pinks, cascading with the showers of dry dirt through the autumn air.

'Jesus! Jesus! Jesus! Give us rain, Lord!' we cried as we stooped our aching backs and bent our knees to lift the scattered potatoes.

And then, as if by a miracle, shortly before we were due to have lunch, it did rain. Scoot pulled up his tractor, looked up at the sky and said, 'It'll not last long, but we'll stop for the mornin',' and we retreated to the Walling House to have our tea and corned-beef sandwiches. The Walling House was the place where the gathered praties were separated into different sizes, the smaller ones being set aside for the following year's seed.

My memories must have merged into a dream then, as I drifted off to sleep.

I dreamed it was later in the day, after an afternoon of back-breaking agony worsened by the rain not returning, and the three of us sat on sacks outside the Walling House waiting for a lift back to Galliagh. A spud-fight broke out. Boiler dashed into the Walling House for cover, and Conor and I stayed outside. Boiler opened the Walling House door to throw and I caught him square on the nose with a spud the size of a tennis ball. The door snapped shut and there was no sign of him for several minutes. I gently opened the door and saw him lying on top of a mound of praties with his hands over his face. When he took his hands away his face had turned into a giant pratie with sandy hair on top. His eyes weren't eyes at all but bruises, sad and dark, seeping tears down his face in clean rivulets through the dirt. And then his spud head fell to one side, rolling off onto the mound of praties and he was dead.

I woke up covered in sweat, thinking I'd killed Boiler with a mucky spud, until the mustard lights from the yard brought me back to the top bunk in Cell 5. I could feel the memory of pain in my back and legs as it dawned on me that I might never suffer pratie-gathering again. I looked down at Anto as he lay on his bed out for the count, sleeping peacefully through another night of his long stretch away from his beloved Strabane town.

2

Days of their Lives

The screws escort prisoners out to the yard in small, staggered batches so there are never enough of them on the open wing to constitute a security risk. There is a sliding gate to the yard at the top of the wing controlled by a screw. On my first journey through it to get outside to the fresh air, I was struck on the side of the head as the screw suddenly slid the gate across. The screw, sitting behind a metal and Perspex screen, looked the other way through his UDA-issue, blue-shaded glasses as I banged on the Perspex with my fist in anger.

'What the fuck are ye at there, hi?' I shouted in shock and fury, cupping my right ear, but he wouldn't turn round.

'C'mon on out to the yard, Dutchie,' called Seán Mack from just outside the doorway.

'That fucker in there slapped me on the head wi' the gate!' I said, still glaring in the direction of the screw.

'I know he did, but he's nothing but a, but a … a big shitass!' he giggled. I could see that the screw was now looking in our direction and had heard.

'A shitass?' I laughed. 'Who d'ye think ye are? Clint fuckin' Eastwood?' Both of us knew that shitass was the most perfectly denigrating word he could've used in this situation.

So it was with a red ear and a satisfied grin that I stepped out into the yard of C Wing for the first time. The gate slid back open behind me to let Anto and some other prisoners through.

I took my first steps on the anti-clockwise circuit around the triangular yard. B Wing was full of petty criminals, many of whom were looking out of their heavily barred windows as we dandered by.

'Bullroots. On the threes,' said Seán. 'Don't even look up at the fuckers,' and I looked away, unsure as to what I was averting my eyes from.

'What are bullroots?' I asked.

'Sex offenders. Dirty bastards so they are!'

Bullroots, I said to myself as we continued along the window-barred wall of C Wing, passing the closed window of my own cell and the many closed windows around it set in neat rows in the thick stone walls. The yard had started to fill up as other prisoners trickled out, all taking part in this strange anti-clockwise procession like we used to do at the Shantallow Community Centre and the Marian Hall disco, walking round in groups eyeing the talent. It was clear that the younger ones stayed mostly together, as Jap and Mickey from Ardoyne began walking with us. Jap had a ball of curly brown hair and a round, pudgy face, always grinning a knave's smile and ready to take the hand out of someone. Mickey was taller and skinnier, with a shock of jet-black hair and the makings of a black moustache. Jap and Mickey were both twenty, so had two years' wisdom over me.

'How long are yous in?' I asked.

'Since August last year,' said Mickey.

'Do ye know that Anto in my cell has been in since August *1979*?' I asked, still finding it difficult to comprehend.

'Sure half of the yard is in since '78 and '79,' said Mickey, adding, 'You can spend up to three years on remand, so you can.'

'And what are yous boys charged with?' I asked.

'Murder,' said Jap.

'Aye, murder,' repeated Mickey.

'Murder? Who ...?' I asked hesitantly.

'There was an attack on an RUC jeep and a woman was shot dead. We're charged with murderin' her,' said Mickey.

Of all the things you didn't want to be charged with, killing an innocent bystander was high up on the list. Killing an innocent woman was higher still.

'What do yous reckon yous'll get?' I asked.

'Life,' said Jap.

'Aye, life,' repeated Mickey. 'It's automatic life for murder, so it is.'

'And what about you, Seán?' I asked him, for he had gone a bit quiet. 'What are ye in for?'

'Possession of a rifle,' he said.

'What are ye expectin' to get?' I asked.

'Probably around twelve to fifteen years,' he said. It still sounded colossal, even after Mickey and Jap's expectation of getting life.

'What about you?' asked Jap.

'I dunno. I could get around the same,' I said, hoping they would disagree and downgrade me a bit.

'Aye, for bombin' a shop? Probably the same as Seán alright,' said Jap.

'And how long d'ye think life is?' I asked.

'Dunno,' said Mickey and Jap in unison, before Jap added, 'Could be sixteen or seventeen years. Nobody knows.'

'Jesus, seventeen years, hi! That's nearly the next century!' I said, finding it hard to take in.

And we dandered on round, me feeling the full weight of my situation. Today was Tuesday. This day last week I was a free eighteen-year-old with, unknown to me at the time, less than twenty-four hours of freedom left. Much had happened in only six days. Six days which actually felt more like six weeks, beginning with the burly RUC man looming darkly at the foot of my bed in Brookdale Park, the journey from Derry to Castlereagh Holding Centre, the incessant waiting in cells, the long interrogations, the dry, desert heat of the cellblock, the appearance in Derry Courthouse, and then the long weekend in the Annex cell with Tommy Carlin, who I was charged with, both of us feeling a deep sense of disappointment in ourselves for admitting our part in the bombing. We had nothing to do except talk. When we stopped talking there was only silence.

Remembering that weekend, I told Jap and Mickey, 'When I was in the Annex on Saturday night, I found a blade of glass in the curled-up bacon.'

'Is that right?' said Mickey. 'That's them fuckin' orderlies; never trust them, half of them are bullroots and they'd slit their granny's throat to please the screws.'

'Anto, who does Dutchie remind you of?' asked Jap,

ignoring my news from the Annex.

'Who?'

'Bette Davis. "He's got Bette Davis eyes",' sang Jap. 'Bette Davis Eyes' was a pop song, at the time high up in the music charts.

'What are ye on about?'

'Look Mickey, hasn't he got Bette Davis eyes?'

'Aye, he does OK,' said Mickey, smiling.

'Bette Davis eyes me arse. What's that supposed to mean?' I asked.

'Nothin',' said Jap, 'it's just that "you've got Bette Davis eyes",' he sang the last few words again.

'And what are you not like with that haircut, ye fucker ye. Yer like Mungo Jerry!'

Just then, two fellas approached us from the shed and one said to me, 'You have to come wi' us to see the Sinn Féin doctor.'

'Aye, dead on. You think I came up the Foyle in a bubble?'

'But ye have to see the Sinn Féin doctor.' The taller one smiled a black moustachioed and white-toothed grin.

'I'm seein' no Sinn Féin doctor. All right?' I grinned back and they knew then that I was on to them.

'No joy there, Glit. Hard luck, Smurf,' said Jap as we continued on our journey, a single bunch among the other groups of men and teenagers all travelling in the same direction and moving between groups to swap stories or join in a bout of slagging. There was a difference, though, in how the various groups walked round the yard. The countrymen lurched forward as if their half cowboy boots were sprung like a mattress, wearing jeans – hands in pockets – and checked shirts, with their jackets thrown open. The most typical of the countrymen was actually called Springs, and he bounced and lurched forward at a frightening pace, his wide shirt-collar flying high up around his long sideburns and him grinning like a schoolboy on a day's excursion.

The Belfast men, mostly smaller in stature than their country cousins, rounded the yard in a hybrid, head-first dander, somewhere between a shuffle and a swagger, their turned-up flared jeans flapping over Dr. Martens or Oxford brogues, scanning the yard to determine where the next laugh or piece of verbal abuse would be directed. Whereas the countrymen appeared propelled by springs, the Belfast men's walk appeared to be controlled strangely by their shoulders, which swung forward alternately, causing the rest of the body to glide along, their feet splayed outwards in a ten to two position. The result of all this was that the cheeks of their backsides bobbed vigorously inside their jeans with each shuffle forward. By comparison, most of the countrymen hadn't a backside worth talking about.

As geographical groupings tended to stick together around the yard, you could easily pick out the countrymen – their sprung feet caused their heads to bob up and down as if practising the breast-stroke at swimming, whereas groupings of much smaller Belfast men resembled a waddle of penguins, arms for wings, bobbing from side to side.

Any feature, facial or otherwise, could be enough to merit attention from two of C Wing's main protagonists: Piggy O'Neill and Fra Collins from the New Lodge Road. Both were in their early thirties and had already been in prison in the 1970s. This time around they had been charged together in connection with a bombing. Piggy was slightly smaller than my five foot seven and a half inches, but was as broad as he was long, swarthy, with a balding head of black hair with middling sideburns and a facial shadow that told you he would probably need to shave at least twice a day.

Piggy eyed me as he passed us sauntering along and his first words to me were: 'Jimmy Durante! Look at the size of the schnozzle on this boy here!' he gestured to his bobbing-arsed walking group. 'Did they stretch it off ye in Castlereagh or somethin', son?' Before I could say that I was very proud of my fine Roman feature, he stuck out his huge, hairy-black hands, fingers wide, and sang in a deep, gravelly voice, 'Sitting here, playin' on my old piano!' He then began petting my schnozzle with his huge mitt as if I were a dog, uttering in a Bronx accent, 'It's da only ting dat calms him down!' Such was my introduction to the yard.

Of course, things could've turned out much worse, as a short while later Glit and Smurf sidled up to someone else who was just in – a tall, thin fella with short, black hair – and you could tell that he had no notion of what was about to befall him. They led him to the toilets or 'stalls', built along the wall of B Wing and, after a few moments, he started passing his clothes out to them over the red half-door. When he was naked behind the door, Glit and Smurf casually walked away with his clothes without him even realising. He simply stood behind the half door in the cold waiting for who knows what to happen next.

Oh, gentle Jesus, that could've been me! I thought, as I watched Glit throw his clothes and shoes onto the roof of the open shed, feeling sorry for the poor fella as he stood shivering and confused, observing the looks of mirth and pity from the dozens of men as they walked by. Eventually, Eugene, for that was his name, poked his head over the half-door and looked around, like a morning chicken from a henhouse, wondering where the Sinn Féin doctor was, and then the whole yard erupted in laughter.

'How am I goin' to get my clothes?' he mouthed to no one in particular, still protecting his naked dignity behind the door, his face a deep shade of purple. Not a soul responded. We just waited for the inevitable as we walked. Eugene stood, contemplating his options. A few minutes later he emerged slowly from the stall and tiptoed the short distance to the metal pole holding up the end of the shed and looked up, wondering how he was supposed to climb up there on his own to retrieve his dignity and pride.

'Hairy Hole!' someone shouted across the yard. 'Black Hole!' someone else called in support. He did actually have a black hairy hole, like most men. But Eugene's hairy hole was jet black against his white, shivering skin.

'Up the pole, Bouncy Ballicks!' called another. And while it was excruciatingly funny to watch, I was only glad that it wasn't me and that Anto had forewarned me of the danger. So I too hurled 'hairy-holed' abuse at the critter, like everyone else.

After a few exhortations, Glit approached him and offered him a handshake, which he took, and then gave him a leg up, the skinny black and white backside a sight, as he shimmied up the pole and stretched over, throwing his shoes and clothes down to Smurf, who collected them, a wicked smile across his face. Of course, when Eugene climbed back down, Smurf darted off with an armful of clothes, like a thief at a marketplace, and Eugene had to sprint after Smurf with one hand covering his dicky, to shouts of 'Run, Hairy Hole, run!' Eugene's bare feet were no match for Smurf's shod hooves as they dashed literally from pillar to post underneath the shed and out around the yard, Eugene's dicky and balls bouncing in front of him as he decided to sprint unhindered until he at last trapped the laden Smurf over at the gate to the wing. A few minutes later Eugene emerged fully dressed to the laughs and a full round of echoing applause from everyone in the yard. The redness of his embarrassment eventually left him as he was invited by a group to join them in the meander around the yard.

'What's the score wi' the cockroaches?' I asked as we dandered.

'Dirty bastards,' said Jap. 'They're everywhere in here; some the size of mice. Ye have to shake yer bedclothes out at night and shake your own clothes out in the mornin' in case ye get a bite on the balls.'

'A. C. Doherty for court! A. C. Doherty!' called the screw over the loudspeaker. The screws had an observation post lodged high on the wall in the corner between C and B Wings, so they could see everything going on in the yard. As I dandered towards the gate a fierce wind blew up, almost carrying me through the gap. Jap told me later this vortex in the corner of C Wing was called 'Liam Hamilton's Mini-Cyclone' as, due to his highly suspect combed-over crazy-wave, he had to get his footing and timing right as he entered the doorway, otherwise there'd be heavily oiled hair swinging everywhere above and beyond the baldy head he was rumoured to have. While very few had ever apparently witnessed the full effect of the cyclone on Liam's hairstyle, many would delay their exit from the yard to see if he would slip up. It was, of course, far worse on windy days, which must have been a nightmare for him.

Once in the wing, I was directed again to stand near the grille and wait for others going to the remand court. We were then taken out of the wing and down a flight of steps before being placed in a cell that smelled of mould and damp.

Tommy Carlin was already in the cell, along with another fella from A Wing who was a few years older than us. In prison, finding out about the man opposite you begins with an initial exploration of how he came to be there, whether his prospects were grave or his imprisonment fleeting, and whether he was guilty or innocent. While most situations were easy to ascertain, with others you had to read between the spoken words and the eyes as you discreetly discerned the truth. This fella said he had been arrested the previous year after an SAS man and an RUC man had been shot and killed on the Antrim Road in Belfast.

'Was that the M60 Gang?' I asked.

'It was, but I'm innocent. I had nothing to do with it,' he quickly added and looked away. Tommy and I exchanged knowing glances, acknowledging the likely opposite of what he had told us.

The cells were staffed by RUC men in mint-green shirts, who also escorted prisoners through the dimly lit underground tunnel running under the road between the prison and the Crumlin Road courthouse. The tunnel smelled of ancient overheated dampness as we were taken, handcuffed in pairs, in groups of ten. It reminded me of the millipede of boys holding hands on the journey between the Long Tower School and Our Lady of Lourdes Hall in the Brandywell for indoor football. Once over on the other side, the handcuffs were removed and we were placed in more cells to await our remand court appearance, which was very brief. After being taken up a steep flight of stairs and through a doorway, I stood behind an iron grille with Perspex windows, peering out as men in white wigs spoke in muffled tones to one another before the RUC man with me said, 'Right, let's go', and I turned and went back down the steps to the cells.

'Well, young Tony Doherty from Derry!' exclaimed Francie Gormley, sitting on a fixed wooden bench among a number of others unknown to me. I had met Francie the previous night in C Wing and, him being from South Armagh, he was among the group of countrymen who had earlier been bouncing round the yard. A tall, brown-haired man, he could easily have passed for a Country & Western singer in his short-cut cowboy boots and jeans. We were handcuffed together for the journey back through the tunnel. He bent to the side to half-whisper in the direction of my ear.

'Ye know, Tony, I'm completely innocent of killing that man.'

'What man, Francie?'

'The UDR man I'm charged with shootin'.'

'Did you sign a statement admitting it, or what?'

'I did and I'm gonna get life for it,' said Francie, making a gulping sound in his throat. I could feel him tense against the handcuffs.

'Jesus, Francie!' I whispered. 'Ye OK?'

'Aye, it's just very hard to get used to. Mother's breakin' her heart. Our whole family's destroyed by this. I put a brave face on it every hour of the day, especially at visits.'

'And are ye definitely goin' down for it?'

'Definitely. Life it'll be. Nobody even knows what that means yet; could be twenty years,' said Francie as we came to the end of the tunnel and had our heavy cuffs removed.

***

My early days in prison opened my eyes to a lot of things, principal among them the fact that many of the inmates were innocent. They had been conned and pressurised into making admissions that their interrogators must have known to be false. And while they all fell under the IRA structure in the wing, many had nothing to do with the IRA on the outside. Another revelation was that of time, not just the passing of it, but the routine guessing as to what time could mean for any of us, how long we all might be in prison for, and that no one knew what a life sentence meant in real years.

The yard thrummed with both the talk of time and the loose talk of past exploits on the outside. And while loose talk was officially frowned on by the IRA, you could say it was rampant in certain quarters. Hessie Phelan came on the wing charged with possession of a pistol. Hessie was quite small and slight, as if he had stopped growing on reaching fourteen. He was from the Lone Moor Road in the Brandywell, near me da's first cousins, the McCallions. He had short, blond hair, swarthy skin and small, wrinkly hands. A few years older than me, he had also been in prison in the 1970s and was seasoned to prison life, or so he would have us believe. He told stories of his exploits in Derry, where he was a member of the INLA, and seemed to know a lot about guns, or 'weapons' as they were universally referred to in 'army' parlance, and appeared wise to the world in other matters, if his tales of sex were anything to go by. Even as a raw eighteen-year-old novice to all these matters, though, I concluded that, if his stories were all true, he should have freed Ireland long ago and his middle name should have been Casanova!

Being from Derry, Hessie hung around with other Derry wans, including me and Colm Carey from the Waterside. Colm too had been in the cages for several years in the 1970s with political status, which the British government had removed in 1976. The hunger strike in the H-Blocks was directly related to republican prisoners now being treated as common criminals. Colm had longish, browny-grey hair and a beard of a similar hue. He had adopted a fella from Twinbrook by the name of Sam Wilson and the four of us walked the yard listening mostly to Colm's or Hessie's prison stories of escape attempts, tales of Free Derry, and visions of ghostly figures gliding through the corrugated tin skins of their Nissen huts.

As we strode, hands in pockets, puffing a rollie or a Regal, Colm often led us in song. He'd pick the trendiest of pop songs and lead out on a version that bore little resemblance to the notes or melody. The pop duo Dollar's songs were his favourite. Taking the opening lines or verse, he'd reduce the sugary, slick 'Who Were You With in the Moonlight?' to the back end of Country & Western in the style of Merle Haggard or Red Sovine, and then have each of us follow after him, while other groups traversing the yard looked on as if we'd lost the plot!

At the end of one such musical reduction session, Colm turned to Hessie and asked him if he remembered the escape from Magilligan Prison, when someone hid inside an old pool table. When Hessie said he did indeed remember, Colm took him to one side and whispered something in his ear. Hessie's eyes widened and his mouth rounded open, looking slightly upwards at Colm, who wasn't much taller. When they caught up with us again, Hessie had a spring in his step, almost bounding around the yard like a countryman, with a wide grin on his face. Sam and I looked at Colm and then at Hessie, but were none the wiser as lock-up was announced. It was to become clear that Hessie wasn't as wise or as seasoned as he reckoned, though.

The next evening in the canteen there was a lot of whispering and heavy-heading amongst those in the know.

Hessie was in the midst of it, as were Glit and Smurf. Word eventually found its way around that Hessie had been told he was to be smuggled out of the prison overnight inside the pool table, the red fabric of which had been worn and torn for some time and needed replacing. The orderlies were to have it removed as soon as the canteen was finished at 7.30 p.m.

Everyone was to behave as if nothing was going on and to go about their normal business. Hessie was in his element, winking confidently across at us as we supped our tea. What Hessie didn't realise was that the whole wing knew that he was being set up and that the screws too were in on it! It was the scheming Smurf who removed the panel on the pool table, heaving Hessie into the opening. Smurf had to remove Hessie's shoes and someone made a joke about *The Elves and the Shoemaker*, such was their tiny size! Once inside, the panel was replaced, clicking back perfectly into place.

'Lock-up, C Wing! C Wing, lock-up!' came the call from the loudspeaker.

'*Faoi ghlas anois! [Lock-up now!]*,' someone else called out as we filled our mugs with tea from the urn before heading back to the cells.

Several minutes later, as we stood in our cells expectantly, one of the screws on the wing called out: 'Does anybody own this wee schoolboy? We found him playing with his balls inside the pool table!', and the whole wing rocked with whooping, shouting and banging doors as Wee Hessie was led back to his cell.

He received a loud round of applause the next morning

in the yard. He took it well except for the huge redner that stayed on his cheeks every time someone called over.

'Hi, Hessie – Steve McQueen, *The Great Escape*!'

'Hi, Hessie – *Escape from Colditz*! Ye'll be diggin' tunnels next!'

'He wouldn't need a tunnel. Sure he's wee enough to slide into a drainpipe!'

'See yous fuckers,' laughed Hessie, 'I'll get ye's all back! Ye only think ye have friends!'

'Aw, Hessie, we were all sworn to silence! There was nothin' we could do!' And we all laughed and giggled at Hessie having made a total reel of himself in front of the whole wing, including the screws!

***

It was a windy day. We all got mauled in the vortex when exiting the wing through the gate. Better still, word had it that Liam Hamilton was due a visit! And sure enough, out he came to the yard in his finest, his head bowed to the swirling vortex, head and hair all held together with the spread of both hands. By around 11 a.m. the wind had worsened, and the East Tyrone prisoners were being called in ones and twos for their visits.

'P. MacKearney 326 for a visit; P. MacKearney. G. O'Callaghan 324 for a visit; G. O'Callaghan,' called the loudspeaker as both broke away from their walking group and made for the exit gate. We knew that Liam would be called soon, our anticipation rising with each call. It would take some doing for him to negotiate the mini-cyclone unscathed on a such a day.

'S. Campbell 274 for a visit; S. Campbell.'

'He must be goin' next,' muttered Colm from under his beard as Campbell headed for the doorway, 'for they all come up on the wan bus.'

'Shouldn't be too far now,' agreed Hessie, coming round from his ordeal.

'S. O'Neill 260 for a visit; S. O'Neill. L. Hamilton 261 for a visit; L. Hamilton.' All eyes secretly diverted towards Whitey O'Neill and Liam, who had been walking together round the yard, and all locked on his imminent exit. And you could tell from Liam's face that he was aware of this, and why. The wind howled round the cauldron of the yard as Whitey and Liam headed for the gate. Whitey was first to enter the vortex, his snowy white hair flapping up with the long wings of his shirt-collar. There was a five-yard gap between the two men and as Whitey disappeared through the gate, Liam stumbled with the pressure of knowing that a hundred pairs of sneaky eyes were on him, his hands lowered to steady himself and then the sharp gust of the mini-cyclone caught him full blast, sending pleats of oily hair straight into the air! He had a split second to check behind him to confirm that the whole of the packed yard was following his movements as we caught a fleeting glimpse of his bald, pinky-white dome disappearing in through the gate, with wisps and straggles of dark hair in tow.

Very few laughed out loud. This *was* the OC after all. However, a jocular hum flew round the yard, conveyed by a hundred or so satisfied grins and nods to one another as at last the OC's most obvious secret had been uncovered by the howling wind.

Just then, a young, recently arrived rioter from north Belfast fell to the ground directly below the screws' observation post and appeared to be in the throes of an epileptic fit, throwing his head of the blackest hair in all directions, his arms and legs jerking out of control. No one seemed to care, simply walking past him as his writhes and shakes continued with what can only be described as extreme youthful energy.

'What's goin' on?' I enquired.

'D'ye really need to ask?' said Colm.

'Stay down! Yer playin' a blinder!' whispered Hessie to the young epileptic as we sallied by. 'Yer doin' great!' and the prostrate critter kicked and twisted with renewed vigour.

'He thinks he's creatin' a diversion for the screws so that somebody on the outside can throw a rope-ladder over the wall for a big escape,' said Colm. We were on our second lap as the young rioter continued in his endeavour to distract all the screws in the wing with his fit.

'How long d'ye reckon he can keep it up?' asked Hessie.

'How long is it from Derry to Buncrana?' Colm replied. 'I've seen them down for ten minutes or more. Ye canny fault their enthusiasm!' he laughed, placing a hand over his bearded mouth to stifle himself.

Glit and Smurf passed swiftly in front of us and Smurf called out in a loud whisper, 'The ladder's comin' now. Stay down!' before casually dandering onwards, hands deep in his pockets and a wicked grin on his face. The young man became a powerhouse of uncontrolled movement, legs and arms kicking as a bluebottle would after falling on its back.

'Lock-up C Wing; C Wing lock-up!' called the screw over the loudspeaker. The young fella stopped momentarily. Then, at someone else's encouragement, he began his extended fit again! Head, arms and legs wriggling and flinging like a boy demented on the hard, open ground.

'Lock-up C Wing; C Wing lock-up!' called the screw again. The boy continued on the ground.

'Jesus, this boy'll be gettin' an Oscar for this performance!' laughed Colm, as we awaited '*Faoi ghlas anois*' to be called by someone in charge, several minutes after the command from the screws. This was to convey to the prison authorities that we had our own structure and rules.

'Lock-up C Wing; C Wing lock-up!' repeated the screw over the speaker. 'And that includes the chronic epileptic on the ground! Epileptic, lock-up!' And the young rioter froze where he had frantically writhed, eyes still closed, as if totally paralysed. The yard erupted. The young man opened his eyes only to realise that there was no ladder, no escape, no plan and that he'd been on the hard ground in an epic fit of contortions for more than five minutes for damn all. Apart, that is, from entertaining the troops. Laughter echoed around the stone walls of the yard. His next move was to put his hands up to his face, which he held for a moment before springing to his feet and making a go for Glit and Smurf, both purple-faced, as they dodged and ducked his frantic advances around the pillars of the shed.

'*Faoi ghlas anois!*' the voice of authority called as the

guffaws came loudly at the slapstick comedy unfolding before us.

'It's great to see that there's always someone else next in line for ridicule,' mused Hessie, glad that the centre of abusive attention was no longer himself.

'Don't kid yerself, Hessie,' said Colm. 'Don't kid yerself. The difference is that, for one, you should have known better as an oul hand; two, even the screws were in on it; and three, your great fuck-up last night with the pool table will be recounted in history someday. It was monumental!' he grinned, silencing Hessie, whose fair head hung low again in shame and disbelief, as we ploughtered a final circle round the gusty triangle of the yard.

3

SOLID GONE

'I'm in for stiffin' a cop,' said Ivor, sitting on the hard wooden chair in Cell 5. He had been standing near the bunk bed as I had several months earlier on my first day, unsure of what to do next. His options were extremely limited. I'd made him a cup of orange cordial and told him it was OK to sit down.

Ivor looked younger than my eighteen years and six months. He had bounded into my domain in a bustle of brown bags as if he were in a rush to get somewhere; a boy suddenly turning into a man, fresh from Castlereagh Holding Centre, where his life had been set on another course. Amid the many stories of rioting and chaos following Bobby Sands' death on 5 May 1981, it had been reported on Downtown Radio News that an RUC man had been shot dead.

Killing a member of the RUC carried an automatic life sentence. Ivor had signed for the killing and he would in all probability get a life sentence, convicted by the single judge without a jury. At that time no one really knew what a life sentence actually meant in years as no lifer had ever been released. Ivor was seventeen years old and lived with his mother and sister on the New Lodge Road.

'Did you sign in Castlereagh?' I asked, already knowing the answer.

'I did. I admitted everything. They battered the shite out of me. They even let the dead cop's friends come into the cell, squealin' and gulderin' that they were gonna kill me.' His hand shook as he steadied the white plastic mug against his bottom lip.

I quickly worked out that the 'dead cop's friends' were probably a ploy to put pressure on Ivor to co-operate, to get it over with, to pay back his debt to society and sort his life out again. I didn't tell him that, though. He'd be feeling bad enough that he'd signed a statement, never mind being disabused about the ploys that he fell for. In Castlereagh anything goes. We were in lock-up that day, which meant we had plenty of time to talk. He told me his father had been interned without trial in the early 1970s and he knew quite a few already in 'the Crum', such as Piggy O'Neill and Fra Collins, who were friends of his da.

I had been in Cell 5 on my own for a week or so, after Anto moved out, having been sentenced to three years for membership of the IRA. On commandeering his single bed, I discovered the delights of having a bed-board underneath the mattress, bringing solid comfort at night without springs creaking and moaning below me. I had pictures up on the cork board of Maire and of 15 Brookdale Park in all its sun-bleached summer glory, with me ma's tulips, red and yellow, standing proud around the front garden, and me ma, Glenn and Colleen happily squinting in the sunshine by the front door. I was fearful at first after Anto left, but I quickly realised the benefits of reading when I wanted to, or listening to the radio when I wanted to, or simply doing nothing.

When you live in such close quarters, politeness and respect for your cellmate are vital attributes, and you quickly learn the basics of accommodating others. And so, as Anto had become my mentor when I entered his cell in March, it was naturally determined that I would be Ivor's as he followed in my exact footsteps into Cell 5 in June. But Ivor was far more familiar with prison life than I had been, because of his father's and other relatives' imprisonment in the 1970s. Referred to as internment, this arbitrary process of imprisonment without trial of hundreds of nationalists had led thousands to march on Bloody Sunday in January 1972. My father and twelve other men and boys had been shot dead that day, marching for the freedom of Ivor's da. And here we were, nine years later, the next generation, pitched against the same state.

That evening, after the canteen, Ivor lay on the top bunk, propped up on his elbow sipping his tea and smoking. The arched window behind him lay open flat on the sill, letting the heat and light of high summer into the cell. Both he and I lay in our jeans, bare-chested and barefoot.

'Did you ever use a Woodmaster?' he asked, puffing his smoke up towards the ceiling.

'I think I did once, on a camp.'

'That's what I used when I shot the cop; a Woodmaster with a telescopic sight. A single shot through the back of the head.'

Even at eighteen I was surprised at his candour, and silenced by the revelation that my cellmate had actually killed someone and was talking to me about the details.

'He had no chance at that range. They call the Woodmaster the elephant-killer, ye know. It's the hunter's favourite weapon for killing elephants in Africa.'

'Is that right, Ivor?' I asked, for I had never heard that before.

'Aye, it's some weapon, so it is. I couldn't miss at that distance. I knew the cops were behind the high fence searchin' for somethin', and when he crossed the gap in the corrugated sheeting, I walloped him in the back of the head.'

As he spoke, I wondered if I would have had the guts to pull the trigger in the way Ivor clearly had. And, while I reckon I could have done the deed, I both admired and felt slightly embarrassed by his nonchalant attitude as he bragged, lighting fag after fag, about the New Lodge Road and the IRA, out defending his streets against loyalist gunmen and the British Army.

Later, as we lay listening to the pop music on Downtown Radio, Ivor sat up in bed and said, 'I was a punk, ye know?', and I laughed because he didn't look like a punk rocker, more like a rocker into Status Quo or Led Zeppelin.

'I was the only punk in the New Lodge. I had blue hair spiked up like a Mohican.'

'Aye, dead on, Ivor!' I laughed, disbelieving him.

'I was! My spiky hair was the talk of the New Lodge and me ma and da didn't know what to do wi' me. They even brought the priest round to the house, but I ran out the back door in me studded leather jacket, blue spiky hair and pins in me nose!'

'Jesus, Ivor, you're a wile man.'

'Stiff Little Fingers. We used to go mad to "Alternative Ulster"; the best openin' riff of any punk song in the world. Even better than the Sex Pistols with their "Anarchy in the UK" shite. But my favourite band are The Nipple Erectors,' he smiled in my direction, testing me, for he knew I still didn't fully believe him.

'The Nipple Erectors, my hole!' I laughed. 'You're takin' the hand outa me now!'

'No, I'm not, Dutchie. It's true; even The Nipple Erectors. It's all true. I *was* a punk!'

'So you're in here for killin' a cop and now you tell me you were a punk rocker?'

'Yes! But nobody says punk rocker, by the way. It's punks; we were just called punks. We used to hang out at the subway near Great Victoria Street. The punks all gathered there from all over Belfast. Prod and Catholic punks all hung out and went to the Pound Club together.'

'And The Nipple Erectors? The fuckin' Nipple Erectors?'

'Aye, their lead singer is a boy called Shane MacGowan. He's brilliant, so he is. He's mad, so he is. He just doesn't care, so he doesn't,' he said, smiling down at me blue-eyed from the top bunk, while I smiled back trying to imagine his shoulder-length black hair, now neatly parted in the middle, in his former blue Mohican spiked haircut.

A day or two later, as I walked around the yard, I was called to one side by Pete Ryan, the wing intelligence officer.

'I have something to tell you and I want you to keep it to yourself. Can I trust you?'

'Aye, ye can.'

'The young cub Grogan from the New Lodge. He's a bit vulnerable and a bit of a Walter.'

'What do you mean by that?'

'Well, he signed for a killing that he's completely innocent of.'

'What? He's innocent?' I asked, my jaw dropping.

'In more ways than one, I'd say.'

'He signed for killin' a cop that he didn't kill?'

'That's the story. My interest in this is that he's highly vulnerable, and the Branchmen in Castlereagh have turned his head into him believing that he really did kill the cop.'

'Jesus Christ! He told me the whole story the other night about using a Woodmaster with a telescopic sight. I believed every word!'

'I know. He told me that as well, but the information from outside is that he had nothing at all to do with it. He wouldn't know a Woodmaster from a ray-gun!'

'God of almighty! So you're tellin' me that the two people I've shared a cell with so far are both completely innocent?'

'That's it in a nutshell. Can you keep an eye on him – make sure he's OK and let me know if anything happens?'

'I'm not sure what ye mean, but aye, OK.'

A few days later, Pete stood at his cell door across the landing from me as we slopped out. Slopping out was the process of emptying your pisspot and cleaning your cell. Early morning saw a procession of prisoners carting their pots up the landing to empty and wash them. On my way back, Pete called me over and asked with a broad smile, 'All OK wi' young Ivor, then?' Ivor was returning behind me, pisspot in hand.

'Aye, he's repeated the story a few times,' I whispered, slowly shaking my head, 'and added more detail each time. God love 'im.'

'Good man,' said Pete as the screw called for me to move on.

Later that morning, Pete Ryan and the whole of the M60 Gang, three of whom were on C Wing, shot their way out of the prison as they were being taken to visits with their solicitors, and blasted their way across Crumlin Road under fire from the British Army guards in the look-out posts, before disappearing in cars speeding into Belfast's republican strongholds. The escape was a huge boost for morale at the time, as three more prisoners had by that stage followed Bobby Sands to their deaths in the H-Blocks: Francis Hughes from Bellaghy in South Derry, Raymond McCreesh from Camlough in South Armagh, and Patsy O'Hara from Derry city.

Over the next few days, Ivor continued to talk about his imaginary IRA career in the New Lodge and the killing of the RUC man. But I had little time to properly digest the news about his innocence and Pete Ryan's dramatic escape, as soon afterwards in popped a new arrival. Gerry Boy, as he was known, stood where Ivor and I had stood beside the bed, at the end of one journey and the beginning of a new one, with the cell, the yard, the court and visits being the sum limitations of the new existence. Gerry Boy was a rioter from a small rural town.

The Crum was full of rioters by this stage, coming in from almost every previously unheard-of townland, village, town and neighbourhood, where angry insurrection fired the air at the death of each man on hunger strike. Boys from Swatragh, Loughmacrory, Loughgiel, Kilrea, The Shambles, Tattyreagh and Castlewellan came in their droves, increasing the average cell occupation from two to three. Most took the dramatic change of life in their stride. However, one broad and tall lump of a fella sat with his dark head in his hands for thirty minutes at the powder-blue canteen table before someone went to his aid. I could see the fella look and speak through his fingers until he was eventually coaxed to rest his hands on the table. He was in shock. His whole life was destroyed as far as he was concerned. He got out on bail two days later.

The obvious sense of compassion towards those in greater need didn't put a halt to the ongoing shenanigans in the yard on a daily basis, though. The jokers had their hands full, with C Wing resembling a nudist camp with so many young men sprinting naked in pursuit of their clothes! You could tell the cut of the farmers as their faces, necks and arms were bronzed in contrast to the rest of their exposed, pearly-white bodies and legs.

Gerry Boy was twenty, a full two years older than me, had a page-boy cut of shiny brown hair, a round smiling face and was slightly chubby, whereas both Ivor and I belonged to the stick-insect family. As soon as we had the newcomer seated on the bottom bunk with his mug of cordial and custard creams, I was called out on a visit. My younger brother, Paul, and Benny McLaughlin had come up to see me. Paul was looking splendid in all of my new clothes, including my brown duffel coat and Dr. Marten boots, and Benny was almost ecstatic that I was sharing a cell with a punk rocker. He confirmed that there was indeed a band called The Nipple Erectors, and I was relieved that there was at least some truth in Ivor's story, even if it was only about punk rock!

On my return to the wing and out to the yard, it immediately became clear that Ivor hadn't passed on the friendly warning about the Sinn Féin doctor, as Gerry Boy and his two co-accused companions were standing there naked, clothes and shoes strewn about the roof of the shed, and laughter was rising decibel by decibel as the whole yard giggled like schoolboys or guffawed like cowboys at their discomfort. All three eventually took their humiliation well and simply fell in to the triangular walk, glad that their naked embarrassment was over. The event became known in the history of C Wing as 'The Day that Glit, Smurf and Jap Doctored Three in the One Go'.

Nakedness returned that night as the three of us lay in our beds in the darkened cell. Gerry Boy told us that he was married and he and his wife had the most fantastic sex life. I, being only eighteen, and therefore not having had much of a sex life, was all ears. I knew what all the parts were for and where they were supposed to fit. But this was almost purely theoretical. I had never even put the words 'fantastic' and 'sex' and 'life' together in the one sentence! I reckoned Ivor, with one summer less than me, didn't have much to go on either. He was all ears too.

In prison your sex life is by and large your own business, requiring (if you're sharing a cell, which was normal in 1981) darkness, the dead of night, discretion and a vivid imagination. Discretion, however, was not always the order of the day as I found out, almost to my horror, from Tommy on one of our tunnelled visits across to court. A friend was sharing a cell with another slightly older man of twenty.

'Every time the door closes, Dutchie, he's fuckin' at it!' Tommy grinned and then laughed out loud.

'You mean, pullin' his wire?' I asked, almost laughing too, like schoolboys.

'I swear to fuck, Dutchie. Every time the door shuts behind them yer man has the blanket over the head and the bed shakin' like the clappers.'

'And what does yer mucker do?'

'What the fuck can he do? He said he just has to pretend it's not happening, hiding himself behind a newspaper or a book or somethin'.'

'Jesus Christ, Tommy. That must be really cat for him.'

'Wan day he counted the blanket routine six times!' said Tommy, shaking his head.

'Six times in the wan day! He'd need to watch he wouldn't pull himself into a coma!'

'I know!' giggled Tommy, 'and that was only in the day-time! But it's no joke all the same. Me mucker's nerves are wrecked sometimes before goin' back to the cell wi' yer man. Spillin' tea out of his mug and everything.'

The more we pitied his plight, the more we cackled, while at the same time trying not to let the screws overhear the conversation.

'You're right there, Tommy. It's all right for a laugh, but it's no joke!'

'Six times a day, Dutchie. Six fuckin' times!'

'The dirty hoor!' I concluded, nonetheless secretly ad-miring the stamina of this notorious wanker.

In our own cell, Gerry Boy, the older man of twenty, talked as we two teenagers listened happily in silence, conjuring images of writhing figures as they did it on the sofa, over the arm of the sofa and over the back of the sofa. They were at it in the hall with the light off, and her wearing suspenders and stockings, and they were at it on the stairs on the way to the bedroom, pausing briefly to go at it again against the banister on the landing. He got a loan of his brother's car and drove to a lake where they did it on the front seat and in the back seat, before going into the woods with a blanket where they did it again.

'Jesus, but she's mad for the stockin's and suspenders, boys,' said Gerry Boy as he neared the end of another epic and highly graphic tale, the finale to which I was glad of as I feared the onset of a sex-induced fit, this time in Ivor. And so, for many nights afterwards, Ivor, for the dirty brute that he was, thankfully asked Gerry Boy to tell us another story about the wife and her suspender belt. Gerry Boy was only too happy to oblige.

Gerry Boy, it turned out, was not only highly sexed and highly talkative about it, he was also a disco-dancer. Downtown Radio broadcast a live disco from a club in Lisburn every Saturday night with DJ John Paul. John Paul styled his voice somewhat on Tony Blackburn, the BBC Radio 1 DJ, but with an American twang thrown in for added effect. He also spoke too close to his microphone and all you heard was an impossibly confusing accent with the odd word from a song title or artist converted into the sound of a fart or a burp midway.

When John Paul introduced 'Making Your Mind Up' by Bucks Fizz as 'Makin' You Minzap by Bucksh Fushz', helped by two tipsy teenagers who giggled loudly into his microphone, Gerry Boy jumped up from the bottom bunk in his boxer shorts and T-shirt and began spinning around and swinging his arms about.

'Watch where yer swinging them mitts! Ye'll be puttin' me eye out!' cried Ivor from the top bunk, as Gerry Boy continued, eyes closed and apparently gliding and swivelling his way in perfect step to the Euro-clang of Britain's successful entry to that year's Eurovision Song Contest. When it was over he stayed on his feet and Ivor said, 'You're not waitin' for another shite disco song, are ye?'

'Fuckin' right I am,' Gerry Boy puffed, his chest heaving and feet tapping.

'Bucks Fizz! Bucks fuckin' Fizz!' cried Ivor with his hands over his face, shaking his head in mock derision. And Gerry Boy laughed and winked at him, his rounded body springing lightly on his feet, waiting for the return of the disco beat. And sure enough, on came 'Funkytown' by none other than 'Lippsh Enk' according to John Paul, and Gerry Boy began another dance of dangerous-looking swivels and twirls, almost falling into the table, while Ivor groaned and writhed in feigned agony on the top bunk. But Gerry Boy could fair bop it out, sir.

'I can nearly taste the Harvey Wallbanger, so I can,'

grinned the boogieing Gerry Boy, his mop of page-boy hair bouncing and flopping on his sweaty head. 'What did you drink, Dutchie?' he asked without breaking his step.

I was almost tasting the Harp lager, feeling its sweet coolness as I lay on the single bed enjoying the live entertainment, when the flap opened on the door revealing a pair of screw's eyes. He stood on longer than the usual cursory check and then said, 'Are you trying to dance yerself dizzy, or somethin'?'

Gerry Boy continued his merry dance, giving the screw the thumbs up as he undertook an amazing disco equivalent of the triple Salchow ice-skating move on the tiny dance floor, emitting a quick 'Holy fuck!' before crashing loudly into Ivor's top bunk and flopping his fat hole on the hard stone floor!

'Stay down, ye fuckin' dickhead!' laughed the screw, before snapping the flap closed with a crack, laughing out loud as he walked away. 'Dickhead in Cell 5!' he called down the landing.

Gerry Boy retired to bed, a bit shaky after his graceless tumble, while the disco rumbled on but had somehow lost its funky appeal. We all lay without a word, our thoughts filled with some musical place on the outside, full of women. Ivor reached over and turned the radio down.

'What d'ye think ye'll get, Ivor?' asked Gerry Boy.

'Life.'

'What does that mean?'

'Nobody knows yet. Could be twenty years.'

'Twenty years! How d'ye just lie there facing twenty years?'

'What d'ye want me to do?'

'Ye must regret it all now, do ye?'

'Regret what, Gerry Boy?'

'Shootin' the cop.'

Ivor hesitated, then, 'Fuck 'im. Black enamel bastard!'

'How can ye say that about killin' another human being?'

'I said, "Fuck 'im." Fuck 'im and all belonging to 'im. Did ye not hear me?' said Ivor with anger, peering down towards Gerry Boy's bunk.

Just then, a voice from the cell window above us called, 'Gerry Boy! Are ye there?'

'Who's that?' I asked.

'Oh, it's Seany from up above on the Twos,' said Gerry Boy climbing up on Ivor's bunk. 'He said he's some hot steak for us and that he'd swing it down.' Ivor looked at me and I looked back at Ivor.

'Gerry Boy,' I said, 'he's taking the –'

'Is that you, Seany?' called Gerry Boy through the open window.

'It is, Gerry Boy. I've that steak for ye heated on the pipe! Ye ready?'

'Aye, go ahead Seany, lower away!' said Gerry Boy, turning to us and rubbing his hands in glee.

'Gerry Boy, listen! He's taking the hand –' Again I tried to stop him.

But it was too late. Gerry Boy had his head at the bars and the hand out waiting for his parcel of hot steak being lowered to him on a string of torn white sheet from the cell above. It came in a brown parcel bag and Gerry Boy grabbed it at the window and in through the bars.

'Hi, thanks, Seany, yer a star!' he called. 'Did one of yous boys fart?' he asked in his next breath, putting a hand to his mouth for cover.

'No bother, Gerry Boy!' called Seany.

'Gerry Boy! For fuck's sake will ye not list–?' I implored.

'Fuck! One of yous is hummin'!' said Gerry Boy, hopping excitedly down from the top bunk to the floor, the bed-frame trembling in his wake. 'Hot steak just off the pipe, boys!' he said as he opened the brown parcel bag on the table.

'Aw fuck! Aw fuck! The dirty bastard!' he cried, pulling his face away, and then looking in astonishment at me and then Ivor.

'He's a dirty bastard!' he repeated, as if we didn't believe him the first time.

Ivor was writhing on the bed in convulsions.

'I did try to warn ye!' I squealed as the foul particulates polluted the air in the cell. It's hard to squeal with laughter as you're breathing in such a stinking hum in huge gulps, but we convulsed at the sight of Gerry Boy in his shorts and T-shirt standing with the brown bag in one hand, his mouth open and the other hand covering it to keep the smell out!

'What the fuck am I gonna do with it?' he cried in disgust, holding the offending article, now crumpled closed again, at arm's length.

'Get it off the table! The fuckin' custard creams'll be contaminated!' I squealed through my fingers and tears of laughter.

'Fuck it out the winda!' cried Ivor through his cupped hands.

'Fuck it out the winda?' cried Gerry Boy in disbelief. 'Fuck it out the winda?'

'What? Are ye gonna keep it under yer pilla' 'til the morning?' squealed Ivor.

'Throw it out the fuckin' winda, Gerry Boy! For fuck's sake!' I muffled loudly from behind my protective pillow.

Gerry Boy jumped up on Ivor's bunk, stuck the parcel out through the bars and flipped it away to crash-land in the yard.

'Is that you, Gerry Boy?' called Seany from the cell above.

'Fuck off, Seany, ya dirty bastard!'

We laughed ourselves to sleep under the sheets as it took hours for the smell to clear.

***

The next morning Gerry Boy received a letter from his lovely wife, who was due to visit him the following day. He seemed anxious, hardly speaking to either Ivor or me. He puffed and sighed in his bunk, reading the letter over and over again, folding it, sliding it back into its envelope and then dropping it lightly on the floor. Ivor caught my eye from the top bunk and I gave him a knowing look back. Gerry Boy's sighs could only be about one thing: his sexy wife who was mad for the suspender belts and stockings. Something was wrong. He usually read out a line or two alluding to their 'fantastic sex life'. Not this time. Not a word.

'Ye OK, Gerry Boy?' I asked, knowing that he wasn't at all. Ivor's eyes grew large and round at my questioning.

'It's the wife. She says she's very lonely,' he replied, stretching down to pick the envelope up from the floor.

'Sure she's bound to be lonely if you're not about,' I advised.

'I know, I know,' he sighed, rustling the pages in his lap. 'She's comin' up tomorrow to visit me but she's saying it'll be the last for a while. That she needs a break.'

Ivor and I exchanged looks again as the cell fell silent except for Gerry Boy's deep sighs and the turning of pages as we retreated into our novels. We were glad to get to the canteen later to break the tension.

The following morning Gerry Boy returned from his visit, sat down on the edge of his bunk and put his face into his hands. It was hard to tell if he was crying or if he just wanted a bit of darkness or some heat from his hands. Every minute or so he'd open a hole in his hands to exhale loudly and breathe in new air before closing it again. And there he sat while Ivor and I went out to the yard, Ivor patting him on the shoulder as he jumped down from the top bunk.

'No yard for you, McLaverty?' asked the screw holding the door.

Gerry Boy didn't respond.

'Naw, he's a bit under the weather, so he is,' I said and the screw gently closed the door.

'The wife's finished wi' me,' said Gerry Boy as we sat down after the yard. He hadn't moved. His eyes red and tearful, his dark-brown hair matted to his forehead.

'I thought she was only takin' a wee break from visits?' I asked.

'She met someone at a disco. She said she was only letting me down gently in the letter.'

'Right. I see,' I said.

'Holy fuck. I'm for bail in the morning and the solicitor thinks I'm gonna get out! You'd think she woulda held on for another while,' he said with another deep sigh.

The next day Gerry Boy was gone from our lives. We wished him the best of luck as he left for court, as we knew he wouldn't be back. Rioters almost always got bail within a few weeks. Later we gathered his clothes, photos and letters in a brown parcel bag to hand to the screw. It was just Ivor and me again, all the worse without the sexy stories, the disco-dancing and the craic. The bottom bunk lay empty.

'Lucky bastard,' said Ivor as we lay over lunchtime, a quiet time in prison.

'Well, he was only in for rioting. They could hardly keep 'im in for that long when they have boys like us to keep!'

'I suppose you're right!' laughed Ivor.

'Have you a visit the day?' I asked, noticing him dressed in his best gear.

'Aye, me mother and sister are comin' up, so they are. I can't wait to see them,' said Ivor, rubbing his hands in anticipation.

'You're goin' out there like Lipton's dummy,' I said, meaning how well attired he was.

'Lipton's what?' he asked.

'Doesn't matter; it's a Derry thing. You're lookin' well, that's all,' I replied.

'Aye, like your German buns; where in under Jesus did

ye's get German buns outa?' he smiled.

'A few years in Derry would put a bit of culture on ye, ye boy ye!'

'German buns? German buns? They're bloody Paris buns, for Jesus' sake!' he laughed.

'I'd like to see the girl's face if you walked into McDaid's Bakery and asked for two Paris buns. She'd probably hand ye two cream tarts or somethin'!'

Ivor jumped up when our door opened, still rambling on about German buns and Derry wans as he left to meet his family. He returned an hour later and lay quiet with his eyes closed on the top bunk still wearing the good clothes: a cherry-red Fred Perry shirt and his best jeans.

'How was your visit, Ivor?'

'Aye, it was great, so it was. The craic was great. Piggy and Fra were out too and they were gulderin' back and forward wi' me mammy.'

'That Piggy's a wile man,' I smiled.

'Never a dull moment wi' him, so there's not,' said Ivor. 'Salt of the earth.'

'Your ma OK, then?' I asked.

'Aye, she's grand.'

Ivor dozed while I half-read and half-dozed. After tea-time on the wing was a quiet time, with hardly a sound apart from a low whisper in the corridor or the light jangle of keys. This was a reflective time, for reading or listening to music down low. Or just staring up at the brickwork on the ceiling wondering what they'd had for their tea at home, or how the garden was. I loved the photo on the cork board of me ma,

Glenn and Colleen beaming sunny smiles into the camera from our front door.

'A woman has been knocked down and killed after a car mounted the footpath in Belfast's Carlisle Circus,' the newsreader announced on Downtown Radio News at five o'clock. Ivor opened his eyes, sat straight up, looked down at the transistor radio on the table and held his stare until all the news and weather had been dispatched. He then glanced at me looking at him.

'Did ye hear that?' he asked.

'What?'

'A woman was knocked down in Carlisle Circus.'

'And?'

'She … Ach, nothin',' he said, lying down again, this time with his eyes open. Silence followed. I observed him over my book as he lay still, lighting roll-up after roll-up from his snout tin, the smoke cascading in furls down the length of his body from his nostrils, dissolving in rolls into the fresh air from the open window above. Between each roll-up Ivor lay with eyes closed, making not a sound, but I knew he wasn't sleeping. While Gerry Boy had been in residence in our cell I hadn't had the chance to talk to him about his murder charge, and after Pete Ryan had asked me keep an eye out for him, I felt I couldn't raise the question of his innocence until Ivor himself felt able to discuss it with me. In recent weeks, however, he had hardly mentioned his charge, never mind the detail that he had killed the RUC man with a sniping rifle.

As 5.30 p.m. drew near, Ivor reached down to turn the

sound up for the news again. 'A woman has been killed after a car mounted the pavement in Belfast's Carlisle Circus. Police have not yet released her name. The accident is causing serious traffic disruption in north Belfast.'

Ivor repeated his movements of five o'clock, lying back again on the mattress, eyes fixed to the ceiling and with one arm behind his head as he smoked his roll-ups. Silence followed each deeply puffed cigarette. It was a heavier, thicker silence this time, though, full of foreboding. It allowed me to clearly hear the opening of metal grilles and the shuffle of feet approaching the cell door. And whispered voices. Then the clink of keys and the heavy lock turning in the door of Cell 5.

As the door swung slowly open onto the wing, there stood a white-shirted Principal Officer (PO) and a white-collared priest, whose nickname was the only name I had for him – Captain Black, a much-hated figure in Crumlin Road Prison, him red-eyed, smelling of drink and wringing his pasty hands. 'Can we see you for a minute, young Doherty?' said the PO, more of a statement than a question. Ivor sat bolt upright and swung his feet over the edge of the bunk, facing the doorway. This had never happened before.

'What's up?' I asked as I stood on the wing with the cell door tilled behind me.

'We have some very bad news for young Grogan,' whispered the tall and burly PO. 'His mother has been killed in a traffic accident just down the road from the prison.'

'Dear Jesus, Mary and Saint Joseph,' I heard myself say, repeating the holy mantra of my parents and grandparents.

'We have to go in to break the news to him,' said the PO. 'You'll have to keep an eye on him till we arrange a visit with his family in the morning. Is that OK?'

'OK,' was all I could say, hardly able to believe it myself. To be frank, you have little choice but to be mindful of your cellmate in the best of times when living in such close quarters. This was different, though. Hugely different. This was the death of Ivor's mother. Where would I even start? As the priest and the PO entered Cell 5 I stood alone on the empty wing with only one blue-shirted screw standing away at the far end. Ivor had feared it was his ma as soon as he heard the first news report. He knew the path she took heading for their home in the New Lodge. He had walked it with her many a day as a child to visit his father in the same prison.

'Do your best with him, young Doherty,' said the PO when they came out. 'We're arranging a visit first thing to-morrow morning.' And with that, I walked back into the cell, finding Ivor sitting on the edge of my bed, his light-blue eyes staring at the wall as the cell door bolted smoothly behind me.

'Are ye all right, Ivor?' I said, sitting down on the bed, a slight gap between us. He didn't answer.

'I'm wile sorry about yer mammy, so I am.' Silence.

'D'ye want me to get ye a cup o' tae?' Silence.

'Is there anything ye want me to get ye, Ivor?' Silence.

Both of us sat quiet. I stared at the wall in front of me too, my mind racing to figure out what I should say or do. The silence continued, broken only by doors opening in the wing.

And then: 'Me mammy's dead, Dutchie. Me wee mammy's dead,' he said, holding his stare.

'I'm wile sorry, Ivor. I really am ... D'ye want a Regal?'

'Aye, gimme one,' he sighed. 'I'm browned off smoking them shite rollies.'

I pulled two from the twenty box, gave him one and then sparked the lighter. Both of us dragged the smoke into our lungs and exhaled towards the wall. Silence. Ivor pulled deeply on the fag. Great long drags of more than five seconds, before freeing the smoke like a geyser over the next three breaths from his mouth and nose.

'Me mammy's dead, Dutchie. Me wee mammy's dead.'

'I know, Ivor, I know,' I said, placing an awkward hand on his shoulder for a moment.

'What am I gonna do? I'm stuck in here, fuckin' no good to nobody.'

'I'll help you, Ivor. I'll be here to help,' I said, fully realising the serious limitations of my words.

'But what can *you* do; me mammy's dead. Some fucker killed her with his car. There's nothin' *you* can do, is there?' he said, an angry challenge in his words.

There is fuck all I can do, I thought, *but say what I'm saying and be here to say it.* The pair of us sat in silent contemplation for a while until Ivor got up and lay on the top bunk on his back, eyes fixed to the ceiling. Long and loud sighs emitted every few minutes into the heavy, smoky air of the cell, some almost quivering to a cry. His eyes pooled tears, overflowing now and again in rivulets down the side of his face, soaking his long locks of jet-black hair. But he didn't cry out, or buckle or contort in the agony of his sudden loss. Thus he lay for a long time, not moving or taking me on, except to light another Regal, the box of which I'd pressed into his sorry hands.

'Ye want a wee cup o' tae, Ivor?' I said, probing gently into the thick silence.

'The PO said I could see the MO if I needed to,' he replied, still staring at the ceiling.

'What for?'

'What d'ye call that stuff? Argackil or something.'

'Argackil? Is that the red stuff ye see the line of crims queuein' for in the mornin'?' The dispensing of drugs was an open affair carried out by the MO several times a day on the wing. The deep crimson medication was served in small, clear plastic cups, thrown back like a straight Jameson, delivering the taker to a parallel reality. Or so word had it.

'I don't know. Me head's fucked.'

'Sure I'll press the buzzer and get ye a wee cuppa, eh? The screw'll let me out.'

'Aye, that'll do,' said Ivor.

The screw lifted the flap and I told him through the gap of the door that Ivor needed a cup of tea. He let me out to fill two plastic mugs from the urn in the servery. As we sat in silence again, with Ivor slurping his tea and dragging on a Regal, he seemed to relax, resting his back against the wall, though clearly lost in thought. He even started smiling and giggling to himself as he struck a pleasant memory.

'What are ye laughing at?'

'Me ma at me, and me a punk with me blue Mohican head o' hair,' he smiled. 'Ye shoulda seen her face the first day I walked into the living room. "Hello Ma, hello Da!" I said as the two of them sat watching *Scene Around Six*. Their chins nearly hit the floor! Me wee sister was gigglin' into her homework books on the sofa!'

'God, it must've been a shock for them, all right.'

'Me and me blue spiky hair!' he laughed into his mug, but then stopped himself and fell quiet again. As the night wore on I drifted in and out of sleep, fully clothed. When I woke I would find Ivor sitting up in bed, lying on his back or pacing the short strip from his bed to the door. The screw lifted the flap more than usual, turning on the light to check on Ivor. Once when I woke, Ivor was sitting up on his bunk smoking and began giggling when he saw I was awake. It was a warm summer night and Ivor had taken his red shirt off, revealing his skinny white torso, haloed by the orange glow of the security lights on the high walls outside.

'You OK, Ivor?'

He didn't answer but sat staring at the door smiling between drags on his fag.

'Are ye all right, Ivor?' I repeated, but he just sat there smiling to himself, the smoke misting the orange glow from the open window.

'Me head's fried, Dutchie. Me head's fried,' he said after a long silence.

'Can I get ye anything?'

'I need somethin' for me head. The PO said I could get Argackil. What d'ye reckon, Dutchie?'

'It's up to you, Ivor. I don't like the sound of it, but … Does it not zonk ye outa yer head or somethin'?'

'I think that's the idea!' he laughed. 'Me head's in a mess. I keep hearin' the words from "Alternative Ulster" when I lie down and close me eyes. An alternative Ulster! An alternative Ulster!' He shook his head forward to the words, as if at a concert, his hair falling forward.

'Yer not doin' too bad then. It's a great song,' I joked.

'I know, but it's every time, Dutchie. I think I'm goin' mad in the head. An alternative fuckin' Ulster!' he repeated, shaking his head again.

'I'd be careful wi' the Argackil if I was you, Ivor.'

'I need somethin' to slow me head down. It's racing all over the place.'

'Take another wee Regal, sure.'

'I've them nearly all smoked on ye,' he said, waving the navy blue and white box with the gold royal seal.

'That's OK, Ivor; you smoke away at them.'

The next time I opened my eyes the cell window was a rectangle of sky blue and the pigeons were cooing early in the yard. Otherwise the world was silent. Ivor lay in the shadows of the bottom bunk, from where Gerry Boy had opened our eyes to his sex life, night after night. I jumped up on Ivor's top bunk to take in the pleasures of the morning from the window. Pigeons, crows and seagulls winged across the yard, the gulls flapping and chasing the smaller birds. A small horde of mice scattered along the wall of B Wing behind the toilets. I never knew that mice could climb walls, but there was not a bother on them, straight up the dark grey stonework to their wee holes and straight down again. Dozens of them. Ivor joined me. Two faces at the window.

Dark rings moated his tired and pained blue eyes. Turmoil simmered below the skin and bone of the brave face he had put on.

'That's where I live; down that way,' he pointed to somewhere in the middle distance to our right and over the wall topped with coiled barbed wire. 'That's the New Lodge.'

'Did ye see the mice?' I pointed over towards the toilets.

'Fuck, look at that; they're scootin' right up past the windas!' he laughed.

'But they don't go in; I've been watching them. They just run past.' We stared out the window for a while in silence, the mice racing and darting around like sugared-up children in a playground.

'Wee Ellen's dead, Dutchie,' said Ivor, gazing down on the grey yard.

'I'm really sorry, Ivor. It must be terrible for ye.' I paused. 'Ye know, my ma's called Ellen as well? Ellen Teresa; me granda calls her by her full title but everyone else just calls her Eileen.'

'Ellen Teresa,' Ivor repeated. 'Ellen Teresa Doherty.'

'That's her. Quigley was her own name before she married me da. We call her The Big E, but she's only five foot two.'

'What time d'ye reckon it is?' asked Ivor.

'I'd say about five.'

'I might lie down to see if I can get an hour's kip.'

Both of us awoke to the sound of screws coming onto the wing for the morning shift. The PO would be doing his rounds shortly, the screw scribbling down the lists of requests from each prisoner such as a letter, making an appointment with the doctor or a request to see the governor. You can hear them coming from the adjacent cells and you must be up and dressed for them to accept your request. Ivor jumped up as our door opened to reveal the white-and-blue-shirted pair.

'Any requests?' said the PO.

'I need to see the doctor,' said Ivor, and the screw wrote this down on his chart. The door closed and Ivor sat on the edge of my bed.

'I'm goin' for the Argackil, so I am,' he said, rubbing his weary face with both hands. 'I need somethin' to slow me head down; it's goin' a mile a minute, so it is.'

'You do what ye have to do, Ivor. Just be careful, won't ye?'

'Jesus, Dutchie, it's only Argackil ye know, not fuckin' heroin!' He laughed and so did I, but I was concerned about him and the effect it might have. As well as that, I'd be sharing a cell with someone zonked off their head on stuff! Not the best of prospects.

As we slopped out later in the morning, carrying our pisspots to the chamber, Fra and Piggy called to Ivor through the metal grille at the top of the steel stairs of the Twos. 'Are ye all right, Ivor? Can we get ye anything? Dutchie'll look after ye and sure we'll see ye in the yard later.'

Ivor stood, pisspot in hand, calling up to them that indeed he was OK and that he had an emergency visit in a wee while. Ivor lay on his bunk as I cleaned the cell, brushing and mopping the floor till the cell stank with disinfectant. That green tub of disinfectant was the only thing that kept the cockroaches in check, especially if you poured it in the groove under the heating pipe, where they often roamed from cell to cell in the dead of night.

'The doctor wants to see you, Ivor,' said the screw behind me as I mopped the floor, and Ivor had to tiptoe over the wet surface. Placing the mop back in the metal bucket, I hopped back onto the bed to allow the floor to dry, while the screw slid the bucket with his foot up to the next cell before closing the door of Cell 5.

Ivor returned a short time later, climbing onto the top bunk where he laid his head on the bed pack and closed his eyes. Not a word was said. I watched him over my book, wondering if he was just tired with being up all night … or was he asleep because of what the doctor had given him? Or a combination of both?

'Ye OK, Ivor?'

I waited a few minutes more. 'Ivor, ye all right?'

He didn't budge. Like a corpse himself, he lay on his back with his hands folded on his belly. Not a sound. He was out cold, and breathing in a deep, deep repose. I watched his chest rise and fall in perfect and peaceful rhythm and thought about his ma, whom I had never met, now dead, and me own ma, widowed at twenty-nine with six children. Two Ellens. I wondered if they had been named after a film star of the early 1940s or something, but no name sprang to mind.

The screws began unlocking several cells around Cell 5. It was our turn for the yard this morning. They let prisoners out in batches to lessen the security risk of a wing takeover or a riot. The bolt shot in our door and the screw called 'Yards!' as

I rose to put on my shoes. Ivor didn't move. He hadn't heard a thing.

I decided to try to waken him in case he'd want to meet Piggy or Fra or any of the fellas from the New Lodge. 'Ivor, are ye coming out?' I called from the doorway. Nothing.

I walked the few steps to his bunk and put my hand on his shoulder. 'Hi, Ivor, ye want to come out to the yard?'

He stirred this time, slowly sat up, half-propped on an elbow, and squinted right into my face, like an old man searching for a familiar feature. His pale-blue eyes smiled lazily through a glaze and his mouth, I'm sure, wanted to follow but his bottom lip drooped helplessly to the one side, revealing several teeth. He lay back on the mattress, sighed deeply and closed his eyes.

Ivor Grogan, at seventeen, was gone; solid gone.

4

THE LONELY BANNA STRAND

In January 1982 Tommy Carlin and I were sentenced to eight years in jail. With the remission system, this meant we would serve around four years each. My father had been dead almost exactly ten years when I received the sentence. Ten years of his loss often created a distant vagueness and I sometimes had difficulty remembering how he looked and sounded, but the way in which he was executed and the callousness of the British government's disregard for justice remained fixed and stark in my mind.

I was now nineteen and one of the Young Prisoners in the YP wing in the H-Blocks of Long Kesh, to which I had been moved after an initial six weeks in H6. H6 was where all the blanketmen were ending up in the aftermath of the hunger strike and blanket protest. There were even a few from Hamilton Street: Thomas Starrs, whose older brother John, an IRA man, had been picked off and killed during an exchange with a British Army sniper in 1972, and others from the wider Brandywell and Bishop Street, such as Pius McNaught, Gerry Donnelly and Phil Nolan. They all looked incredibly young and clean for men who had spent the past four to six years in tiny cells pouring their pish out the doors and spreading cack on the walls. One morning at breakfast one of them told me that the worst of it, apart from the beatings and the abuse, was waking to the acrid smell of stale pish every morning of life. They all agreed that Bloody Sunday was instrumental in their decision to join the IRA.

'Ye see that red-haired screw on the gate?' Pius asked, nodding backwards. I looked towards a slightly built screw whose short, reddish hair battled an invasion of grey. I looked back at Pius. 'That's *An Capall*, The Horse; a brutal ignoramus of a man. He was also known in other blocks as The Red Rat.'

'I'll tell ye what type of a man he is,' said Starrsy, still known by his old Hamilton Street nickname. 'We were in H4 and someone had heard that the boys in H5 were getting jam wi' their bread. Someone in our wing made a request for jam. The following day the *Capall* came round the doors wi' the breakfast. "I hear ye's are lookin' for jam; here's yer fuckin' jam!" he said, plopping a spoonful of strawberry jam into the cornflakes and milk.'

'And the same day,' said Pius, taking his story back, 'he came round again wi' the dinner. "I hear ye's are mad about the strawberry jam in this block; here's more of the fuckin' stuff for ye!" he said, slopping more strawberry jam onto the spuds, meat and gravy, and him laughin' like a man possessed. A total ignoramus of a man! A real *fear dona*,' hissed Pius.

I knew from the Crum that *fear dona* meant a bad man and I could smell vengeance in the air.

'But then there was a big screw,' said Pius with a smile in his eyes, '"Big Hank" we called him. I'll never forget this, but one evening in 1979 he came in and played both sides of ELO's "Greatest Hits" on the record player. Every song he played, and ye could hear it all over the block. I stood at the door with me blanket around me so I could hear better. When "Mr Blue Sky" came on it was like a magical spell cast over the whole wing. God, it was great to hear! There wasn't a sound on the whole block. And when it was over, someone jumped up to the door and called: "Hi, Hank! Ye wouldn't have any of the Nolan Sisters on ye, would ye?" and the whole wing erupted in kinks of laughter!'

Most of the blanketmen had hardly seen a newspaper or a television screen since 1976 or 1977. They wore their hair long, down past the shoulders, parted in the middle in the mid-1970s style. Some even had flicks! Looking like the leftovers from a Bay City Rollers concert, they paraded the yard in bell-bottom flares, turned-up parallel Wrangler jeans and Gilbert jumpers, preserved in tagged brown bags in prison property since the day they were sentenced and had refused to wear a convict's uniform. They often spoke to each other in Irish in the yard, the canteen and when going to visits.

From the steel door to the concrete-barred window, the cell was seven and a half shod feet long and six and a half across – slightly more in stocking soles. The walls were a light cream colour, the door bottle-green, the same colour scheme as our house in Hamilton Street, freshly painted before the Battle of the Bogside but now demolished. The floor and the two parallel heating pipes at the rear shone with a black gloss. On my first night I discovered a name deeply gouged into the top heating pipe. I got down on my knees to read it.

Thomas McElwee. He had died on hunger strike the previous August and was buried in his native Bellaghy in South Derry. In my nineteen years I had never once been to South Derry and barely knew of the existence of Bellaghy or anywhere else in that area. I had been in Belfast only once, and that was in 1979. McElwee was only six years older than me. I ran my fingertips over the letters and into the rough-hewn gouges the dead man had left. *Did he scratch this out before he went on hunger strike? Or was he already on it? Was he afraid he'd be forgotten if he died?*

An H-Block is a self-contained prison within a prison. Each of the four arms and legs of the H is a wing, lettered A, B, C and D, with their own separate yards for walking, playing football and other games. The belt in the middle of the H is the administrative 'circle' where the screws, PO, MO and block security are lodged, controlling all movement between the wings and from outside the block. All the blocks were serviced by vans and lorries for food delivery and bin collection, and escorts for visits to the prison dentist and hospital.

If you were in A Wing you could see right to the end of B Wing, and if the steel door at the end was open the brightness rushed through the gap, bouncing off the glossy black floor and shiny bottle-green doors and brasses. Like a bright light at the end of the tunnel. Every wing was exactly the same. Showers, a single bath, toilets and sinks on your left as you came through the gated steel grille, the canteen on the right, accessed through another steel grille near where the screws usually gathered to take charge. Cell 1, next to the

THE LONELY BANNA STRAND

canteen, was for administration purposes, the numbers then continuing, ending with number 26, a cell built for four but not always occupied.

On my first night, after discovering Tom McElwee's name on the pipe, I lay back on the single bed looking around me. The cell was sparse and its walls were bare. The round, plastic-covered light on the concrete ceiling shone down on the four walls around me. I got up when I thought I could see vague scribbles on the wall opposite the bed. After studying under the poor light I could just about make out a series of pencilled verses scratched across the wall before realising that I was looking at the full eleven irregular verbs of the Irish language. I had begun to learn Irish in Crumlin Road from a Tyrone man. The words had been painted over, but it was a lazy, single-coat job with cheap emulsion.

The first one was the verb 'to be', written in full in past, present and future tenses, for example:

An raibh tú	Were you?
Bhí mé	I was
Ní raibh mé	I wasn't

This was followed by the verb 'to hear' in the same past, present and future forms:

Ar chuala tú	Did you hear?

Chuala mé	I heard
Níor chuala mé	I didn't hear

When I was learning Irish in the Crum, huddled in a corner of the canteen, competing with the noise of the TV, the pool table and the general craic, one of the other learners in the class couldn't say *chuala mé* (pronounced '*hula may*') in the singular form as his only previous reference to hula was the hula-hula skirt worn in Hawaii. So, when he tried to say *chuala mé* he would say '*Hula-hula mé*! ['I heard heard']! Or, '*Ar hula-hula tú* [Did you hear hear]?'

My only two prior encounters with Irish had both been in 1980. The first was with my girlfriend, Maire, as we lay on the beach in Buncrana picnicking on cheese baps and a carton of milk between us. It was the All-Ireland Fleadh Cheoil, and the sand was warm and pleasant from the sun.

'Does that say *banny*?' I asked, pointing to the carton of Donegal milk.

'No, it's *banya*,' said Maire, pronouncing the word *báinne* properly in her fine Thornhill College accent.

The second encounter was just before the first hunger strike in October 1980, when someone had written a slogan on a wall in Leafair Park, not far from Brookdale. *SCRIOS NA BLOCANNA H!* it said in large yellow letters. 'Smash H-Block!' it meant, as we learned afterwards, though no one could pronounce it.

During my time in H6 I got a 'Dear John' from Maire. I knew before I opened the already censored letter what I was about to read. I didn't expect her to wait until March 1985, the earliest I could be released from prison. It was never mentioned but sort of understood between us that she would go her own way after me being sentenced. I was now nineteen and single. I kept her photos for a month or two, as they were cute, but mindfully left them under my bed pack of white sheets and brown and grey blankets when I was later moved to the YP wing along with a few others, including Tommy, Glit and Smurf.

'YPs my arse!' the older prisoners would exclaim when looking across the grilles between the wings or meeting us at mass. 'Look at the size of that brute! He must be forty!' referring to Glit, who was tall and broad with black hair, a black moustache and toothed like Freddy Mercury.

In the Kesh even the heathens went to mass. There were many of them and numbers were growing as a result of the stance of the Catholic Church during the hunger strike. Mass was held in the canteen, and prisoners from other wings were allowed to cross over to attend. For most, it was about meeting up with friends and, in some instances, family to catch up on the *scéal* from inside and out. The heathens amassed at the back of the canteen, maintaining a whispered hum of news and events. Many whispered in Irish and spoke it in the Belfast vernacular. When mass ended, the throng erupted in a gabble of voices let loose between the hard concrete walls, and the screws had to shout to indicate that mass was over and to get ready to go back to the wings.

One spring morning, as I waited at the grille to be taken on a visit, looking casually from the YP wing, then in H3, up the long, glossy corridor of the opposite wing at the sunshine pouring through the open door from the yard at the top, I saw a tall, brown-haired man emerge shakily from his cell, gripping the door posts, and turn in my direction. I was transfixed as he clumped one foot out, followed heavily by the other, arms out and fingers stiff to steady his trembling frame. His head falling onto his shoulder and his eyes rolling in his head, he shuffled inch by inch up the wing and was let into the canteen by the attendant screw, who closed the grille gently behind him. This was Laurence McKeown, who had spent seventy days on hunger strike up to September 1981 when, on his lapsing into a coma only hours from death, his mother had given the medical authorities the go-ahead to provide life-saving nourishment.

The contemplation of death, either taking someone else's life, or taking your own, was a constant revolving door of questions and conundrums for me in 1981 and 1982. Ever since Ivor had told me of how he had blasted the RUC man to death, the subsequent farce of his claim aside, I had asked myself could I kill, or could I have killed? The answer, of course, is that I had no real way of telling. Now, since I discovered Tom McElwee's scratched name and witnessed a former hunger striker stagger and sway slowly back to life from near death, I silently contemplated what type of person was I in all of this? Was I cut out for life as an IRA man? Could I starve myself to death for my friends and comrades? For principles? Was there something special in a man who could do this? Or were these people just like me, full of doubt and not really knowing until they got there?

The YP wing was a mixed wing. 'Mixing' in prison terms meant there were loyalists and some criminals on the same wing. Integration was the formal policy of the Northern Ireland Office (NIO) and carried out by the prison authorities. It was to prove a highly dangerous and ultimately unworkable policy. Whereas community and society on the outside were largely segregated and did not mix, the NIO in their wisdom felt that integrating prisoners who belonged to organisations established on the one hand to annihilate and on the other to prop up the state of Northern Ireland was a good and sensible thing. And so we young republicans found ourselves living cheek by jowl with young loyalists, one of whom had rather thoughtfully remembered to drop a concrete slab on the head of the Catholic man he had just shot. A lifer, he was a big, empty-headed galoot who loved himself and preened each day in the mirror in the ablution area at the top of the wing. During exercise periods, we walked around the yard in the Crum at different times on alternate days, but here in the Kesh we stuck to our own in groups, but were often followed by this man at the head of a pack, and we could hear him cocking his air-machine-gun before 'mowing us down' from behind. The 'bullets' flipped from his blubbery mouth as his confederates giggled under their chins. They were in the majority on the YP wing at the time, and word from above was not to antagonise them. This was to change, however, over the months ahead. Tension would grow in many blocks as loyalists became the minorities, a status they were unused to in life.

Inky was an INLA man from the Falls Road in Belfast serving twenty years. For a fella his age he spoke with great authority on the subject of revolutionary warfare on the streets of Belfast, Saigon, Havana and Managua. He was also into pop music; Kid Creole and the Coconuts were among his favourites. He was able to recite 'Stool Pigeon' at whim and dance the 'arse-dance' of the Coconuts while belting out verbatim the words to 'Annie, I'm Not Your Daddy', twirling round, hands clasped high above his smiling face with its slightly bulbous nose. He had a dark moustache and kept his sideburns half-mast down his cheeks. He was for getting ripped into the loyalists at any time, often staring them out as they passed on the wing or in the canteen, even the lifer, until they were cowed and looked the other way. Word had it that Inky could fair handle himself.

Danny McGarrigle was from Strabane and was also doing twenty years, for attempting to kill a member of the UDR. Of course, like many Strabane men, he had been arrested and had signed a statement for the offence but was completely innocent. Not only that, but he had been in borstal from 1978–80 for another, relatively minor, IRA-related offence of which he was also completely innocent. He seemed, though, to accept his fate with good grace, his permanent grin forever drooped by the rollie dangling from the corner of his thin red lips. His dark, coppery-red hair grew in natural pleats around his thin, pale face, rising like a pony's mane when he dashed around the yard chasing a ball. He was built like a greyhound, wiry and sinuous, perfect for the sprint, his ribcage and spine sculpted onto his white frame.

There were around forty young men in total in the YP wing in the summer of 1982. As each wing had twenty-six cells, with the larger Cell 26 capable of taking up to four prisoners, many prisoners doubled up; I shared with Tommy. Glit and Smurf shared too. Prisoners came and went, either being moved to other prisons, mainly Magilligan up the coast from Derry, or to other wings on reaching the age of twenty-one.

As the summer progressed, hundreds of republican prisoners had been moved into integrated wings throughout the H-Blocks and were minibussed to undertake prison work in the various workshops within the camp. We made office desks, gluing and stapling their chipboard tops with a rubberised fabric. It was a professional job. The workshops were mixed too, but each group worked separately, their tasks devised by screws employed as technicians. On leaving the factory one day on the bus, someone pointed out Lenny Murphy as he gardened with his hoe and wheelbarrow just outside the factory gate. Lenny was one of the leaders of the notorious Shankill Butchers Gang, who slaughtered dozens of Catholic men and teenagers in north and west Belfast in the 1970s. A bronzed and evil-looking hoor he was too, as he grinned and stared at us young ones gliding by him each day.

It was clear to me that there was something strange behind the willingness of the former blanketmen to undertake prison work – one of the fundamental exemptions demanded during the hunger strike. Communication between the blocks was heavily facilitated by prisoners bussing here and there to this factory and that. The workshops facilitated communication throughout the whole prison. All prisoners became part of a clandestine postal service, secreting dozens of tiny, tightly folded communications wrapped in cling film that were passed from block to block through the workshops. A message sent from H7 in the morning could be answered from H1 in the afternoon.

One morning, the screws went round the YP wing handing out large, brown bin-bags to around a third of the prisoners. Tommy got one with his name written across the top with a thick, black marker. They were all for Magilligan. Like Tommy, I had also requested a move, but I was to stay put. By the afternoon he was gone. It was as sudden as that. I was on my own for a few days until Danny McGarrigle and I agreed to shack up in the same cell. New YP prisoners arrived: Kevin 'Two-stroke' Lynch from Fermanagh, sentenced to eighteen years; and Brendy Shannon from Belfast, sentenced to sixteen.

Two-stroke got his nickname from the moped that wouldn't start and caused him to be captured. Wearing his feelings on his rosy cheeks, you could tell from the cut of him what he was thinking. Almost like a Times Square headline gliding across his forehead, and him with his black, curly hair around his face, hardly ready for shaving. Animated was the word for him as he lilted his story up and down like the soft Fermanagh hills, and the more animated he became the squeakier his voice pitched, to the point where he would need to rush his last words in case they descended into nothing but squeals of laughter or shrieks of indignity. He must have spent a lot of time riding his moped from Donagh to Newtownbutler, Lisnaskea and surrounding districts, as his legs, long and thin, were bandied like a film-star cowboy, and him with hardly a decent backside to his name. A great talker he was, though, and you could hear him and Brendy gab, giggle and guffaw well into the night as the rest of us blinked in the darkness till sleep came.

'Give over now, Two-stroke!' someone would call, probably from next door or nearby, where the murmur we could hear further down the wing was echoed and amplified by proximity. The guffaw belonged to Brendy, though, not Two-stroke, whose laugh was as high-pitched as the end of his yarn. Brendy was a great laugher. When he was sentenced he was told that, because of his age, he would be separated from his co-accused, Dermot Finucane, and sent to the YP Wing. There was only six months separating him and Dermot.

'That ballicks Finucane fair rubbed it into me the night before I was moved. "Don't you worry now, Brendy, son, they take very good care of you down there: when you arrive in the wing they give you a big box of Plasticine to make farm animals with, and a huge box of giant crayons of all beautiful colours so ye can write your name in big giant letters on your door and send big giant letters to your mammy, telling her how happy you are and how good a boy you've been. The screws are all dressed up like Big Bird and Elmo and Miss Piggy and they bring you big giant bags of marshmallows if you eat up all your dinner!"'

He stood the same height as Two-stroke, slightly higher than me, his angular face squared like Kirk Douglas. For a young man, he had trouble with his hairline, his sandy hair shorn like a soldier's and shallowing at both sides of his forehead. One day he shaved the lot, down to the wood-work, and in his shorts, bare-chested, he proudly marched his shiny head from the shower cubicle up the wing. As it happened, a Mrs Applegate from the Board of Visitors, a wee granny-like woman in her late sixties, was doing a tour of the wings, handing out Christian prayer cards from cell to cell. 'Mrs Applegate! Mrs Applegate!' called Brendy, as she was about to exit the wing. As Mrs Applegate turned around, peering up the wing through her wee round glasses, Brendy pulled his shorts down, baring his hairy buttocks in her direction. Mrs Applegate's tiny Christian face turned a grey colour and her thin-lipped mouth turned slowly to a frightful O as the screw accompanying her, Big Chang, practically manhandled her through the grille, his own face a purple contortion as he fought hard not to laugh. Brendy's loud guffaws echoing down the wing, combined with the laughs and roars of twenty others, made keeping his cool even more difficult.

Big Chang, an ex-soldier, stood at six foot two and cut an imposing but affable figure standing sentinel at the top of the wing.

'Served in fackin' Londonderry, I did,' he told us one day, gathered at the grille waiting on transport. 'I reckon I shot one of you lot,' he said, referring to the IRA in Derry, but wouldn't be drawn any further.

He stood in equal height to Big Archie, who was friendly and talkative, but more of a stickler for the rules. Big Archie was from around Belfast. There were no reports of him having abused prisoners during the blanket protest. Nor was anything untoward ever mentioned about Big Chang. The two tall screws had two somewhat smaller colleagues as regulars on the YP wing: Dinger, an Orangeman whose hair even appeared to be of an orange hue in his younger days, and Wee Willy, an oval-shaped critter in his early forties who spent most of the day click-clacking in his steel-tipped brogues up and down the wing, denying his baldness by patting his comb-over crazy-wave every few seconds to keep himself decent. Finally, there was Old Ricky, a once tall, but now rather bent-over man with a friendly, grandfatherly face. Some years later, I came across a photo of him armed with a stout cudgel, marching with his RUC comrades towards William Street during the Battle of the Bogside in 1969. He didn't look as much the friendly grandfather then. Everything in good time, it appears.

There were a few non-political prisoners in the wing, otherwise known as hoods. All from Belfast and several hailing from the Divis area. By and large they kept to themselves but were on friendly terms with the rest of us. One of them was the wing barber, but he hadn't a clue about barbering and created many a disastrous head, causing several, me included, to resort to a tight skinhead or to take it right down to the woodwork on occasion.

Christy 'Badger' Mallon, from near Dungannon, could turn even the most brilliant of pop songs into Tyrone Country & Western. 'We're the boys from Amerikay!' was his favourite, belted out in his best Killeeshil accent in a single, repeated line as he dandered from the cell along the wing to the ablutions. Not quite as Kim Wilde had intended, but maybe something that Big Tom or Philomena Begley could be proud of. Badger talked of Philomena as if she were his aunt. As he walked, sprung-footed, round the rectangular yard, a careful eye on the young loyalists, he'd give a good go of 'The Shoe Goes on the Other Foot Tonight', clicking his fingers and chanting in the monotone of south Tyrone.

Inky was joined on the wing in the autumn and winter of 1982 by several other young INLA prisoners from Belfast. As well as this, in early October, the wing numbers were further boosted by five newcomers, from Camlough in South Armagh. Charged with a variety of things from IRA membership to possession of explosives, their sentences ranged from five to fourteen years. Two were brothers, Declan and Conor Murphy, the others being Tony Jennings, Peter Lynch and Paul Graham. The last two had been given the very uninspired nicknames Lynchy and Grahamy. Declan was the oldest of the group, at twenty, while the rest were nineteen. I'd known Declan and Lynchy from C Wing but had never met the other three.

Around the same time, the campaign for segregation from loyalist prisoners was heating up – heating up quite literally, as firebombs were exploding under loyalist beds on almost a nightly basis, with reports that several prisoners had been badly injured. It was strange hearing on the radio news in the morning about the firebomb explosions when the event had taken place in the wing across the way or in the next block. As if things weren't bad enough for them, wasn't it the loyalist lifer's idea to plant a hoax firebomb under a young loyalist's bed to take the hand out of him? The critter squealed and battered the door like someone demented when he discovered the device, consisting of two batteries tied to a tube of toothpaste, as he fluffed up his pillow. Another got head-butted on the nose one morning in our wing for chanting sectarian songs out his window the night before. His next-door neighbours were the Murphy brothers and it was Declan who delivered the early morning message. Eventually the loyalists refused to leave their cells except for visits, and many broke up their cell furniture in protest. And then, one day soon after, they were all brown-bagged and gone, moved into their own wings, leaving us largely to our own devices. The transformation was immediate as we teenagers set about making a home for ourselves in H3.

When you were on remand in Crumlin Road you missed out on the sole source of pop culture updates and novelties, as lock-up always came before *Top of the Pops* was on. The lock-up times in the Kesh were different, adding a crucial half-hour to the evening. As 7.30 p.m. approached, there was a rush to fill cups with tea, get the biscuits for a dip and find a good position around the TV, which was placed six feet up on a shelf in the corner of the canteen. When Boy George sallied forth across the stage in his kimono, dreadlocks and make-up for the second Thursday in a row singing 'Do you really want to hurt me?', the Camlough boys didn't know quite what to make of him, or her. A hush fell upon the throng, gazing over their white plastic mugs and chocolate digestives. On seeing this, I turned to Tony Jennings and asked if he fancied having sex with *her*, or cruder words to that effect, to which he replied, 'Fuckin' right I would, ya boy ye!' And of course his face fell on being told that Boy George was in fact a man and that there was an obvious clue in the name! The canteen erupted in laughter as Tony sat trying to smile his way through his purple redner hidden under his cupped hands. There was nothing else he could do.

Lynchy looked and walked like John Wayne fresh off his horse. More advanced, musically, than the rest of us, he was the first in our block to play Harry Chapin, the American folk and pop singer and philanthropist who had died the previous year, putting a name and a face to 'Cat's in the Cradle' and 'W.O.L.D.' for the first time. Shrill notes emanated from the battery-operated record player in each wing and each prisoner was allowed two LPs. Lynchy had a Harry Chapin album and 'The Best of Gordon Lightfoot'. I had 'Tonic for the Troops' by the Boomtown Rats, and 'Black Sabbath – Volume 4'. Other musical fare available included Bob Dylan, The Furies, Queen's Greatest Hits, Bob Marley and, of course, Philomena Begley. Music filled the air at lunchtime, teatime and into the evening, when we could take the record player into a cell, having been charged up in Cell 1. A maximum of four prisoners was allowed to gather round the record player at any time in one cell.

Despite the recent move of young loyalists out of the wing creating a more settled state of affairs, the prison authorities suddenly placed four new ones on our wing, apparently reversing the original decision that was to all intents a sensible one. Our group met that evening in a cell at the top of the wing to discuss the matter and agreed that any response should be swift but discreet. However, first thing the next morning discretion was immediately abandoned as Declan smacked one of the unfortunate young loyalists on the jaw as he headed towards the canteen. The result was the four being moved out again, and Declan too was removed from the wing and sentenced to a draconian fifty-four days in solitary confinement on the Boards. This meant that the date of his return to the wing was Christmas Eve. It would be a long, dark, winter stretch.

The Boards was a punishment block located deep within the huge concrete sprawl of Long Kesh Prison, or HMP Maze as it was officially called. I had been there once after an altercation with a Scottish soldier convicted of stabbing someone at a disco in Lisburn. Being on the Boards was a stark and meagre existence, the meagreness designed to help you appreciate the normal, everyday luxury of prison life and to make you realise how lucky you actually were. In the cell, in a block of ten, the bed was a hard mahogany board fixed to the ground. There was another small mahogany board attached to blocks for a seat. Apart from your pisspot and water-gallon, that was it. The bed pack was removed at 7 a.m. each morning and the day was broken up by meals served to your door, not unlike hotel room service, except, of course, the food wasn't exactly hotel standard. If it wasn't raining or snowing, you were allowed a half-hour's exercise on your own in the tiny yard, boxed in by high, corrugated fences. A neat square of sky above, blue, grey or white, put the lid on the box, across which the odd bird would dart, the flap of its wings clearly audible in the quiet.

One evening when I was on the Boards, as I lay back on my bed, which consisted of a thin mattress, starched white linen sheets and rough brown blankets, it dawned on me that in the ten years since Bloody Sunday, the event had been reduced to just another tragic event of the Troubles, now surpassed by the hunger strike and mentioned only at the anniversary each January, as sodden and thick-coated wives, fathers and mothers, sons and daughters trudged the hills of the marching route through freezing blizzards, wreaths held like shields against the elements. It was now history to be studied in years to come. And here was I, doing 1,240 days in prison for an offence which very few would remember because of its insignificance, a tiny speck, hardly even a stitch on the tapestry of history since 1968.

And yet, while Bloody Sunday was a massive event, causing many to conclude that the violent path to bring down the state was the only path, nothing had happened. *Nothing had happened.* The planners and killers weren't lying prostrate, wrapped in prison linen and rough brown blankets on either side of my punishment cell, or in any cell for that matter. Chances were that one of them could even be handing me my breakfast tomorrow, grim and grey-faced, as his job was to service one of the quietest inhabited places on earth. It was like a monastery here. There were many English and Scottish ex-soldiers among the screws. I wondered if one of them had been in the Paras. I wondered if they knew me from the details in my file as 'Tony Doherty, IRA bomber, son of Paddy Doherty, killed on Bloody Sunday'. Or, did it just say 'Tony Doherty, IRA bomber'?

The latter, of course, Tony, dumb-ass! Rumour had it that the Queen decorated the killers afterwards. They accepted the medals with a salute. The case against them had never opened, never mind the closing of it. It was done and gone. Solid gone. And the medals and citations added the gilded touch.

Very recently I had read about the Sharpeville Massacre in South Africa. It was exactly the same. Dozens of poor people killed for peacefully opposing the state. And South Africa was a *strong* state. Like here. Like the British one. All sealed up by the army, the police and then higher still. 'I bet there was a Paddy Walsh in Sharpeville,' I concluded in the darkness. Someone, a labourer or a painter, with a house full of wains, risking his own life to save someone he didn't know, stemming blood with a torn shirt. I would sip a drink one day in Mailey's Bar, I thought, and sit with our Patrick, Paul and Glenn at Paddy Walsh's table and thank him for being unbelievably brave and for bringing some comfort to me da in his final moments.

***

Wing moves happened without notice. Shortly after Declan had departed to the Boards, our whole wing was brown-bagged and minibussed through several high metal gates to A Wing H1. When we arrived it was evident that several of the cells were still in a state of disrepair, having been damaged by loyalists. Workmen came and went until eventually all the cells were liveable again. Everyone simply moved into the same cell number as the one they had vacated, or as close as they could get.

In the short period since the Camlough boys had come onto the wing, I had clicked with Conor. Conor was dark-haired, while Declan was dirty-fair like me. We took turns to stay in the canteen over lock-up to clean up after lunch, which ran from 12.45 to 2 p.m., and teatime, from 5 to 6 p.m. Conor and I stayed out over teatime one evening to undertake cleaning chores around the huge hotplate, the dishes and brushing the floors. We were all very interested in each other's lives and families, especially if they had sisters – Conor and Declan had five, plus two other brothers. The dark evening took hold of the cold through the canteen window as we two nineteen-year-olds began our first friendly information exchange about our lives and times.

'Jesus, but that grub was shite the night again, wasn't it?' I asked, making more of a statement than a question.

'Blackened lumpy spuds and spot-the-meat; thank God for the oul Pot Noodle and Cup-a-Soup or we'd starve!' said Conor.

'How the fuck can ye set out to make a dinner and end up with that shite?' I asked in exasperation. The food was regularly of a cacky standard. There was really no other way of describing it.

'So, when are you due to get out, Conor?' I continued.

'Next December. I got the shortest sentence of us all.'

'That's not too far away; and how did that happen?'

'I shouldn't have got a single day. The cops verballed me in Castlereagh. I never said a single word to them but the judge accepted the word of the cops, of course, at our trial. What was the craic with you and Tommy?'

He knew Tommy from A Wing in the Crum.

'Both of us signed on the first day in Castlereagh, which is the usual story. Most people who sign do so on the first day. That's what I heard anyway. They reckon if you get over the first day, you're elected,' I replied.

'Ah well. Better luck next time! Our Dec told me that the cops had him against the wall screaming into his face. One of them spewed breath like a sewer and Dec reached his hand up to his mouth and nose to wave away the bad smell. Like you would a fart. He says yer man nearly went ape-shit on him!' laughed Conor.

'That's what ye call takin' control,' I said, with more than a hint of jealousy.

The wing goes deathly quiet at the teatime lock-up, so we spoke in hushed tones across the canteen as we brushed and cleaned and wiped down. Having set the balls up for a game of snooker on the seven- by three-foot table, the crack of the break echoed round the neat rectangular canteen, which sparkled after our cleaning endeavours. It was clear that we had both wasted some of our youth in snooker and pool halls as the quality of play was quite good.

'I'm from Quarter Road, one of the main roads through Camlough,' Conor announced. I could tell that this meant something dear to him. 'Camlough means Crooked Lake in Irish. Cam Loch.'

'I'm from Brookdale Park in Galliagh, near Shantallow, but I'm originally from the Brandywell,' I said, aiming a shot.

'That's where Davy McKinney's from, isn't it?' he asked.

'Me and Davy grew up in the same street – Hamilton Street. A great place. It's knocked down now. What did he get? Sixteen years?'

'I think it was sixteen, OK. Him and Busty. Busty's your cousin, isn't he?'

'He is, indeed. Me da and Busty's ma, Maureen, are brother and sister.'

'Have you any sisters?' he asked with a grin, chalking his cue near my ear, anticipating my miss. I missed. It was an awkward shot.

'Aye. Two. Wan's married, and Colleen would be too young for you. She's thirteen.'

'That's a pity.'

'Have ye no girlfriend of yer own?' I asked.

'I do and I don't. There's a girl from Camlough who writes and comes up to visit once in a while,' he said, placing the cue onto the groove of his thumb and forefinger, his hand spread wide on the smooth green surface of the table.

'So what's the craic with all these sisters of yours? And gwon hurry up and miss,' I said, harassing him and chalking the cue over the pocket to put him off his shot.

'Mind your own effin' business. None of them would even look at you!' he replied, burying another red.

'Oh, I don't know about that, now! I saw the photo you have up on your board; a fine bunch of girls they are too!'

'Right enough. They were all dolled up for a family wedding. Who else is in your family?'

'I've two younger brothers – our Paul, who's a year

younger, and Glenn, eleven – and an older brother, Patrick, who's over in London. He's gay, Conor. Yer man out of Soft Cell wouldn't have a look-in wi' him.'

'Jesus, sure they're all gay nowadays. Even on *Top of the Pops*!' he laughed, missing the blue and giving me a chance to catch up on points.

'That Tony Jennings was well caught the other night wi' Boy George, wasn't he?' I said, taking aim at another red.

'Typical Jennings; two feet in first!' he laughed, shaking his head.

'So what does your da do, Conor?'

'He owns a chemist shop in Newry. Dessie they call him. My mother is called Maeve. Your father was killed on Bloody Sunday, wasn't he? Tommy was telling me.'

'He was, aye,' I said, never knowing how that conversation could be sustained. It was always something to be acknowledged but not elaborated upon. We went quiet as I feigned sole attention to sinking the pink.

'What age were you when he was killed?' asked Conor.

'I was nine. Just turned nine.'

'God, it must've been rough on yer ma; her left wi' six of yous.'

You always think of your mother as old. That's the nature of things. She was forty now. She was old and angry when she opened the tin of Quality Street on Christmas Day in 1971 to discover that her greedy brood had devoured the lot but left the shiny wrappers and then taped up the round lid again. She was old and gorgeous when she gazed into me da's eyes as he sang 'The Black Velvet Band' to her, and him with a beer in him. She was old and pale at twenty-nine when she came into the sitting room on that bitterly cold and dark evening to tell the six of us that our father was dead. Two were too young to understand. And she was old and beautiful with perfect white teeth when she sang 'Sunshine On My Shoulders' at a party at our house in the summer before my arrest.

'I have a photo of her in the cell; I'll show you later. Tell me about the Quarter Road,' I said, changing the subject, but taking back control of the game. Down another black went.

'It's a country road coming out the village in the Armagh city direction. The Black and Tans torched our house after they came looking for my grandfather in 1921. He was on the run. Me ma has a photo of him standing outside the burnt-out shell the following day.'

'Did they? The Black and Tans? And do yous still live in the same house?'

'We sure do!' said Conor, proudly standing with his chest out, his cue a spear, like a Roman soldier standing sentinel. 'It's the house where all nine of us were born and reared. Now, hurry up and miss till I teach you a lesson!'

'Did you tell your ma about Declan gettin' the fifty-four days on the Boards?' I asked him.

'I did and she was a bit upset. But she knows Declan. She said he's unbreakable. We're gettin' a joint visit with her and me da next week.'

'I did five days on the Boards during the summer. For smackin' a Scottish Brit. Two of them were on the wing for a while before they moved them out to England or somewhere.

Five days was a blink of an eye; but Jesus, fifty-four days I wouldn't fancy!'

'What were they charged with, the Scottish Brits?' asked Conor.

'I think they stabbed someone outside a disco in Lisburn or Larne or somewhere. I'm not sure. That'll be good for your ma and da to see the two of yous together, all the same.'

'It will, all the same,' said Conor, adding bitterly, 'Dec was saying it was that wee ballicks of a governor who grinned and smirked as he gave him the sentence of fifty-four days.'

The governor was a small, doll-eyed, smartly dressed man, who would often parade himself down the wings, invariably accompanied by tall and burly POs and screws. Of course, this had the effect of making him appear even tinier than he actually was. Distant, aloof and smirky he was indeed, with his steely stare and soft, manicured hands. A man who clearly loved his small self, but his own mother must have found him difficult to love.

'Sure listen, it'll not be long in passing and it'll give us somethin' to aim for at Christmas,' I said, as the steely echoes of the screws bustling on to the evening shift broke the peace. I guided the cue between my left thumb and forefinger on the snooker table, taking aim, and sank the final black without mercy.

***

It snowed several times in the weeks before Christmas, but it didn't settle. Lucky for us, as we loved our football in the yard, crunching our young bones on the hard tarmac and firing against the green-painted goal on the corrugated tin. Each wing got a new, black and white leather ball every month, whether it was needed or not. We always did need it, though, as the leather wore away quickly on the tarmac, or someone would kick the ball over the fence to kingdom come. To retrieve it, we formed a human pyramid of six: three, two and one, the one usually being the smallest and most agile who could climb up the bodies and shout to a passing screw to boot the ball back again. H1, however, didn't have much passing traffic, which meant that when the ball was kicked over it was rare for it to be booted back.

We'd gone without a ball for several weeks in November, as it disappeared over the fence after only a few games. A new one was due on Saturday morning. There was great excitement as Inky and Danny McGarrigle picked the two teams in the canteen on the Friday evening. Fair and balanced, we all thought. It was going to be a great match! As usual, we changed into shorts and trainers the following morning after breakfast. The floors and ablution area of the wing were quickly cleaned and we waited patiently for the new ball to arrive around 10 a.m. Like greyhound pups anticipating their daily walk, we circled around and hung hopefully on to every sound emanating from the circle. And then it came. Black, white and shiny, it was bounced and paraded up the glossy floor of the wing and into the yard, where we took great care not to boot it over the fence as we waited for the last of the stragglers to show up for the game.

Inky, Danny, Two-stroke, Brendy, Grahamy, Tony, Lynchy

and a few others took turns stretching, feeling the newness of the ball, all very eager to get the game under way. It was quite a bouncy ball, we agreed, so we would need to impose a head-height restriction, like indoor football, to keep it low, so that it was unlikely to get kicked over the fence.

Conor was the last to show up in the yard in his T-shirt, shorts and trainers. And as he came through the gate, bursting with joy and eagerness like the rest of us, didn't the spanking new ball bounce high in his direction and didn't we look aghast, mouths open in horror, some calling, 'No, Conor, don't …!' as he connected a wild swipe with his boot, and didn't it rise high as the Rossville Flats, eyes and mouths following it in shock and disbelief, and didn't it disappear over the wire! Silence followed as the fence and high wire captivated our stares before we turned to glare at the hapless Conor, his offending right leg frozen in mid-air. Then:

'For fuck's sake, Conor!' Lynchy roared.

'G'won ya stupid fuckin' wanker!' I roared.

'Jesus Christ, Conor! What the fuck are ye at?' Danny roared.

'You're the stupidest ballbag out!' Tony roared.

And then it was too hard to say who was roaring what, their faces burning red with anger and frustration, baying for blood. Conor stood open-mouthed, rooted to the spot from where he had booted the ball, his arms raised so that his hands gripped his head on both sides in a crude attempt to squeeze the stupidity out through his skull.

After the abuse had abated, our only hope lay in the formation of the human pyramid. Three of the tallest lined up facing the fence, two more clambering to stand on their shoulders, followed by another one at the apex – Sandy Patterson, a small Belfastman, though he was almost as broad as he was short. Conor was not allowed near the pyramid, shunned for the time being.

'Not a living soul,' called Sandy from his position of observation. 'Not a single being. Hi, Murphy, there's our ball down there!' he pointed into the distance, 'ye stupid wanker ye! It's in no man's land, boys. I'm comin' down.'

We shivered in our shorts and T-shirts before returning en masse to the wing to get dressed. Conor followed from a safe distance, his head hung low with the shame of it.

'You're a total moron, Murphy. A total moron!' I called from the cell door.

'A total moron; the very word!' called Lynchy.

'I think you'll find that is, in fact, three words. Put that on your stupid list!' Conor retorted.

Danny laughed from our cell and called, 'Ye fucked up there, Lynchy. *The very word*; that's an official balls-up!' and Lynchy ran the length of the wing as Danny was inscribing the latest balls-up into the list he kept under his bunk.

'It's not a balls-up!' Lynchy called as he reached the door.

'Aye it is, Lynchy. *The very word*? It's monumental! It has to go in,' responded Danny, pen in hand and rollie dangling from his lips.

'It's not a fuck-up. It wasn't a slip of the tongue. Don't put it in!' implored Lynchy.

'Sorry, Lynchy. It's a massive fuck-up. Ye just need to accept it,' said Danny.

'Aw, for Jesus' sake! That stupid hoor Murphy boots the ball over the fence and it's me that goes on the list?' he replied.

'Ye fucked up, Lynchy,' I agreed, getting ready to head to the yard again. 'Simple as that.'

And as Lynchy trudged back to his cell to change, Conor, feeling brave again, called to him, 'Hi, Lynchy! Ye fucked up; the very word!'

'At least I'm not a total fuckin' moron,' Lynchy snapped. 'You and that fuckin' clubbed foot of yours. Ye should be banned for six months!'

'The very word!' called Conor as Lynchy disappeared into his cell, cursing and kicking the table.

In our wing you became known for your mistakes made in speech – slips of the tongue, in other words. Danny McGarrigle it was who started the trend, probably in all innocence, before it took hold. They were officially referred to as 'balls-ups', and Lynchy and Danny were joint custodians of the Balls-Up List – the official A Wing record, sometimes referred to as the Fuck-up List. Someone once referred to Cliff Richard as 'Criff Lichard', for example. It was Conor himself who enquired as to the whereabouts of his Bob Dilly LP. Someone else ballsed up when recounting the pleasure of a jow-blob from a former girlfriend, even if no one actually believed him. Inky converted Two-stroke to Two-strawk and made Glarry Gitter out of Gary Glitter. A scone became a scrone, pop band The Buggles became The Boggles, and the Falkland Islands became the Franklins. When a morgue attendant appeared on the news having been charged with necrophilia, Brendy Shannon enquired, 'So you're telling me that he's charged with stiffing the stuffs!' According to Sandy Patterson, 'scruffles' broke out in the Belfast courtroom, presumably as irate families turned up to scream abuse at the maniac who had stuffed the stiffs, as Brendy had wished he'd said it. It pays in certain circumstances to get your *U*s and *I*s in the right order!

The worst, though, was yet to come. Tony Jennings sat quietly in the canteen reading the *Irish News* as we dipped bread into Cup-a-Soups and Pot Noodles, having rejected the trays of sub-standard gruel on offer. 'What's a Thalley Domide?' he enquired out loud.

'A *what*?' Lynchy queried through furrowed brows as others looked on.

'A Thalley Domide,' repeated Tony. 'It says here, look: Thalley Domide,' offering Lynchy the paper.

Lynchy exploded in laughter: 'It's Thalidomide, ye stupid wanker!' Tony's face changed from slightly quizzical to deeply mortified in 2.5 seconds and remained a crimson red from the neck up for long after. Not surprisingly, Thalley Domide became Tony's nickname until someone pointed out that it wasn't exactly PC.

***

It was around this time that our minds began to race on in anticipation of Christmas, Declan's return on Christmas Eve and the possibility of making hooch. Grahamy and Tony both worked in the prison kitchen and had heard that the 'yeast buns' were as good as yeast in the making of hooch. Who were we to know better or argue otherwise? So the plan fell into place that the hooch could be made in water gallons with apples, water, sugar and yeast buns, and the reckoning was that there was enough time between then and Christmas for it to properly brew.

Since a peaceful air had descended on the H-Blocks after segregation, we had access to the handicraft room each evening where, six at a time, we carved rough mahogany into decorative harps and Celtic crosses, using chisels, saws, planes and bradawls. There was a brick-built box with a mahogany lid in the corner of the room, standing two feet tall. Inside was the heating regulator for the wing. With the screws gathered near the grille, we prised the lid off to reveal the perfect (and only possible) hiding place in the whole wing for four water gallons of hooch. As the heating pipes connected into it, it had its very own microclimate in which the ingredients would ferment into a drinkable cider.

Conspiratorial smiles beamed hither and thither along the wing, and in the ablutions, canteen and yard the following day. The mahogany lid had been stuck down using wood glue. We left no sign that anything had been disturbed as we left the handicraft room gleaming and dust-free just before lock-up. The screws would never know. It was the perfect plan, well executed.

After smiling and grinning at each other for around a week, we levered the lid off one evening to get a measure of progress and were delighted to see that the four water gallons had expanded, one bloating to almost bursting point.

On loosening the tops there was a rush of gas and some of the hooch ran down my fingers, which I licked, and to my surprise it really tasted of cider, or maybe a beer shandy. I wasn't sure. Drink of some sort anyway!

'Jesus, this room is hoachin' wi' this stuff; light up quick!' said Danny McGarrigle, the wing OC, and we puffed our heads off, filling the room full of smoke, left the tops loose, wiped around the water gallons to remove the smell and again stuck the mahogany lid down with glue. Perfect. The handicraft room looked and smelled as it should, all the tools locked in the huge cupboard bolted up on the wall, the bench and floor brushed down and dust-free.

Christmas was just a week away. On the Sunday before the big day, after the doors were opened, Conor showed us that he had decorated his cell overnight with strips of newspaper looped and Sellotaped together and drooping from the four corners onto the plastic light-cover in the centre of the ceiling. 'It's for Declan coming back; he's only a few days left on the Boards!' he said, rubbing his hands, as we took in the view. His and Declan's Christmas cards were looped on a string above the table, like you would over the hearth at home.

That morning and into the afternoon the whole wing set to work, converting the drab cells into Christmas home-places. Even the canteen got a touch. We pulled the tables together in the centre of the floor, placing our personal supply of chocolate and biscuits in the middle of the new arrangement. It was communal, someone said. Perfect. We young prisoners buzzed around from cell to canteen and canteen to cell, tip-toeing past the handicraft room so as not to draw attention.

The Christmas buzz, though, became increasingly accompanied by a Christmas hum. A sweet, appley hum. From the handicraft room. Like apple tarts. Our smiles and grins changed to furtive looks of concern as the day wore on. The wing smelled like a fusion of bakery and brewery. If we could smell it, so could the screws, although none of them seemed to take any notice.

'Maybe if they're drinkin' at night, they canny smell it in here the next morning?' mused Danny. It sounded plausible. Dinger, for one, had a nose on him like Rudolf the Red-Nosed Reindeer. The rest of them would chat about drinking in the screws' social club and sometimes you could smell the beer off them after lunch and teatime.

We eventually got the handicraft room opened in the afternoon. Big Chang, it was, who opened up, grinning widely as he slotted the key into the lock. *A knowing grin*, I thought. The brick-built box might as well have had a flashing light and siren by this stage. Again, with Big Chang and Dinger hanging around the exit grille to the wing, I prised open the lid to reveal several of the water gallons bursting at their seams, swollen almost transparent by the fermenting gases. All we could do was clean up with cloths steeped in disinfectant before gluing the wooden lid back down.

As the week progressed, so did the hum. It was really quite pleasant, its fruity sweetness an agreeable contrast to the floor polish and disinfectant of the circle. If it smelt that pleasant, we mused, what would it not taste like? And if the screws knew it was there they didn't seem to mind. We thought that maybe they thought, *Sure, what odds is a bit of hooch at Christmas? Sure, what harm could it do?* And thus we had ourselves convinced. They're turning a blind eye. Not a bad shower after all, sure they're not?

That was until Wednesday after teatime. In marched Big Archie and Wee Willy with a white-shirted Senior Officer (SO) in tow. Straight into the handicraft room, screwdriver under the lid and out they marched again with a badly swollen water gallon at the end of each arm. We looked on forlorn as they disappeared out through the grille, while Dinger and Big Chang smiled nervously at the throng of young prisoners gathered at the canteen grille. It might as well have been the discovery of an escape tunnel! Declan would be back in less than two days and not a drop of hooch left to welcome him.

'Would turn you fackin' blind, that stuff,' said Big Chang later when we stood chatting at the grille. 'Or give you the serious shits!'

'We hadn't thought about that,' I said, seeing the philosophical side of it.

'I could've spent the whole of Christmas Day leading you lot up the wing by the hand to shower the shit off you!' he laughed.

Declan returned to the wing on Christmas Eve morning after doing every one of his fifty-four days on the Boards. He was greeted by handshakes and hugs as he came through the grille, and was genuinely happy to be back.

'This must be what it's like to get out of jail!' he laughed later in the canteen, where we celebrated with slices of currant cake and mugs of tea. It was some stretch. Almost two months in solitary confinement. It was great to see him back and unscathed. Just as we were divulging the news about the captured hooch, the grille opened and in breezed Tony and Grahamy, returning from a shift in the prison kitchen. It was obvious they'd both been drinking.

'There was vodka. Some screw brought it in,' grinned Tony, exhaling the fumes, after greeting Declan. 'Grahamy's full as a tick; look at him!' And sure enough, Grahamy could hardly sit straight in his chair, and he smiled broadly, droopy-eyed and burping, as we gathered around the communal tables in the canteen.

'Hey Declan; gis a cheughklit biccy!' grinned Grahamy in an exaggerated South Armagh accent.

'"A cheughklit biccy!" Are you for Creughssmaglen for the dance?' laughed Declan.

'Creughssmaglen? We're for Carrickmacreughss. Creughssmaglen's not worth a feughk!'

'Hope ye have yer songs ready for the concert the night,' I said to Declan.

'What ceughncert?' he replied.

'The ceughncert we've planned for your return, minus the hooch, of course, thanks to that big hoor Archie.'

'Well, I've had plenty of time to practise!' laughed Declan, clearly glad to be back in the land of the living.

'What about that wan, Jona Lewie, "Stop the Cavalry"?' I said and, as someone turned the radio up, we sat around the block of tables, more than a dozen of us, trumpeting, bugling and tromboning, and giggling like school wains. It was a magical moment. Declan was back. Conor's face was lit up, cheery as a Christmas tree. In the centre of the tables was enough cake, biscuits, sweets and cordial to see us through Christmas and into the New Year. Perfect.

Grahamy was almost falling onto the table by the end of the song. If he was caught drunk he'd be waking up on the Boards. As we worked out how we were going to transport him from the canteen to his cell, Big Archie appeared at the grille.

'Young Doherty,' he called, interrupting the craic, 'the governor's looking to see you.'

'The governor? What about?' I asked, as the others looked on, shuffling towards the grille to block his view of Grahamy, now clearly palladic. It was highly unusual for a governor to ask to see a prisoner and was usually the other way round.

'I don't know. But he's in the circle waiting,' replied Archie, appearing not to notice the drunk prisoner.

The governor sat small behind the large table in the PO's office. I stood in front of him, looking down, wondering what stroke of badness he was about to pull. He had shafted Declan by sentencing him to fifty-four days on the Boards for assault. Could it be about the hooch, I wondered, as he opened a large envelope?

'We received these a few days ago and we've decided to let you have them. They're from America,' he said as he slid the contents across the table: dozens of Christmas cards hand-painted by children. All addressed to me. 'To Tony at Christmas', read one in red and blue paint and a sprinkle of glitter. Another read '*Feliz Navidad a Tony Doherty!*' which I now know means 'Happy Christmas to Tony Doherty!'

Later, when we were locked up again, I spread the few dozen cards across the top bunk. 'They're from a primary school in Harlem, New York.'

'What the fuck did you ever do to get these?' enquired Danny McGarrigle as we sifted through them.

'Dunno. But it could be that their gorgeous young female teacher has heard of my good looks and outstanding personality!'

'Fuckin' cretin! They're takin' pity on you 'cos you're an ugly beast!' he laughed, an unlit rollie hanging from the corner of his lips.

'Well now, jealousy will get you nowhere!' I replied, as I proceeded to hang the cards on the cord above the table, reading out the names of each young Hispanic artist, placing some in the gaps between the concrete bars in the window.

'Enriqué, there ye go wee lad.'

'Dominica. In between the bars there, daughter dear.'

'Rosa. You in beside her, dearest ducky doo.'

'Pablo. Up on the cord, wee man.'

'Isabella. Up there too.'

'Lorca. Lorca? Strange name, but up ye go anyway on the wee cord.'

The children's cards in the window, on the table and along the Christmas card string brought great colour to the wee cell, interspersing with the more traditional scenes, like red robins and snow-covered cottages, on the cards sent by family and friends.

'What d'ye reckon, Dan?' I said gesturing at the view.

'Neat,' he said, 'really neat. But why you, ya cretin?'

'I have huge international appeal and you, dear man, are from Strabane! ... But, seriously, I haven't a clue why I got them, I really haven't,' I said and I fell silent. I never did find out why they chose me over everyone else in prison at that time.

***

The whole wing was hushed, now that it was Christmas Eve. A light fall of powdery snow drifted aimlessly across the orange security lights in the block forecourt, some nestling on the thick wire fence. Danny and me stood quietly observing. This was Danny's fourth Christmas inside, with six left. It was my second, with two more to go.

'This is a great wing we're in, Dan,' I said, almost in a whisper.

'The best, Dutchie. No better bunch of boys have I ever been with,' said Danny, as we stood in silence watching the snow falling.

'Hi, boys!' called Lynchy from his cell nearby. 'We ready or what?'

'You start, Lynchy!' called Danny from behind the cell door, '"Cat's In The Cradle!"'

Everyone fell into complete silence as Lynchy took off in song from behind his thick metal door, his voice echoing softly along the wing. Verse after verse and word perfect, several of us joining him in the final refrain as the father promised the son a better time to come. The doors banged loudly in appreciation as Lynchy tailed off; the H-Block equivalent of 'Bravo!'

Our Christmas concert was matched by a series of similar events in other wings in other blocks. Some had set up in the canteen, singing songs and reciting poetry they had learned at school or during the years of prison protest. I heard after Christmas that, in one wing, they had used a hairbrush for a microphone tied to a mop, which they all sang into, and that a screw, a Dutchman, had joined them, beginning with Frank Sinatra's 'My Way' in Dutch, and that they couldn't get the hairbrush out of his hand as he wove seamlessly, in English and Dutch, from one song to another. The whole wing was in uproar, apparently, as prisoners rolled in laughter on the floor of the canteen, watched by screws in their own fits of laughter in the corridor through the grille as the Dutchman belted it out.

'You're next, Dutchie!' called Lynchy, relieved for sure that his performance was done. I had the words of 'Wichita Lineman' written out on a page, ready for the call. It was the first time in my life that I sang to any audience. My heart thumped in my chest as I took to the door, my mind comforted as I eased the first line out: 'I am a lineman for the county ...', and the rest just followed, with only a few minor vocal casualties on the higher notes. The metal doors banged as I brought it to a close. *Perfect*, I thought as I sat down, with Danny giving me the thumbs up from his bunk. I'd done it. I'd sung my first song to an audience!

'I think I'll do "The Lonely Banna Strand" next. What

ye reckon, Dan?' I asked, sifting through the pages of handwritten songs.

'Go for it, ya boy ye,' Danny replied, puffing smoke in plumes towards the mattress above him on the bunk.

'Right, Fred! Up ye get!' called Lynchy to Conor. Fred was Conor's nickname from his schooldays.

'Hi, Fred!' called Tony Jennings.

'Yes, Tony.'

'Andrew Gold, "Never Let Her Slip Away". Sing it for Geraldine, ya boy ye!' Geraldine was an old girlfriend of Conor's.

'Piss off. None of that oul pop stuff for me,' countered Conor, and with that he began a credible rendition of 'The Bold Fenian Men', the 'Glory O's gliding like ghosts along the smooth sheen of the darkened corridor. As doors were beaten in appreciation, the flap on our door opened to reveal a pair of eyes belonging to the screw on duty. Diamond was his name.

'Young McGarrigle,' he called through the flap. Danny, the wing OC, rose to meet him. 'I've been asked by your friends in B Wing to ask you to keep the noise down a bit,' he said.

'Tell them it's Christmas Eve and we're havin' a concert,' said Danny through the slit. No hesitation.

'Are you sure that's your message?' asked Diamond.

'That's the message.'

At that, Diamond squeaky-booted out of the wing. I was bristling to sing again by this stage and had the words of 'The Lonely Banna Strand' on a page gripped in my hand.

'Who's next?' called Lynchy and without a word of introduction I sallied forth with the opening lines of the ballad:

'Twas on Good Friday morning, all in the month of May,
A German ship was signalling, beyond out in the bay,
We had twenty thousand rifles all ready for to land,
But no answering signal did come from the lonely Banna
Strand.

However smooth and neat it appeared on the page before my eyes, though, I knew I'd started at the wrong pitch and was far too nasal into the bargain, but I stood at the cell door, the scribbled words of the song in my hand, and belted it out as best I could. I was aware that the pitch and tone were all wrong, but I didn't know how to fix it, to tone it down, so I just continued, verse after verse, until the end, sometimes losing control of my voice in the highs and lows, emitting squeaks and grunts instead of the words of the song. I held it well, though, through the first and into the second verse, losing vocal control only momentarily here and there. I was sure no one had noticed as I ploughtered into the third, realising belatedly that it takes a lot of voice to hold a good ballad. But I was holding it, I was holding it, even after a word or two got lost somewhere up my nose, refusing to budge. Danny McGarrigle lay on the bottom bunk smoking his rollie, voicing the odd word of support and encouragement between puffs. At one stage, towards the end, I could sense movement behind me on the bunk and glanced at him but he'd rolled over to face the wall. *What the fuck was McGarrigle doing?* I couldn't turn round fully to look as it would have broken my concentration, but it did put me off. *What was he doing? Why were the bed-springs rattling?* There was also something about the silence on the wing, where the only sounds to be heard were the words of my lovely ballad. However, whereas the earlier silence was appreciative, the longer 'The Lonely Banna Strand' continued, the more lifeless and echoing I sensed the wing becoming.

But I was holding it as I approached the final verse, even though I wasn't sure which part of my face was producing the words of this song, sacred as it was in the litany of glorious defeats in Irish history. Like a good death, the end was quick. There was a momentary silence on the wing. *Were they all asleep?* And then Conor called across 'Good man, Dutchie!', the doors banged loudly, like they did after all the singers that night, and there was a round of applause from behind the closed doors of the whole wing, plus shouts of appreciation, and I stood back from the door and took it all in. Danny turned back towards me with a huge grin on his reddened face. *Was he laughin' at me or somethin'?* I wondered, and then immediately dismissed the thought. *Of course he wasn't. What would he be laughin' at?*

I felt hurt when I heard the next morning that Declan had had to use a pillow to stifle his fits of squealing laughter, and that his hilarity, and that of his brother, Conor, had continued well into the night. I had heard them both giggle sometime after I'd finished singing but had just assumed that it was about something else, a really funny story from home in Camlough, in South Armagh, or something. But no, it was me they found funny. And it being the first time I had ever volunteered to sing on my own, after fretting about it for hours! They didn't find it funny just for a minute or two, mind you, but the whole blessed night and into the next day!

I had sung at last, though, and that was that. I had made my contribution to the 1982 Christmas Concert in A Wing of H1, Long Kesh. I could sit back and relax, and even abuse others for not having the Henry Halls to get up and sing themselves.

As the noise of applause abated, a van appeared in the forecourt of the wing and a screw dressed as Santa Claus got out, staggered a bit, found his footing again and entered the block by the main door, his bag swinging on his shoulder. A few minutes later we heard cheers from across in C and D wings as Santa walked the yards, ringing in Christmas 1982 with his bell. A short while later he appeared in our yard, out of sight of those on our side, and was greeted with applause and whistles until he passed the cells just across from ours, where Brendy Shannon and Two-stroke shared next to the two Murphys.

'Hi, Santy, Conor Murphy said he wants an inflammable sheep for Christmas!' called Two-stroke, excitedly high-pitched.

'Go and fuck yerself, Santa, ya bullroot!' shouted Brendy, before collapsing in stitches.

'Would ye ever fuck off and catch yerself on, Santa!' called Conor, followed by other well-chosen expletives and commands from Declan. By the time that Santa came back to the block forecourt he was a broken man. He threw his sack into the van and flung the bell across the tarmac, where it ding-a-linged for a frantic few seconds before resting on the powdery snow below our window. He sat, head in hand as the van pulled slowly out through the high gate of H1, leaving dark tracks in the snow. His Christmas effort had been ruined. The wing fell to silence.

'Hi, Two-stroke!' Conor called into the dark quiet. 'Two-stroke!'

'Yes, Conor?' Two-stroke replied.

'Ye's listening, Lynchy and McGarrigle?' Conor called from behind his door.

'Yes!' both replied from their doors.

'Hi, Two-stroke!'

'Yes, Conor?' Two-stroke repeated.

'Inflammable sheep?'

'And what?' Two-stroke replied.

'I think you'll find that the appropriate word is, in fact, *inflatable*. As in, an inflatable sheep, Santy,' laughed Conor.

'Ach, would ye ever fuck off, Murphy!' retorted Two-stroke.

'An inflammable sheep; the very word!' called Lynchy as the final bout of the evening's laughter rose and fell, and as time delivered us merrily from Christmas Eve to Christmas morning in our darkened cells, the snow thickened, glittering amber, silver and gold as it cascaded through the glare of the tall security lights around the block forecourt.

PART TWO

5

SAY HELLO

In Derry, our rain comes from upriver, aided and abetted by the deep glacial scar of the Foyle itself, colluding to blur and blight our view of the sun. When we were children in the Brandywell below, we sniffed it first on the breeze before raising our eyes westerly as the misty clouds stole the horizon of the shining confluence, its wooded banks and a hopeful blue sky. All gone. We'd lift our goalpost jumpers, squatting in hope under the drippy hawthorns that it was 'only a sun-shower'. Sometimes the sun-shower could still be there belting down the following day.

On this big day of mine, mizzle wafted east in greying drifts, mottling the ivy-green hill of the Kittybane townland and the straight rows of grey-roofed houses of Top of the Hill, eye-level to my gaze, past the rain-darkened limestone of Patsy Doherty's Celtic cross. Below Kittybane, lipping the river, the bare branches of Derry's oak wood rose at Prehen; a place name that comes from the Irish *preachán*, meaning 'crows', and pronounced almost the same in both languages.

I had come to meet him again. On my own. I *wanted* to meet him on my own. Our Paul asked to come with me, but I told him I had to see someone else about something else. A nod and a wink. To see a man about a dog, I joked,

THE SKELPER AND ME

ye know the craic. A white lie to a younger brother who was now a father. Ciara had been born in January past, on my birthday, the first of January. Me ma had a field day with this one, as she had when our Karen was born on the same day as me granda Connor, 31 October. A witch from the day she was born, we joked. We stood in our home for the first time together as men, Paul and I, after everyone had gone back to school or away to work. It was Friday morning and I had been released on the Wednesday.

I went the whole way on foot from 15 Brookdale Park: from the extreme north of Galliagh to the extreme south of Creggan. That's the way I planned it. Up the steep Sticky Pad into Carnhill Estate, hands deep in the pockets of my younger sister Colleen's grey combat coat, hood up in the rain and down again with the sun. Racecourse Road at a canter, hadn't changed a bit; neither had the red-brick walls and huge smoked windows of Pennyburn's Youth Club, where we had shaken our stuff, young and heavy, to Gentleman Tramp blasting 'Dearg Doom' and 'Smoke on the Water' in 1979. The lead guitar man had even played it behind his head like Jimmy Hendrix. Those memories now seemed to come from a long, long time ago as I bounded the long hill past Duncreggan Barracks, where the fresh-greened British soldiers had first set up camp in the sun-stroked summer of 1969.

Cars, buses and lorries sped by, causing me to walk on the inside, the heavier vehicles trembling the pavement underfoot as I let Magee College glide by, stately and aloof behind the high walls bordering Northland Road, the length of which delivered me to the cathedral and the Middlette Stores at the crossroads on the top lip of the Bog, passing Bull Park, the wall of which was made famous by The Undertones in 1978. The high flats of Rossville Street sprang out of, and dwarfed, the smoky terraces, a windowed barricade to the centre of the city, where the British Army squatted on top for well over a decade behind their sandbags, fed and watered by helicopter. And finally, the New Road, carved and curved out of the steep hill of Creggan, drawing in deep puffs of misted breath as I took the route that hundreds travelled, eyes lowered and blighted by the sight of their school pals or Training Centre friends being mown down in Glenfada Park, Rossville Street and Abbey Park in the valley below.

I had come to meet my maker, among the rows of dead on Creggan Hill.

He had been gone thirteen years in January past. It was now 12 April 1985. In recent times I'd lost the memory of his voice, except him calling 'Hi, boy!' to us children, either in jest or as a warning.

The tall Celtic cross marked his spot in the world. Cut from limestone out of another Irish hillside, it stood bearing down at me like me da used to. But I was grown now. I swore that I'd come. I made him a promise after realising I couldn't remember him much any more. Me da was a full ten years older than me when he was killed, and now, here I was, a twenty-two-year-old veteran making up for lost time and lost memories.

The white lettering etched on the plinth had faded and peeled off in parts, but it was still easily read:

IN LOVING MEMORY OF
PATRICK JOSEPH DOHERTY
21st Sep. 1939–30th Jan. 1972
AGED 32 YEARS
MURDERED BY BRITISH PARATROOPERS
ON BLOODY SUNDAY

After leaving a large gap below for the names of others, some of us even, at the bottom of the plinth it reads '*Go ndéana Dia trócaire orthu*'. By now an Irish-speaker, having mastered it gradually since 1982, I can tell you that this means 'May God have mercy on them'. I had forgotten there was a line of Irish on his headstone and wondered whether this was a considered act of resistance on me ma's behalf. For there was no Irish in Derry in those years. Not that I remembered anyway. Was it the stonemason's idea to use a line of Irish, fadas and all, from his repertoire of eternal words? God only knows. For there was no Irish in our house either.

Beside me da, to the right, was the grave of William Nash, nineteen years old, and to the left were Pius Gilmour, Michael Kelly and Kevin McElhinney – all aged seventeen and all lost in that twenty-minute fusillade around the Rossville Flats. *Mercy?* I thought, almost out loud, on the damp hill. He'd hardly be asking for mercy before entering heaven after the death he got, and having had to go find work in England because nationalists couldn't get work in their home town. If they couldn't tell from your name, they asked you what school you went to. Then they knew. And coming home to Moore Street to share a double bed with his four wains and me ma! No, his eternal repose should have been instant and in luxury with all the trimmings and trappings of a 4-star hotel. Mercy, my backside! No effin' purgatory for Patsy Doherty!

On the base stone, before staking its claim to this piece of stony earth, it read:

> WHILE IRELAND HOLDS THESE GRAVES
> IRELAND UNFREE SHALL NEVER BE AT PEACE

Fresh from a long communal experience in Long Kesh, I was intrigued about the plurality of both the reference in Irish to 'them', rather than him alone, and to 'these graves'. Bloody Sunday was a communal, almost tribal, massacre. Collective punishment and communal suffering among Derry's big nationalist families in the Creggan, Bogside and Brandywell. Everyone felt it because those killed had gone to the dances in Borderland, were their cousins, near neighbours, going out with the shopkeeper's daughter, or used to be in their class at school.

The base stone quote is by Patrick Pearse, from a speech given at the graveside of Jeremiah O'Donovan Rossa in 1915, and shot straight from the hip of republican politics decades later, initiating a long war against the British after 1972. This was a quote for a dead rebel and I felt proud at that moment that me ma viewed her husband's murder not just as a huge personal loss to her and to us as a family, but connected in history to the Easter Rising of 1916, before the foundation of the northern state in 1921.

Anyway, what am I here to say to this man I have largely forgotten? I thought to myself. For, while I had planned to visit him, I hadn't worked out what I was going to say. Like going to a wake and gazing, empty-headedly, at the corpse when you're supposed to be saying real prayers. And then it came to me. It was his death. The way he was killed. The way they were all killed. Dying boys of seventeen swung like bags of chaff into a Sixer, leaking blood onto the road. Sunday suits and Wrangler jeans. Gleaming winkle-pickers and Dockers' hobnails. The dead shod, tossed in, heads and thraws. His black Mexican moustache on a cold, waxy face, and stiffened fingers latticed with the black death of the Rosary. The little blue book of black lies that lay on the telephone table for weeks in Hamilton Street below. No telephone. Mammy in her bed. Karen in charge at the age of twelve. Maisie McKinney bringing kindness, toast and tea, as outside in the dark all had changed in Derry, a city of guts knotted tight in anger and fear. Oiling ancient guns in cold kitchens.

'Hello, Daddy,' I whispered, hunkering down, below eye-level with his name: Patrick Joseph Doherty. 'I got out the other day and I'm here to see you … I was away in prison for four years and I'm twenty-two now … You were never a gunman, sure you weren't; you were your own man; you worked hard and enjoyed your pint on a Friday. And you stood up for what you believed in. I want to say, Da, that I'll, ah, I'll ah … I don't know what I'm goney do yet, Da, but I'll sort it out sooner or later. You OK with that?'

The grey limestone cross, darkened in the rain, gazed blankly back. Water dripped from its arms onto the grass of the tended grave. *Patrick Joseph Doherty, 32*, in its chipped, off-white lettering, in places only the sunken furrow of the stonemason's chisel remaining, gave nothing away. I stepped forward to the side of the cross, running my fingers along the lettered grooves to see if the worn paintwork would give further. Not a bit, not a smidgin came away with my scraping nails. It's the weather that takes its toll: driving wind, rain and snow on this most exposed hillside above Derry's deep valley.

I stood scanning the horizon misted by the rain, my mind fuzzing blankly in the wet morning. There are no horizons in the H-Blocks. You had to set your own imaginary horizons in your head. This was my first real one in over four years. In the distance, the sun struggled through the greyness here and there, spotlighting the green slopes and bare hedges across the river.

This is a different kind of revenge than before, I thought. Not an oath but a son's promise to a dead father he can hardly remember. My hand patted the smooth, hard stone of his broad shoulder, and I left it there in the puddled rain till I reckoned it was time to go.

I didn't say enough, I thought, as I walked along the pathway stretching out between the graves spaced toe to toe, so that the etchings on the headstones spoke across to each other in perpetuity. In case people forgot about them, they had themselves. Their own wee community with names on their doors. Names of my childhood, of my class and of my street.

I didn't say enough to him, I repeated as I headed out

through the main gate into Creggan Estate, on the road to my next mission, feeling I could have done more.

St Mary's Chapel has a commanding view of the city, the wide gorge and high banks of the river dividing it. I remembered we were at a wedding there in 1968. It was me ma's sister, Mary, marrying Jimmy Doolin, the shit-hot biker and smiler with the fuzzy hair, shorn tight for the big day. Me, our Patrick and Paul; all dressed up like Lipton's dummies in black polo-neck jumpers, grey shorts and white socks. Paul, still wearing a nappy, with it bulging white from the inside legs of his shorts. Karen was there too but escaped being shepherded by me aunt Siobhan, who wore a light-blue coat and matching hat. Siobhan's job was to keep us out of bother and permanently silenced with threats where promises had failed. As Mary and Jimmy were about to speak their vows, Jimmy collapsed backwards, like his tree had been axed, thumping his head off the marble floor.

'Jesus, Eileen, Doolin's down! Doolin's down!' me da whispered out loud to me ma, who took a fit of giggling as the best man and others tried to revive my uncle-to-be, his head rolling on his chest as they sat him up against an oak pew in his wedding suit.

As I walked on I wondered how on earth the British had got away with killing all those men and boys and then telling the world those lies about them. How did all this happen in full view of television cameras, get reported across the world and yet it's the dead and their families who have been criminalised? Saint Mary's was the chapel on which the whole of Ireland descended to bury Derry's thirteen sons on that cold, grey morning all those years ago. Bishops and Irish government ministers aplenty, but what had happened since? Not a thing.

***

As I pressed the push-button handle to open the front door in Mulroy Gardens, me granny lifted her head from the hall carpet she had been closely scanning.

'Jesus, women of the world! Would ye git off yer knees!' I called and she said, 'Stay there! Don't come in! I dropped that len o' his and canny find it!'

'Ye dropped what, Sally?' I asked, thinking that 'a len' was obviously something invented since I went to jail.

'A len!' she repeated. 'I dropped his len on the carpet and it's buckin' walked.'

Me granny seldom cursed. Buck wasn't really a curse, though, because it starts with a B. On the odd occasion she would describe someone as a bastard, though, spat out of her mouth the way a good sin should be. And then she would cross herself, asking God to forgive her this day.

'What is it, Sally? Sure, I'll give ye a hand. I've better eyes than you.'

'His wee plastic len for his eye. He's two of them and he canny see a thing without them.'

'Ah, ye mean a *lens*, Sally! *A lens*. I see now. Where'd ye drop it?'

'Is that you, Doherty?' called me granda from the sitting room.

'It is, Connor!' I replied as I went into the room, me granda planked square in front of the TV, the back of his broad mustard chair facing into the room.

'How's the oul form?' I asked.

'Still in recovery from your big do; me gut's wrecked,' he said.

'Ye canny just stick to the beer; ye have to make a pig of yerself wi' the whiskey!' called me granny from her search position. 'I'm buckin' workin' wi' him ever since!'

'Jesus, Mary and Saint Joseph, sure wasn't it the young fella's big night!' Connor retorted. 'That buckin' woman there,' he said in a lowered voice, shaking his head.

'That buckin' woman there's the best thing ever happened ye!' I chided.

'Ach, sure don't ah know,' he said, looking from me to the TV and his black-and-white film.

'There 'tis. There 'tis now!' called Sally in jubilation.

'I'm bline as a bat without them lens,' said Connor as Sally approached him.

'Pit yer head back 'til I git these in,' she commanded, and Connor dutifully reared his neatly combed, sixty-nine-year-old, greying head while she fingered both lenses onto his blinking eyes. The black in his hair was shockingly dark against the whites of his sidelocks. Like a magpie. 'I was born in nineteen and sixteen; in the year of the Easter Rising,' he used to tell us, as if he were a direct product of the event.

'Thanks for the money the other night,' I said. I was loaded. Connor and Sally had given me £100, and others, including the local RA, had brought money down as well.

'It's the least we could do, Tony,' said Sally. 'It's great to have me big grandson *and* godson back, and you with your beard 'n' all.' And she came up to me standing at the hearth and hugged me down into the softness of her neck. Holding me tight I could feel her tensing and then I realised she was weeping silently on my stooped shoulder, her breath shuddering slightly.

'Away into the bathroom and rub it off wi' a rough towel,' smiled Connor. 'I grew more between me breakfast and me dinner!'

'It's OK now, Sally. Sure it's all over,' I whispered over the sound of the film turned down low. Connor turning the TV down was reserved for special visitors such as Dr Cosgrove, the local priest, or Otto Schlindwein, the chemist, who sometimes personally delivered his medicine so they could talk horse racing and, waiting for Sally to make the tea, so Connor could slip him a wad of money for his bet. I felt privileged. Connor fell quiet.

Sally eased her grip and wiped her eyes with her hands. 'I've a spud on for the dinner,' she said, turning away. 'Are ye lookin' to get fed?'

'You're right I am! Red fish on a Friday wi' white sauce? Sure, haven't I been waitin' years for it!' I laughed, and Sally laughed too as she exited to the kitchen. In those days you got your dinner at lunchtime and another dinner at teatime called your tea. The only difference was that you actually got a cup of tea at teatime but not at dinnertime. Dinnertime was for milk, water or cordial.

'So, how're ye gettin' on, Doherty?' asked me granda from his chair.

'Aye, OK, Granda. OK. It's a whole new world I'm in now, isn't it? I was down at the cemetery at me da's grave,' I said. 'I wanted to do a couple of things on my first days out; visiting me da was one and coming up here was another.'

'Paddy Doherty was one of the nicest men that I ever set eyes upon. Not a single being ever had a bad word on him. But give him a whiskey and he'd start a row in an empty house,' Connor laughed, shaking his head. 'God, but we had some great craic all the same over in the Telstar and down in The Silver Dog.'

I loved hearing stories about me da. Laughing, drinking, wallpapering, singing with his pals under the street light on the corner of Moore Street; the Teddy Boy with the cool dander and the coiffed hair, the Brandywell man who fought soldiers on the street.

'And then to think of the death that the filth of England gave him.' He spat the words out with bitterness, as if they didn't belong to his mouth. His face had gone red with rage. 'And to think of that man …' his voice broke and tears appeared, which he wiped away with his fingers.

I hesitated, taken aback that me granda was sitting here crying all these years later.

'What man, Granda?'

'Paddy Walsh,' he wept.

'Is that the man who crawled out to him?'

'That's him,' said Connor with a deep sigh. 'That's him; he takes his pint in Mailey's.'

'I'd love to meet him, ye know, Granda.'

'Sure if ye go to Mailey's he's always sitting up at the bar just inside the door. He's as baldy as a coot; ye couldn't miss him. That man shoulda got a medal for what he did that day. For they massacrayed all them men and youngflas. Massacrayed them!'

'And they got off wi' it,' I added.

'They did, son. They did so far,' he said, and then hesitated in thought. 'But you're the boy who could change that, Tony Doherty.'

'That's what I promised me da there now, down in the cemetery. But what can I do, Granda? I've already done four years in jail.'

'I'm not sayin' to lift the gun again, son. Ye've done yer bit, now,' he said, hesitating again. 'Don't be askin' me for the answers; I'm an oul man. You'll work it out, but not the day nor the marra. You're the boy to work it out.'

We fell silent. The American voices from the TV became the only sounds in the room as I gazed out through the venetian blinds at the bluff and bluster of this spring day of all seasons: rain, wind, cold and heat. *A baldy, middle-aged Derry man getting a medal for bravery?* I asked myself. *He was brave all right, but on the wrong side for medals. And what was I supposed to work out? Where do ye even start?* It was all too much for now.

'Would ye fancy a wee night down in Mailey's wi' our Paul?' I asked, as Mailey's Bar was always in my thoughts as somewhere I should go. A hallowed place where stories and singsongs happened.

'Aye, surely, son. Sure, just let me know.'

'Ye all right now, Granda?'

'Aye, I'm OK, son. But ye never really get over it, ye know. I can still hear the rifle shots as loud as hell and me helping yer ma over the barricade to get away. I'll never forget how petrified I was that day. I can still feel it in me bones.'

I didn't expect this. Thirteen years later and people were still crying in their living rooms. I was glad when Sally came in with two steaming plates of dinner. Dinner and tea were both eaten in the living room, the plates or bowls balanced on the arm of the settee. This was despite the fact that there was a table and chairs in the dinette beside the kitchen. The dinette was used for Lorraine's dates and listening to records.

The fiery-orange red fish steamed beside the pounded mound of creamed potatoes and white cornflour sauce. Connor salted his with LoSalt, as the doctor had ordered him to keep his blood pressure in check. A fork was the only piece of cutlery required as the red fish was soft and easy to flake. The taste was incredible. Sally was a genius in the kitchen, her set-piece dinners and teas practised to perfection since the late 1930s when they married and took a room in Nelson Street in the old Bogside before moving to No. 6 Moore Street in the Brandywell, where I was reared thirty years later. Connor's stories of the old Bog were legend and, apart from the standard one of the stranger appearing at a card school with a cloven hoof dangling from his drainpipe trousers, the one of the talking cat possessed by 'the divil' was the most frightening, the way me granda used to tell it.

He said Tommy and Josie, two brothers who lived in Wellington Street, thought their cat was possessed and didn't trust it in the house. The cat was put out every night before they went to bed. During the night the cat sat on top of the yard wall and called up: 'Jooooosssiiieee!', me granda wailed in a ghostly cat-voice, 'Tooooommmyyyy!' Always in the same order.

When neither Josie nor Tommy put the light on to let the cat in, the cat would call again from the wall: 'Jooooossiiieee!' a bit louder this time, followed by 'Tooooommmyyyy!' When we were children, we used to run upstairs together to bed terrified, checking under the bed again and again to make sure there was no cat there.

'And Paddy Stewart died?' I said as we ate.

'Ach, poor Paddy!' said Sally. 'Aye, last year. God but he was a real gentleman all his life. Never harmed a single soul.'

'I would've loved to have met him again. I hear our Paul told him that I was in for the six months,' I said. 'The six months' was a term used in the early 1970s to describe the automatic sentence for rioting.

'That Paul's a deadner! But Paddy was dotin' a bit in his last years. Every time I went down to see him he would say, "Tony's six months must be nearly up now. That'll put the royetin' outa him!" And that was in 1983!' laughed Sally.

'And where did he live when they knocked Moore Street down?' I asked.

'He got a new flat in Coshowen, out the Line. Right beside the river,' said Sally, as Connor sipped the last from his pint glass of milk. I collected the dishes to take them to the kitchen and as I returned Connor let a huge rift out of him; 'one up from the toes' as me ma used to say.

'Ye want a wee fag, son?' asked Sally, offering me the box with a Regal protruding from it.

'Sure I don't smoke any more, Sally. I gave them up a few years ago.'

'They're a buckin' curse, them things,' said Connor as the news came on the TV.

Sally scratched a match and lit her Regal, taking long drags before letting it billow out in plumes from her nose and then her mouth. She flicked her ash into the chrome bowl of the floor-standing ashtray, where she deposited the butt, lifting the chrome handle and allowing the butt to disappear as her smoke hung in slumbering layers across the living room.

'Is Lorraine workin' in Wellworths the day?' I asked, knowing that she was.

'Aye, she's away wi' her overall on her,' Sally replied. 'Never misses a day, that wan.' Lorraine, or Lorny, as she was more commonly known in the household, was the only child left at home, Joe and Michael having married in the early 1980s.

'Have ye still got Michael's records? Or did he take them with him?' I asked.

'There's wans out in the dinette and there's others upstairs under Michael's bed, I think. You can go up if ye want,' replied Sally, laying her head back on the sofa. Connor didn't turn the news up, which meant he had nodded off. The English newsreader's voice broadcast low into this Creggan living room as Sally followed Connor for their midday, postprandial nap. Connor's head was forward and Sally's was back, mouth open and hands folded over her belly, which rose and fell with each deep breath.

When me and our Paul lived with me granny and granda in their old home in Central Drive in 1974, after our house in Hamilton Street had caught fire the previous November, I took the notion that I would become a drummer in a pop band, like Alan Longmuir of the Bay City Rollers. I kept two pairs of drumsticks, as they often broke over the set of pots and pans on me granny's kitchen table, or simply when beating the dust out of the arm of the settee or a cushion on the floor.

'Jesus, youngfla! Yer goney have us all in the conjey-house!' me granda would shout from the foot of the stairs as I moved from room to room so that I could batter something, anything, with my sticks in relative seclusion. I was good at it too! The speed of my delivery was breathtaking as I drummed like a maniac, and could well have been the forerunner to Megadeth or Anthrax for all I know.

Michael tried to take me in hand by playing me his records and telling me to listen to the drumbeat and bass on 'After the Goldrush' by Neil Young and 'The Mamas and the Papas Greatest Hits'. The record player was in his room and I would do my best to listen while Michael gently closed the door to get on with his own business, leaving me to the tame rhythms and beats which were, in my mature view, a paltry selection of the musical youth of the 1960s and early 1970s. Boredom would set in after the first track and, before long, I'd be hammering the fluff off the thick patchwork quilts which covered every bed and were a dead weight and freezing to climb under in the winter.

'Jesus, Mary and Saint Joseph! Preserve us this good day for that racket's damnable!' me granny would shout, after both me granda and me uncle Michael had failed to shut me up. It was only after hearing both Neil Young and The Mamas and the Papas on the radio when I was inside that I began to appreciate their sheer brilliance.

The time-blended scents and smells of childhood rose with me as I climbed the carpeted stairs. And as I pulled the heavy box out from under Michael's bed (for it was still his room as he was the last to leave it), there before me in slightly worn sleeves were the young faces of Mama Cass, Denny Doherty and Michelle and John Philips. *Denny Doherty sounded like a cousin,* I mused as I tilted the record from its musty sleeve and onto the record player, and 'Monday, Monday' crackled into life. As it played I sifted through the box of musical treasures, retrieving 'After the Goldrush' and 'Harvest' by Neil Young, as well as Rod Stewart's 'Every Picture Tells a Story'. These were the sounds and songs that formed the soundtrack of my early days, both in the Brandywell and Creggan in the 1960s and early 1970s.

'*Only love can break your heart,*' sang Neil. It stopped me and I felt a lump rising in my throat. Tears almost followed as the words brought me back to Moore Street and Hamilton Street on sunny days playing tig and chasing rats out the Line with Dandy and Brandy. Brandy had died around the same time as Paddy Stewart. She was such a great wee dog and her with her injured paw in the air. She took refuge in

Mary and Jimmy Doolin's house in 1981 and never returned to Brookdale Park.

'Granny, can I take a lend of a couple of Michael's records?' I asked later when I came downstairs. Sally had woken from the first of several daytime naps and was in the kitchen tidying the dinner dishes.

'Aye, surely, son,' she said as she dried a large white plate.

'It's just these two by Neil Young,' I said, records in hand.

'Not a bother,' she said. 'Sure Michael hasn't played them in years.'

***

I was looking forward to the walk down the town. Sauntering down the New Road is one of Derry's most pleasant experiences. The smoky chimneys of the Bogside, the rust-coloured clock tower of the Guildhall, the walls with the British Army ensconced beside their listening towers, the sparkling river and the Waterside, twinned high with Creggan across the valley, gradually reveal themselves as a picture of magnificent beauty. Even on this day of showers and sun, wet and dry, and the lazy drift of smoke from terraced chimneys.

It's great to be back in Derry, I thought as I walked towards the top of Westland Street and into the Bogside. As I drew level with the gable of Blucher Street, the place where young Damien Harkin was flattened by a British Army three-tonner truck in 1971, I noticed an old man, tall, burly and white-haired, eyeing me from across the road.

'How're ye doin', young Quigley?' he called as I walked towards him.

'Well, I'm Doherty but me ma's Quigley,' I smiled. I'd never laid eyes on the man before.

'Aw, I knew by the cut of ye, danderin' down the street,' he said, grinning to himself that he'd got it right, his snow-white hair poking out from under a flat cap. 'And then there's that,' he pointed an accusing finger right at my nose.

'What d'ye mean?' I asked, knowing fine and well what he was about to say.

'That's a Quigley nose, ever I saw wan,' he said. As I took in the nose on him, I could see the resemblance.

'I'm a cousin of your granda Connor's,' he said.

'Very pleased to meet you,' I said as we shook hands. This could only happen in Derry, the place where your nose, your dander, or the cut of your jaw-blade makes you who you are and the cousin of someone else.

'Here, I'm away into the bookies now, young Quigley! Sure I'll see ye again,' he said, and I walked on down the Bog having not even asked him his Christian name, nor he mine. The school wains were trickling across Blucher Street from St Eugene's primary school up near the William Street baths. On Westland Street the feeling of being watched from the city walls is palpable and real. The army sangar – sandbags and corrugated tin – was at the high corner overlooking the Bogside streets from its place of steep advantage. Many an itchy finger stroked the trigger of an SLR or a General Purpose Machine Gun (GPMG) from the observation slot in front as the people below walked to work, or bought their meat in the butcher's or tomatoes weighed on the scales in Foyes' shop behind the Bogside Inn.

My first walk past the multicoloured panels of the Rossville Flats evoked memories of endless riots in the mid-to-late 1970s, the army clumped behind their tall shields at the junction of William Street as we pelted them till they chased us in their white baseball boots, swinging their long batons behind our stooped heads. William Street never seems to age any more than its ancient self. The Bradley & McLaughlin's undertakers and taxi firm, the butcher's, the newspaper shop, swanky Frankie Ramsey's café, the hairdresser's, Ferguson's Fashions, and then Tracy's Bar on the corner, opposite Littlewoods' gable where the checkpoint used to be, that had become a regular spot for street-drinkers tapping for odds. As children in the Brandywell we often aped the staggering and slurring of the 'alcos' – oul Gurley and Tipperary – as they sat in their dark coats, white shirts and dark ties sipping their half batches of Mundie's Fortified South African Wine.

Looking across the street, one of the alcos looked very familiar in his brown duffel coat.

'How's it goin', Jamesy?' I asked my former classmate, smarter than the rest of us and capable of outwitting soldiers, officers even, when they stopped us on our road to school and searched our plastic bags of books.

'Not too good,' he smiled, the smell of stale Mundie's on his breath. His teeth were clean and his mousy hair was short. He didn't recognise me at first, but then realised who I was.

'Jesus, Dutchie! I haven't seen ye in donkeys; when did ye get out?'

'The other day, just,' I replied. 'I'm only just out the gate.'

'Great to see ye, hi,' said Jamesy, his eyes now downcast.

I hesitated. 'What happened ye, Jamesy?' I asked quietly, the two of us standing head to head on the footpad. William Street bustled with comers and goers, shoppers balancing bags on each arm, and school wains in bunches puffing on shared fags. Cars and black taxis passed by, picking their way through the pedestrians crossing the road at whim.

'The wife left me. Took the wains,' he said, shrugging the truth away with his shoulders. 'Couldn't take it. Here I am now,' he gestured to the tall gable wall and to Sheila and Sammy, a pair of winos and sometime lovers resting their backs against it with their wee terrier popping its patchwork head out of Sammy's fawn-coloured duffel coat.

'Sheila's the best in the world but that fucker Sammy has her heart broke,' he smiled, taking me into his world. 'I have to watch him.'

'Jesus, Jamesy,' I said, almost under my breath, finding it hard to take in. *An alco? At twenty-two years of age?* I thought.

'Sure, what can ye do?' he stated more than asked. Silence followed the resignation.

'Have ye any odds on ye?' he asked and then snapped, 'Naw, it's OK, I shouldn't have asked ye!' before walking away towards Sheila and Sammy. Equally embarrassed, I shuffled the coins in my pocket onto my open hand, kept enough for the black taxi home and followed Jamesy to the gable.

'Here, Jamesy. Take that.'

Looking away in the other direction, he reached a hand out and I placed the coins into it.

'Thanks, Dutchie,' he said.

'Sure, I'll see ye about,' I said. 'Good to see ye, anyway.'

'An' you too,' he said, still looking away from me, his glassy eyes gazing further up William Street, seeing nothing in the distance. It was a sobering moment for me. Here I was on the edge of a new life and God only knows what was in store. But it felt good, not knowing, but expecting things to come over the horizon at me. And here was Jamesy, frog-marched by a failed marriage to Littlewoods' corner to tap for odds. And he had wains and now their da had become an alco on William Street. At twenty-two years of age. His pained, bleary eyes seeing no horizon. His life was now lived at twenty-two years of age.

My journey through the city of my birth continued through Waterloo Square and into Wellworths to see me aunt Lorraine, now busty and bubbly in her overall, as we regaled the events of my big coming-out do, including me singing, me granny and granda singing, the craic with our Paul and what we were going to do that night. I was now looking down at the same shelves and displays I used to look up at as a youngster, when I sallied round the aisles with me ma or me granny. I was also looking down on Lorny too, as she'd stopped growing upwards at sixteen. I was a proud five foot seven and a half; far taller than me ma and even me da, who had stood at five foot four.

Paddy Walsh! I thought as I dandered through the Guildhall Square, the place where me ma with her tanned feet and me da in his Teddy Boy suit and haircut first set eyes on each other. I would go to Mailey's soon with our Paul and me granda for a pint and chat with Paddy Walsh, as early as next week. As I took in the high view of the cannons protruding from the walls, I thought of me uncle Gerard taking us to see *Darby O'Gill and the Little People*, coming out of the picture-house into the dark winter evening, and Gerard scaring the lives out of us, pretending that the banshee lived across the walls or behind the next gable as we walked the steep hill towards Creggan, keeping close together under the street lights. At least, if you were taken by the banshee, physical proximity to your brothers and sisters meant that they would probably be kidnapped too!

The blue and white Ulsterbuses and black taxis competed for space on either side of Foyle Street as teenagers in green, blue, black and maroon school uniforms swarmed the footpads, blowing plumes of cigarette smoke into the diesel-laden air.

***

It was Napoleon Bonaparte who said that the battle plan is only relevant up to the first encounter with the enemy. It's the *planning* that is important. The same could be said for getting out of prison. Except you have little or no notion of what may be ranged against you when you get out. You do your best. You don't have the luxury of planning. No one plans to mortify themselves on a monumental level, but an example from a Derry ex-prisoner, Richard, shows how it can happen.

Paddy Walsh braves live gunfire as he approaches my father, fatally wounded, near the Rossville Flats. © *Gilles Peress, Magnum*

Me and Martin 'Monga' McMonagle, taken at the All-Ireland Fleadh Ceoil na hÉireann in August 1980.

15 Brookdale Park, Derry, flagged and bedecked on the day of my release from prison, 10 April 1985.

Me holding my niece Jennifer, while my ma, Eileen, looks on, just hours after my release from prison.

Paul with baby Ciara, Eileen with baby Paul, me, Glenn and Colleen outside Brookdale Park in 1986. © *Gilles Peress, Magnum*

Aunt Celine and Patrick enjoying the craic at a family wedding in 1987.

Me and Stephanie
with her granny
Annie and granda
James in 1988.

Conor, Stephanie and Catherine Murphy at the wedding do in the
Bogside Inn, September 1988.

Patrick and mum in the Bogside Inn at our wedding.

Me with Pesski
Doherty in the
yard of Lower
Nassau Street in
1992.

Me working in No. 1
Westend Park in
January 1993.

Bloody Sunday March in London in January 1995. *Left to right*: me,
Gerry Kelly, Jeremy Hardy, Diane Hamill, Eileen O'Neill and
Jeremy Corbyn.

Seated: Éamonn McCann and me. *Standing*: Martin Finucane, Johnny Walker (Birmingham Six), Christy Moore and Paddy Hill (Birmingham Six) at a special concert for the Bloody Sunday Justice Campaign in 1993.

Rossa Ó Dochartaigh with Pesski in Lower Nassau Street in 1997.

Maureen and Mickey English holding their grandchild, Oscar Ó Dochartaigh, in May 2005.

Letter from Gaelscoil
Éadain Mhóir giving the
children the afternoon off
because of the publication
of the Saville Report.

GAELSCOIL ÉADAIN MHÓIR

128, Bóthar Lecky, Tobar an Fhíoruisce, DOIRE Éire
128, Lecky Road, Brandywell, DERRY Ireland
Teil / Faics: 028 71 268020 R-phost : gaelscoil@hotmail.com
www.school-sites.org/gaelscoileadainmhoir

Tuairisc Saville
Saville Report

14 Meitheamh/June 2010

A chara

Mar is eol duit tá *Tuairisc Saville* le foilsiú amárach. Tá mórshiúl eagraithe ag
2.30in ó Chuimhneachán Dhomhnach na Fola i d'Taobh an Bhogaidh chuig
Halla na Cathrach a chomhthitfidh lena foilseachán. Tá cead ag tuistí a bpáistí
a ghlacadh amach as an scoil go luath chun freastal ar an mhórshiúl agus beidh
siad marcáilte isteach ar an rolla go fóill.

Dear parent,

As you know the *Saville Report* is to be published tomorrow. A march has been
organised at 2.30pm from the Bloody Sunday Memorial in the Bogside to the
Guildhall to coincide with its publication. Parents have permission to take their
children out of the school early in order to attend the march and the school will
mark them in as present.

Go raibh míle maith agat.

Le dea-ghuí

Mary Nic Ailín

Mary Nic Ailín
Príomhoide

Me embracing Minty Thompson in the Guildhall Square after the
publication of the Saville Report and David Cameron's apology.

It was Richard's second day free from prison after seven years and he was waiting for a taxi at the Shantallow shops. The world had changed in so, so many ways. While he couldn't have known, and anyone who found out later could hardly have foreseen on his behalf, it was another one of those grateful but hugely cringing moments when I thought, *That could've been me. Holy Jesus Lord Almighty, that could've been me!*

The black taxi rounded the bend to pull up to the shops where, years ago, in the mid-1970s, Richard had stood proud in his parallel Wranglers and shiny black Oxford shoes, steel-tipped heel and toe. The shops hadn't changed much. Still the track of the Freedom 74 graffiti and crossed rifles that he and his young pals had painted, standing high on the veranda until the Brits came and chased them, laughing like hyenas and banging the sides of their Rat Jeeps with their batons as they sped across the green. On another day Richard could have been waiting for those same soldiers, rifle in hand. Such were the times; very little had changed.

The black taxi pulled in. Richard was the only one waiting. There was someone in the front beside the driver and three ladies of varying ages filling the back seat. Richard reckoned they were grandmother, daughter and granddaughter. Their three noses and six eyes were exactly the same. There was a wide gap between the three women and the partition separating the driver from his back-seat passengers. The only place Richard could sit, apparently, was on the floor.

'I had thought I was a bit too low down, looking up the hairy nostrils of the granny grinning down at me from her soft seat,' he told me afterwards. I had my face in my hands as I listened to his tale. None of the three women spoke, but each kept a permanent grin as they looked at each other, then towards Richard sitting cross-legged on the floor of the motor, before turning their gaze to the window as they headed down the Racecourse Road on their journey up the town. Richard was on his way to make a fresh claim for unemployment benefit at the Bru on Asylum Road.

He didn't think much about his low position until they reached the taxi stop at Belmont, where a man got in. But before stepping in, the newcomer yanked at the pull-down seat from where it was held, sprung upright and parallel to the driver's partition. He sat facing the three women, looked down at Richard and then looked behind to where the other pull-down seat was: Richard's pull-down seat, against which his head and back rested. Richard gazed up at him, then across at the three women, who beamed wide-eyed down at him, and not a single word was spoken. The journey up the town took about twenty minutes. It was excruciating. Of all the things he had thought about doing when he was released after seven years in the Blocks, including four years on the blanket protest trying hard to maintain his dignity wrapped in a coarse brown blanket and barefoot, making a right dick of himself on his second day out on the floor of a black taxi wasn't one of them. This had not been in his plans. All he could do was sit and grin until the three ladies indicated they wanted to stop outside The Strand picture-house. Richard got out too, his face burning as he tried to cross the busy Strand Road.

'Nobody tells ye about the traffic,' he told me later. 'I was that glad just to get out of the black taxi. Me jumper was stuck to me with sweat. And me like a stray pup in the middle of the road dodgin' cars and buses.'

'Nobody tells ye not to sit on the floor of black taxis either!' I laughed, highly relieved that it wasn't me. Richard was mortified and probably scarred for life.

The day I got out I travelled up the town in a black taxi with old friends, all twenty-two years of age, so I found out about the pull-down seats. Nobody tells you anything. Because they don't know that getting out of prison is as sudden and as comprehensively shocking to the system as going in. There's no manual for any of this, and no Anto to inform you of the dos and don'ts.

I was taken offsides by Benny McLaughlin, Monga Mc-Monagle and Alec McLaughlin. Alec had lost an eye after being struck by a plastic bullet during the hunger strike riots in 1981 and wore a white cotton patch over the gap.

'They gave me a glass eye, Dutchie,' he said as we supped a pint in the Gainsborough Bar in Foyle Street, 'but it felt like a marble rolling round inside my head, and when I saw myself in the mirror I was a cross between Marty Feldman and Quasimodo!' It was easy now to laugh, but four years earlier he had been on the critical list for weeks. Strange how a life or death crisis gets downgraded over time and replaced with the dark humour of survival.

'The last thing I remember was bending down to pick up a stone to throw at a crowd of RUC men who had surprised us from behind the old Shanty Library on the Racecourse

Road. I woke up in the Royal Victoria Hospital about a week later,' said Alec, as if he was describing needing treatment after a fall or something.

'I was there and saw the whole thing,' said Benny from across the table. It dawned on me that we were war veterans at twenty-two years of age.

'The RUC man fired at his head from point-blank range and Alec was blasted into the air. The plastic bullet was stuck in his eye-socket and we carted him to Killen's house and phoned an ambulance. We all thought he was a goner; so we searched his pockets and stole his money!' laughed Benny.

'You're a wee fucker, Benny,' smiled Alec in return, 'but I love ye just the same!'

'He had to be flown by helicopter from Altnagelvin Hospital to the Royal the same night, as they thought he was goney die,' said Benny.

I didn't really want a pint, but me ma insisted I go. I would've preferred to stay at home breathing everything in. My appearance had stopped some people in their tracks. Gone were the long locks parted in the middle. In my last eighteen months I had mown the hair off, letting it grow on both head and face before taking the lot off again when it got too long. Down to the woodwork. I now had a longish skinhead and a reddish beard. The moustache, though, was fair and mostly see-through.

Earlier that morning me ma and our Colleen had picked me up from the gate of Long Kesh in the wee, rust-coloured, two-door Sunbeam Talbot hatchback. Earlier still, the governor had cut a page of prisoners' signatures I had collected out of my leather-bound Irish Bible.

'We don't know what this is. It's in Irish so we don't know what it is,' said the midget, looking up from behind his dwarfing desk.

'It's prisoners' names written in Irish. It doesn't take a genius to work that out,' I snapped.

'Indeed, but I cannot take your word for that, can I?'

'You can if you wish.'

'Well, no. I cannot. I'll have to remove it,' he said.

'Against my will,' I replied.

'Evidently,' he said, reaching into the drawer of his extra-large desk to produce a scalpel in one of his boy-sized hands, then proceeding to slice through the offending Irish page, flipping the leather cover over and sliding the Bible back to me. Not another word was spoken as I gathered my stuff and headed out for the van bound for the front gate. 'Wee bastard,' I breathed in the back, accompanied by one screw only, who pretended he hadn't heard.

I had never worn a seatbelt before. Me ma and Colleen, permed dark-brown and blonde respectively, giggled as I tried to wrap it around my head and shoulders, me ma eventually showing me by example. We had hugged in the car park but didn't hang around. Why would you? Seeing traffic flowing against us was frightening at first, particularly the huge lorries, causing me to stiffen and grip the seat.

'Jesus, would you relax young fella!' me ma laughed. 'You're in good hands ye know!' as we made our way through County Antrim villages, many with the tatty remnants of Union Jacks flapping from lamp posts like ragged waifs.

Me ma looked gorgeous for a woman of forty-three. She wore a pleasant grin on her face and lightly hummed to herself when we weren't chatting. Colleen had sprouted from the plump twelve-year-old Thornhill girl into a shapely sixteen-year-old. Gone was the long, dirty-fair hair, parted in the middle, now replaced by a mop of permed curls set above a pretty face with perfect teeth. It was a fine spring day as the wee rust-coloured Sunbeam slowed and laboured, grappling with the steep Glenshane Pass, the main road from south Derry to north Derry and on to Dungiven.

Me ma was a great driver. She had even taught our Karen to drive, and one day in 1979 she had offered to teach me in the car park of the Templemore Sports Complex. She put me in the driver's seat of the orange, two-door Volkswagen Beetle she had at the time. Glenn was in the back seat. Having explained the clutch, the gears, accelerator and all, she allowed me to start the motor, clutch, put it into first gear and then ease my foot off the clutch while pressing on the accelerator. We stalled a few times, the car jerking forward as my awkward foot hooked the pedals. With great patience, me ma explained the sequence over again until the wee car started to glide forward and into second gear. Second gear must've triggered a signal from my head to my right foot to press hard and the wee car took off like a rocket from the empty part of the car park towards the full part.

'Jesus! Stop! Stop! Jesus Christ!' squealed me ma from behind her hands as the wee Beetle careered through gaps between parked cars.

'Jesus, Ma, calm down; I'm driving!' I laughed as the

wee German engine roared at the height of its second gear capacity. I had sped back out to the empty part to turn her around in the space provided and headed back to the full part like a shark returning to finish off a half-eaten corpse.

'Stop the car! Stop the car, youngfla!' pleaded me ma, gripping the dashboard with both hands. Glenn was laughing in the back seat. Colours streaked by in blurs as I kept the foot down in the only gear I knew.

'Jesus! We're goney die! We're goney die!' me ma screamed as I manoeuvred the speeding orange streak between the ranks of other cars parked in long rows.

It was only after she said, as if I was an attacker pointing a dagger at her throat, 'Please, Tony; please stop the car,' in a calm voice, that I realised that I should probably do as I was bid. The car slowed after I took my foot off the accelerator, promptly jumped forward as it was still in gear, and conked out.

After a few moments of silence, and me looking at her with her face in her hands and at Glenn smiling broadly in the back, she quietly said, 'Get out of the car, Tony.' Which I did, and so did she from her side, until we were both seated again with the doors closed.

'That was the worst experience I have ever had in my life. Never again! Never again will I ever let you take this wheel. You're a bloody maniac, son!' she hissed, in a calm but determined voice. I had never been called a bloody maniac before and, at sixteen, I didn't know whether to feel insulted or take it as a compliment. I chose the latter, chuffed that I had driven a car at last!

The long curve of Derry's Foyle Bridge gives you a view of the city that was impossible before I went to jail. From the mouth of the wide lough looking westwards from a colossal height, the city bustles out in high spires and commercial blocks along both banks of the tidal river and disappears around the distant bend. There was no Foyle Bridge when I left Derry. It was the squat Craigavon Bridge or nothing, with the British Army and RUC camped almost permanently in the centre of its four lanes. We were near home. My heart beat faster as we passed Stewart's car park where Stewart's Supermarket used to trade before it was razed to the ground during the hunger strike in 1981. Word has it that every house in Shantallow had ample supplies of Jeepers trainers and snorkel jackets to last ten years or more. A matter of substance over style which raised few eyebrows on the Racecourse Road.

'Brookdale USA!' me ma announced in a Yankee accent as we took the bend at the top of the street. My heart thumped in my chest. There it was. Our cream-coloured house amid all the rest of a similar hue. Except on ours a bedsheet dangled between the bedroom windows proclaiming 'WELCOME HOME TONY'. The low fence around the garden had been freshly whitewashed and the windows gleamed in the sun. As our wee Talbot Sunbeam pulled into the driveway, aunts, uncles and siblings spilled from the front door like a lava flow, all brimming with joy. I hugged and held them, it only dawning on me then that I hadn't felt body heat for over four years, and now I was hugging aunts Siobhan, Celine and Mary, and me granny Sally wouldn't let me go from her clutch as we embraced in the front garden. She tucked her face into my neck. Granda Connor was there, and so were Siobhan's husband, Seán, and uncle Jimmy Shit-hot too. All the neighbours came out and rushed across the street: Laura and Jim Glenn and their dog Rusty Glenn, and Winnie O'Brien, who used to live near the Creggan shops and who had married and since parted from a tall English soldier. Me ma's John was there too; the two of them had settled down reasonably well over the years, except for the odd break-up now and again.

Our Paul's girlfriend, Fiona, was there holding Ciara, only three months old. The wain was raised aloft for me to hold and was then passed round like snuff at a wake. My old friend Benny was there too and he seemed shy at first for a punk rocker, allowing close relatives to do their bit before him. I caught sight of my wee brother, Glenn, standing on the low garden wall to get a better look, and him raven-haired like me da and with the makings of a moustache on his almost fourteen-year-old lip. It was great to be back. I was the son returned. Broad smiles lit every face and many a happy tear fell as they flashed the fags and puffed smoke into the air on that fine spring day of 10 April 1985.

Later me ma insisted that I go up the town with Benny, and Monga and Alec, so we grabbed a black taxi at the foot of the banking round our back. When we returned to Brookdale Park a few hours later and walked back across the green and down the front street, there approaching us was a full flute band decked out in their grey jumpers with green and orange hoops on their sleeves, dark trousers and black berets. Me ma stood beaming proud with me on the footpad as our Glenn and his friends blew, tapped and swayed their way under the street lights through a repertoire of rebel tunes, and the street was packed on both sides with people, most of whom I didn't recognise.

The welcome-home party started in earnest as the day faded into evening. It could've been Christmas in the early 1970s. The house smelled of new paint, new lino in the kitchen and mint-new carpet in the living room. People landed at the door with beer, and Bacardi and vodka for the women, and took their places in the sitting room, kitchen, on the stairs and even along the low wall out the front. The back hall was commandeered and converted into a bar with three kegs, cooling-gas and pumps, with Glenn appointed as the head barman and me ma's John as chief cook and bottle-washer. There were trays of sandwiches, cocktail sausages, and a threesome of cheese, pineapple and small pickled onions. Crisps and nuts by the square yard.

Me ma was in her element. She swanned from kitchen to sitting room making sure everyone had enough to eat and drink. The whole marching band had come in, delighted to have been asked, and mingled with neighbours, aunts and uncles, drinking beer from the tin, puffing on fags and munching sandwiches, all of which can be an awkward balance while standing up.

The craic really was ninety by the time our Paul pulled himself forward on the edge of the sofa to sing 'The Craic Was Ninety in the Isle of Man':

Well, weren't we the rare oul stock?
Spent the evenin' gettin' locked
In the Ace of Hearts
Where the high stools were engaging …

He had a great balladeer's voice. He had filled out broader than me at the shoulders, but I remained that big-brother inch and a half taller. A father now himself, Paul was the one I was reared with as the six of us were brought up in pairs: Karen and Patrick; Tony and Paul; Colleen and Glenn. Always in that order from the oldest to the youngest and always in the same order if we were called in from the street. Paul, or 'Dorts' as he was now more popularly known, punched the air in the final lines, the house exploding in laughter and applause.

'Give us the wan ye were shot for, Dorts!' called me ma. Even *she* was calling him Dorts.

Dorts, one of the most quick-witted people on the planet, shot back, 'Jesus, Ma, would ye give over! Me ma's the only Derry woman who went to Spain and came back wi' sunburn on her tongue!'

'Give us the song ye sung for the Special Branch in Castlereagh, Dorts!' Dooter bellowed from the kitchen.

'Aye, sure you'd know all about it, McKinney!' Dorts replied. 'The time you were in the barracks they had to send up to Wellworths for a box of biros ye were talkin' that much!' And then, turning to his cackling audience, 'The only reason they let him out was that he admitted to shootin' John F. Kennedy an' the Pope!'

'Will ye give us a wee song, Daddy?' me ma called across the room to me granda.

Smiling broadly after his few beers, Connor sat forward from the soft comfort of the sofa, in his grey striped suit, white shirt and tie, with his suit trousers pulled up from the knee so that his socks and calves were visible. The room fell to silence, the quiet cascading out gently to quell the buzz and cackle in the kitchen:

> Where is the man who does not love
> The land where he was born?
> Who does not think of it with pride
> No matter how forlorn?
> I only know that I love mine
> And long again to see
> Oppression from it banished
> And old Ireland once more free!

His voice faltered slightly as he took the refrain:

> Let friends all turn against me
> Let foes say what they will.
> My heart is in my country
> And I love old Ireland still.

No. 15 Brookdale Park hummed and thrummed with merriment, the clink of glasses and conversations in the kitchen, hall and stairs, and even on the landing. My cousins Checker and Joe Doherty hunkered down on the living-room floor. Grown men they were now, like myself. Their older brother Danny had been riddled to death by the SAS the previous December, and here they were, down to see me on my big night. So was Dooter McKinney, the Brandywell wain who had cast the first boulder onto our Paul's toy bus in 1968; he'd grown taller than me, though his facial features, wing-nut ears included, hadn't changed since the days we marched and trollied along Moore Street and Hamilton Street. The Shantallow IRA were there too, enjoying the banter in the kitchen. Our Glenn kept the supply of beer flowing from his bunker in the back hall, while John kept the supply of clean glasses coming at a steady pace.

'Hi, Tony, they're calling ye for a song,' said me aunt Lorraine from the kitchen doorway.

'Wait till I get me book,' I said as I shuffled past people through the living room and on the stairs. I had the words of several songs written out in a lilac-coloured exercise book that had survived the scalpel on the way out of Long Kesh. My heart raced as I scanned the sea of family faces waiting to hear me sing for the first time ever at a family do. I knelt in front of the fire and sang, in a steady voice, one of my favourite songs in Irish: 'Bacach Shíle Andaí', or 'Sheila Andy's Cripple':

An raibh tú 'gCill Alla, nó Caisleán a' Bharraí,
An bhfaca tú campaí a bhí ag na Francaigh?
Mise 'gus tusa 'gus ruball na muice
's bacach Shíle Andaí, bacach Shíle Andaí.
Ó bhí me 'Cill Alla 's Caisleán a 'Bharraí,
Chonaic mé campaí a bhí ag na Francaigh.

It's a short song about news of the French landings in Mayo in 1798 in support of the United Irishmen. The excitement is passed by word of mouth along the roads and glens about the French soldiers setting up camps in the countryside in anticipation of revenge on the English and of better days to come. Beginning as a shock to the English garrisons, who took flight initially, it ended in slaughter and mayhem as the tide turned against the Irish and French. Another glorious defeat. This centuries-long curse of the Irish has, however, left a potent legacy of excellent rebel songs and ballads.

Even me granny sang. A long line of excited faces and fingers rounded the kitchen doorpost, almost top to bottom. Very few had ever heard her sing before, apart from lilting youngsters on her knee or mixing the words of pop songs in the kitchen. For a brief period in 1977, she took to singing 'Mother in Town' to the tune of the of the clearly titled 'Mull of Kintyre'. No one had the heart to tell her!

'This is for Tony, my big grandson and godson,' she said, sitting forward, presiding over the packed room of sons, daughters, grandchildren, neighbours, in-laws and out-laws. She closed her eyes:

> If you sigh, we hear you
> If you weep, we weep
> In your hours of gladness
> How our pulses leap.
> Ireland, Mother Ireland
> Let what may befall

Ever shall we hold you
Dearest – best of all.

Sally received a rapturous round of applause and sat back
in her soft chair to raucous cheers, as she had held it well,
never missing a word or a breath. She grinned widely under
her soft perm and wiped her misting eyes. Connor dabbed at
his tear-filled pools with his pocket handkerchief and then
trumpeted loudly into it, shaking the merry audience from
the spell Sally had cast with her soft words from another era.
Her words were special. This evening was special; not just for
me and my freedom. It was the happiest state our family had
been in since the black days of 1972 and the hardship that
ensued over that decade and into the next. We had come of
age.

I had the feet walked off myself in the days that followed,
visiting me aunt Maureen in her Creggan home where she
pined after her big son Danny, then only four months in his
grave; Eddie O'Donnell's ma and da, still in their Ardnamoyle
Park home in Shantallow where they had waked him in
the high summer heat of August 1979 after his untimely
and tragic death aged sixteen. Eddie senior and Sally both
worked in Glasgow in the 1950s, where they met and fell in
love, and came back to Derry to have and rear their boys and
girls. Young Eddie and Danny died in the wrong order of
things – one under the limb of a diseased elm, and the other
under fire from the SAS among the pine, ash and oak woods
at Gransha. Sons aren't meant to go before their parents.

There was blue murder at Danny's funeral as the RUC

sought to take control of the cortege of him and his younger comrade, Willie Fleming. The IRA later blasted four automatic rifles over the coffins in the Creggan en route to the city cemetery. This was the city I returned to in 1985. The city where the long war still raged on, the hand-me-down double act of infliction and retribution still the order of the day. There had been little room for much else.

***

Our Paul got me a job on an industrial window-cleaning run with Liam McCartney, brother of my primary school teacher Jimmy. Windows were in the McCartney family, as a fair proportion of them had legged ladders round the town and further afield, rubbing the chamois cloth across panes, panels and see-through doors for generations. There were two squads, one of which hung mainly around the city, while the other chugged around south Derry and Coleraine in a blue and white Ford Transit van. Converted from a poke-van, rumour had it.

As I wished to see more of the world, on my first Monday morning of freedom we headed out on the road to Dungiven, one in the front with Liam and the remainder of us perched uncomfortably on fixed plywood benches in the back. The squad consisted of our Paul, his best friend Paul Brown, nicknamed Browner, Jackie McGonagle, Barry Rice and Harry Brady. The latter three had a variety of speech impediments. Getting stopped along the road by the RUC, British Army, or worse still, the UDR was a common occurrence, because vans were often used as car bombs. Many an April and May morning we would stand spreadeagled against the van as traffic sped by on the main Belfast to Derry road, and rough hands poked and prodded and fingered our pockets. They knew Liam well, but hadn't caught on that I was an ex-IRA prisoner, otherwise the treatment would have been rougher and lasted longer. The disdain they felt for us was palpable, though, while our hatred of them needed some degree of suppression, otherwise there would be no work done.

That first day, Liam asked from the driver's seat, 'Where we goin' the day, Jackie?'

'Squatragh,' said Jackie.

'We're all goin' to Squatragh the day, boys,' called Liam into the back of the van.

'Ye mean Swatragh, Jackie?' cackled Browner.

'Aye. Squatragh. That's what I said,' smiled Jackie, knowing that he couldn't pronounce it right.

Barry and Harry, both in their late fifties, couldn't hear the difference, and couldn't make out what the laughing was about.

The garment factories in Swatragh, where we cleaned the windows inside and out, were full of women, mostly young, crouching behind their machines in their overalls and with their hair tied back in ponytails. It was like I had walked through the door into a whole new world. I had never seen so many women in the one place before! Liam, our Paul and Browner laughed later in the van as they had witnessed me almost falling over the ladder I was holding, mouth agape, as a group of the factory girls sallied by on their tea break!

Around this time, Tommy Carlin, who had been in prison with me but had been released several weeks earlier, was teaching an Irish class in Shantallow in which our Paul, Browner and Jackie were students. As beginners, they were learning the bare rudiments of the language in the form of greetings and brief phrases.

Later that day, our Paul said, 'Hi, Jackie, tell us about the Irish class last night.'

'What. What about it?' replied Jackie, smiling and his face going red.

'Ye want me to tell them?' asked Paul.

'Aye, if ye want,' said Jackie, burying his face in his hands in the front seat.

'The Irish for "that's right" is *sin ceart*, isn't it, Tony?' asked Paul. More or less pronounced as 'shin cart'.

'That's right, Dorts, eh, Paul,' said I, not fully used to his nickname.

'Well, Tommy asked Jackie, "How d'ye say 'that's right' in Irish, Jackie?"' said Paul. 'And Jackie said, "I dunno, Tommy. You tell me." So Tommy said, "It's *sin* something, Jackie; do you remember now? We did it the last night," and Jackie said, "Naw, Tommy. *Sin* what?" And Tommy said, "*Sin* and what comes after the horse, Jackie? *Sin, sin, sin* what, Jackie?"'

Our Paul, as well as Browner, almost in convulsions of laughter by this stage, said, 'And Jackie said, "Aw, I know now, Tommy: it's tail – *sin tail*!"'

'The whole class just fell apart,' cackled Browner, 'including Tommy, who had to sit down holdin' his sides with the laughin'. We howled the whole way through Carnhill on the way home!'

'*Sin* horse-shit, Jackie,' laughed Liam. 'Good to see ye haven't let the side down again!' as he sped the road from Swatragh to Coleraine.

On the same journey, Liam returned to the subject. I was having a drop of tea from the flask in the back, when Liam turned off the radio and said, 'Gwon, say something in Irish, Jackie.'

And in an instant, as I took my first sup, Jackie spoke loud and proud, '*Cá bhfuil tú, mo Ghaeilge, Ó?*' with an unearthly emphasis on the final Ó, and I immediately sprayed Browner, Dorts, Barry and Harry with India's finest without milk, as it shot across the van in the wake of the hoot that had geysered it from my throat. When I recomposed myself, I explained that what Jackie had said was, literally, not to mention poetically, 'Where are you, my Irish language, O?!' God only knows what he was actually attempting to say!

On another day, as we passed Fort George army base in Pennyburn in the van, ready to hit the road south, we were flashed in on the Culmore Road by two RUC jeeps. Me and Browner sat up front while our Paul was the driver. In the back were Jackie, Barry and Harry, and another new man, Patrick Brewster. Patrick too had a speech impediment. The big cop slid the side door open, pulled his black notebook from his dark-green jacket and edged his head in to see who he was going to harass first.

'Where are you going?' he said to our Paul.

'Up that road, there,' he answered, his finger pointing up towards the new Foyle Bridge.

'Where are you coming from?' said the cop.

'Down that road, there,' said Paul, his thumb indicating over his shoulder.

'What's your name?' he asked Jackie, sitting opposite the door.

'Yackie McGonagiggle,' said Jackie nervously.

'What is it?' said the cop, leaning in to hear.

'Yackie McGonagiggle,' stuttered Jackie, louder this time.

'What the fuck is he saying?' said the cop.

'Jackie McGonagle,' called our Paul.

'What's your date of birth?' said the cop, addressing Jackie again.

'Ober twinty-win,' said Jackie.

'Ober twinty-win?' mimicked the cop, taking note that Jackie was over twenty-one.

The other RUC men had by this stage swarmed around the van, rifles crooked in arms, and some checking the certificates on the window and poking at the lights and wipers.

'We all covered?' I whispered to Paul, meaning the van and all.

'Hunky-dory,' he whispered back.

'We gettin' hoisted, ye think?' I whispered.

'Could be for Fort George with these shower,' said Paul, staring straight ahead.

'What's your name?' the cop asked the man next to Jackie.

'B-B-Bawwy Whice, c-c-cuntable,' said Barry Rice. The cop raised his gaze from the notebook, a grin widening his cheeks.

'This is goin' to be a fuckin' pantomime here,' whispered

Browner along the front seat. Paul stared at the curious cops standing next to the van.

'What did you say your name was?' asked the cop again.

'B-B-Bawwy Whice, c-c-c-cuntable,' repeated Barry.

'What the fuck's that supposed to mean?' said he, directing his annoyance to Paul.

'"Barry Rice, constable!" he said,' our Paul called over his shoulder again.

'And are you *ober twinty-win*, too?' the cop mimicked.

'Y-Y-Y-Yes, I am, c-c-c-cuntable,' said Barry.

'And who the fuck is next? What's *your* name?' he said, poking his head round the door to get a better look.

'Haw-Haw-Haw-Hawwy B-B-B-Bwady,' said Harry Brady, eventually.

'Haw-Haw-Haw-Hawwy fuckin' B-B-B-Bwady!' howled the cop, while the others guffawed around the van. 'Hawwy Bwady! I can't fuckin' believe this,' he called out loudly to his other colleagues. 'Not one of these fuckers can talk right!'

'So, Mr Translator,' he said, shaking his head in merriment, addressing our Paul again, 'what's this one saying, now?'

'Harold Brady, over twenty-one,' grinned our Paul, barely keeping himself together.

'Not wan of yous boys better laugh in front of these hoors!' I snapped in a whisper to Browner and Paul. But it was really hard going!

'Ober twinty-win,' repeated the cop slowly, as he scribbled in his notepad. 'And you, tail-end-Charlie; what's your name?' he asked the last in the line.

'Pa-Pa-Pa-Patwick B-B-B-B-Bwewstoh,' said Patrick Brewster from his seated position at the back door. Silence ensued and then:

'Pa-Pa-Pa-Patwick B-B-B-B-Bwewstoh! Patwick fuckin' Bwewstoh!' the cop exclaimed to his grinning friends. 'What's this, the fuckin' Stradreagh fuckin' bus, or something?' he roared. He guffawed so hard that he couldn't write Patrick's name into his book. Along the front row of the van, the three of us kept our heads, not wanting to make the situation any worse for the four with the speech impediments in the back. Objecting to the constable's behaviour, however, would have been a step too far for 1985. We'd have been hoisted for sure.

'And who the hell are you?' he grinned widely to Browner, 'Wudolf the wed-nosed fucking weindeer, or what?' before convulsing in stitches at his own joke. And before Browner had time to answer, the cop held up his hand to stop him. 'I tell you what; I can't take any more of this. Away on about your business!' he chortled, red-faced, shaking his head in disbelief and folding his notebook into his top pocket. 'Away you go outa my way!'

And as we drove up the Culmore Road, the three of us in the front hugely relieved, one of the four in the back spurted in the clearest of voices, 'Black enamel bastards!' and all seven of us exploded in hysterics, with our Paul doubled over the steering wheel of the van on its way to the factories full of young women in south Derry.

6

WAVE GOODBYE

There were two weddings planned for 1988 in the Doherty household: our Colleen was set to marry Decky McGrellis in May, followed in September by me marrying Stephanie English. I met her in the Rockin' Chair Bar at the top of Waterloo Street in November 1985. The Rockin' Chair was a magnet for ex-prisoners, Rossville Flats dwellers, IRA people, Sinn Féiners, loose-talkers, girls from the Bog and their sisters, and girls from Creggan and their sisters too.

After a dance, a chat and drink (lager and lime, she drank!), she was happy for me to walk her home. As we dandered down the Fahan Street steps towards the Rossville Flats, passing the shops underneath the veranda, all closed apart from Tommy Ho's Chinese, we crossed over the spot where me da met his sudden death almost fourteen years previously. While his spot was no longer marked with the green paint and black writing that used to be there, the main feature of the forecourt was the grey stone obelisk of the memorial to the massacre, set on one of the six 'thrupenny bit' stone beds scattered along the open ground between the flats and Rossville Street. As we walked in the cold through the Bogside, passing Free Derry Corner and the Bogside Inn, I felt drawn to Stephanie and had a feeling that I had discovered something precious and charming.

She lived with her granny and granda, James and Annie Doherty, at 6C Dove Gardens, an upstairs, two-bedroom flat. Up we went through the open stairwell, dimly lit from the street. Stephanie took me right into their sitting room when we entered the flat.

'Granny, this is Tony Doherty. He walked me home,' said Stephanie, and the blonde and curly head of Annie turned momentarily in my direction, her keen eyes scanning me over her specs.

'How ye doin', son,' she said, her attention divided between the knitting in her hands and the black and white film on the TV lodged between the open doors of the teak and smoked-glass cabinet. She was sitting forward in her dressing gown, her stockings rolled down to her calves.

'This is me granda, James,' said Stephanie, as white-haired James raised a huge hand for me to shake, puffing from a cigar butt rolled into the corner of his mouth.

'Ye fancy a wee cup 'o tea or coffee?' asked Stephanie over the sound of the orchestra on the TV.

'I'll take a black coffee.'

'D'yous want anything?' she asked, directing her question to her granny and granda, as she headed towards the kitchen, a tiny adjunct to the sitting room.

'Naw, we're gran',' answered Annie for the two of them.

'Jesus, Granny, but that TV's wile loud,' called Stephanie from the kitchen door.

'The buckin' remote slid down the chair and I canny get at it,' said James, poking his large hand down the side of the broad and chunky chair, matching the orange, brown and cream sofa upon which Annie was lodged. The orchestral music boomed around the room. It was a war film. RAF. Airmen were waltzing with their wives and girlfriends.

'Here ye go,' said Stephanie, handing me the coffee in a white cup with red hearts. She sat down on the edge of the sofa.

'What's that yous are watchin'?' she asked, as I took a bite of a chocolate YoYo and my first slurp of the coffee.

'It's an oul British perduction,' said Annie, over her knitting and glasses.

'An oul British perduction,' repeated James.

'But a great cast,' said Annie, overcoming her prejudice.

'Great cast,' added James. 'Great cast,' he repeated for emphasis.

The sound of fighter planes filled the room competing with the orchestra. It was like being at the pictures.

'He was married to yer woman, ye mind the wan wi' the hair and the big eyes?' said Annie. 'What's it ye called her now?' she asked more of herself than James, eyes scanning the ceiling for clues. The clicking needles stopped momentarily as she pondered.

'Wasn't a bit good to her, mind ye,' she said. 'Bastard,' she added, her fingers moving in automation again.

'Bastard,' repeated James.

'Bastard,' said Annie again.

'Bastard,' repeated James.

'Were ye up at Lifford the night, Granda?' asked Stephanie, to change the subject. Her granda reared greyhounds all his life. There were two in the wee shed across the landing from the front door.

'I was. God it woulda skinned ye! I haven't heated up right since. She'll not shift from that fire,' he said, referring to Annie, engrossed in the loud humming planes flying in formation across the sea on screen.

'Ye make a rise?' asked Stephanie.

'Not a hope. Buckin' useless,' he said to her, winking one eye and nodding across to the unseeing Annie. 'I'll sort ye out in the mornin',' he grinned.

'I got ye them square records the day up the town,' Annie called over the sound of the TV, never shifting her eyes from the screen.

'Thanks, Granny. Cassette tapes, she's talking about,' said Stephanie for my benefit.

The shelves in Stephanie's room were lined with 'square records'. Dozens of them. Tape-recordings of every Bob Marley album, a healthy smattering of Van Morrison and Christy Moore, and a range of Top 40 hits taped from the radio. She put Sade on the double tape deck.

I drank the remains of my coffee as we sat together on the sofa bed. There were two photos in matching frames on the opposite wall. They were her two dead brothers, Gary and Charles. Gary had been struck by a British Army jeep in a riot during the hunger strike in April 1981, not long after I'd gone to prison. The driver had reversed the jeep over him as he lay unconscious, his body broken, on Creggan Street.

Earlier, in the Rockin' Chair, her friend had told me that Stephanie was the sister of Charles English, an IRA man who had been killed in August 1985 after he tripped while carrying a loaded rocket-launcher. The explosion that followed, in the confined space of an alcove in William Street, peppered his body with masonry and he died in the back seat of a car en route to hospital.

As I was by then a student of Irish at Coleraine University and living in Portstewart, we arranged to meet the following weekend, in the Rockin' Chair again, naturally. At the end of our second date we walked down the Bog, but this time we headed towards 59 Cable Street, the English family home since the early 1970s. This was the household of Mickey and Maureen English. Maureen was a daughter of James and Annie. I noted the exact same two photos of the two dead sons on the wall.

'This is Tony Doherty, Daddy,' said Stephanie to her father.

'How're ye doin', son. Are you the boyfriend? Nice to meet you,' said Mickey, rising from his chair in front of the TV to shake my hand.

'This is Keith, me brother,' said Stephanie as her skinny punk of a brother came in from the kitchen. He was about fourteen.

'Ye all right?' he grinned.

'Keith, put the kettle on for a cup o' tae,' said Mickey, and Keith went out to fill the kettle. Just as he came back into the sitting room the house was plunged into darkness, as if someone had flicked a switch.

'Aw, Jesus, the meter's gone!' said Mickey, getting up from his seat to open the blinds to let the street light in. 'Yer mammy left 50p somewhere out in the hall; I'll go out to see,' and him already through the door. We could hear him fumbling around in the dark, searching along the telephone table, on the high windowsill and opening the press where the electricity meter was. Stephanie and I smiled through the dark at each other from opposite ends of the sofa. There was no embarrassment. There were meters for the electricity and gas, and many people even had their TVs metered! So running out of coins for this or that meter was commonplace in both our houses and many more besides. It was funny, though, and it made me feel at home right away.

'Keith, have you a torch or anything? I can't find where she left the money,' he called from the hall door while rummaging through drawers. It was nearly two o'clock before the tea came.

Over a long series of weekends, we became boyfriend and girlfriend. As I was twenty-three and she was only just turned eighteen, she pretended to her parents that I was only twenty as she reckoned her ma would think I was too old for her. She pined after her brother Charles a lot as they'd been very close. She had a framed picture of him wearing a mask and carrying a rifle, taken several months before he was killed.

There was another photo in a drawer, of the funeral of Danny Doherty and Willie Fleming.

'That's our Charles there, nearest, with the rifle,' she said, pointing. 'He was killed eight months after that.'

'We were on holiday in Spain when we got the call,' she told me one evening. The two of us were sitting on her sofa bed drinking coffee and listening to a tape of Van Morrison. 'There was me, me sister Michelle, Elaine McDevitt, Jacqueline Healy and Gráinne McCarron. Me granny reads cards and tea-leaves. D'ye know, a few weeks before we went on holiday me granny read our cards. She told Michelle that she'd be in a crowd following a flag, but not in a good way, and she told Jacqueline that, when it came to it, she was goney be the brave one.'

'What do you mean?' I asked.

'We didn't connect it all up until afterwards, when things had settled down a bit. She said she didn't know who the bad news was about, but she told Jacqueline that she'd be the brave one and would take the call.'

'How'd she know that?' I asked, thinking of old Josie Browne in me granny's street seeing a walking vision of me da after he had been killed.

'Me granny sees things that others don't. She has a sixth sense. She's as mad as a March hare too, but she does see things that others don't. She read our cards. We all just laughed and giggled afterwards, but I had a bad feeling in the pit of me stomach. Before we left I knew I'd never see Charles alive again. When we received the knock on the door that morning in the hotel in Torremolinos, I knew that Charles was dead. When we walked down to the foyer with the holiday rep she instructed us that one of the phones in the four wooden kiosks would ring. The call would be from me granny's flat. When the phone rang it was Michelle who went into the kiosk, lifted the receiver, dropped it on its dangling cord and ran out. The rest of us froze as Michelle mumbled something about me granny and then the holiday rep nodded to Jacqueline to lift the phone. I knew before she put the phone down what the news would be.'

The explosion that fatally wounded Charles happened only a few hundred yards from where his brother had been killed in 1981. Both were killed on the same stretch of road four years apart. Their father, Mickey, had witnessed me da's death several years before in the forecourt of the Rossville Flats, very close to where Charles was killed. Derry had become a city long locked in war, loss, fear and retribution. No one expected anything different now. This was the way it was. It was us versus them, and them versus us. Booby traps exploded, home-made grenades were made from plastic explosives, the IRA went on armed propaganda walks through the streets, IRA funerals were attacked, British soldiers' housing estates on the outskirts were bombed, informers were recruited, hunted down and executed, snipers took aim, the RUC took revenge.

The steep walk to me granny's in the dead of night from the Bog up to Creggan was normally precarious. I'd walked the same route several nights a week for a long time now. If I heard the sound of jeeps in the Bog or when I reached Creggan, I would usually stand in somewhere, in an alley or behind bushes, until they'd passed by.

One dark morning, as I headed up Stanley's Walk, I heard shooting in the distance. Rifle shots; a full magazine. *Fuck!* I said to myself, as I knew they would send out patrols from Rosemount and Strand Road Barracks and the helicopter would go up from Ebrington Barracks, across the river. I sharpened my pace and put my head down as I approached the bottom of Bligh's Lane to take the exposed hill. There was not a car or another soul to be seen. I had no choice but to keep going.

While passing the high railings outside St Cecilia's Girls School I heard the distinctive growl of the heavy diesel engines from the direction of Creggan. I was hoping they would head down the New Road, giving me the chance to clear the hill into lower Creggan, but the beam from their headlamps told me they had turned off the New Road and would soon come into view at the top of Bligh's Lane. 'Jesus, please let it be the Brits! Not the cops! Not the fuckin' cops!' I whispered under my breath. I had no choice but to keep walking as they had me in their sights.

It was the cops! The pair of grey RUC jeeps approached on the road and pulled in. I stopped walking. To ignore them now, to pretend they weren't there by walking on would be folly. The chunky metal doors swung open at the front and rear and out jumped six RUC men armed with a variety of weapons. The jeep engines hummed as they approached, guns pointed in my direction. There was still not another sinner on the steep road.

'Name?' demanded the tallest, towering over me by a foot, his face hidden by the shadows of his peaked cap.

'Anthony Doherty,' I replied without any hesitation. He didn't write anything down. This worried me. It was unofficial. No record.

'Address?'

'15 Brookdale Park,' I replied.

'Date of birth?'

'1 January 1963,' I replied. He walked over towards the lead jeep and conferred with the driver, both of them looking in my direction.

'You know what this is?' said a smaller one, dark-haired and no cap. He had stuck the barrel of his military pump-action shotgun right between my eyes. I looked down into the black abyss of the barrel as he fingered the trigger, looked back at him and smelled whiskey from his excited breath. *O Jesus, this is really bad; I'm in serious bother here*, I concluded, while trying to remain calm and not antagonise him. All it would take was one wrong word.

'It's a gun,' I replied, obviously not keen to reveal the extent of my knowledge of weaponry.

'Yes, it's a fuckin' gun. But what kind of a fuckin' gun?' he said, the aggression rising with the smell of whiskey, the muzzle still a few inches from the bridge of my nose.

'I don't know. I'm not sure about guns,' I replied.

'Do you not, now? Well, I'll tell you what I'm fuckin' sure about, Doherty; this is the gun that's gonna blow the top of your fuckin' head off!' he growled, his hands tightening around the shotgun, the muzzle now touching my forehead. The blood pumped from my beating heart as he tilted my head backwards against the railings.

'Take it easy, Trevor!' one of the others called out.

Fuck! Even them boys think he's goney shoot me! I screamed inside, trying not to panic or further aggravate Trevor in any way. Trevor never flinched. I could feel the strength of his grip as he continued to press the hard muzzle into my forehead.

'Do you want me to pull the trigger?' asked Trevor, with the smile of someone who didn't ask silly questions.

'Trevor!' someone screamed in the dark. I couldn't see who.

'Take that fuckin' thing off him!' called another, realising that it had gone too far.

While he was clearly unhinged, the drink had surely made him much more volatile. And then someone opening up on them with automatic fire? *Would all these things loosen or tighten his trigger finger?* I asked myself. A chopper hovered and buzzed above the city, shining its probing beams on the dark streets. I closed my eyes and waited to explode into oblivion.

Just then, I heard the sound of a car approaching, its lights penetrating my closed eyelids. I could sense other cops around me as Trevor eased the muzzle from my forehead. When I opened my eyes, the driver of the car was being searched, spreadeagled upright on the road and all the doors and boot were open wide. One of the cops beckoned me to walk onwards up Bligh's Lane, which I did, very slowly, nodding towards the car driver and he nodding back. My body tensed as I walked away, awaiting the single, aimed shot from Trevor. It never came.

***

Stephanie's mother's name was Maureen. We clicked the first time we met. She told Stephanie afterwards that she thought I had nice teeth – I'd taken great care of them ever since the inspired warnings from the prison MO in 1981. Maureen had nice teeth too, set within a gorgeous face crowned with a head of blonde hair like her mother, Annie. There was only two months separating her birthday from me ma's. She was born on 14 February 1942, and me ma came to be on 16 April that year, during the Second World War.

'God, but your mammy and daddy were the real glamour couple of our day at the dances at the Crit [the Corinthian Ballroom on Bishop Street],' she told me. 'Your father was a handsome man. A beaut of a man! And a great dancer. We all would wait to see them come into the Crit, and your ma with her dress on and him with the Teddy Boy suit.'

'Were you goin' out wi' Mickey at the time?' I asked.

'Naw. I was goin' out wi' Sticky Begley. Sticky Begley was a great dancer too. As good as your da,' she said.

Maureen was a happy woman. Her first thoughts were always for other people, her family, her ma and da, as she bustled from Cable Street to Dove Gardens, to the shops at the Field or down the town with her shopping bags. You wouldn't know to look at her that she had lost two grown-up sons. Gary and Charles smiled down from their twin frames, dusted and polished like everything else in Maureen's living room. She kept a good house and she kept a smile on her face. These were her standards. Her children affectionately affronted her by placing the HP sauce bottle and the tall Saxa salt container on the front windowsill for her to see on her way back from the shops. She'd raise a hand to shield her eyes from the shame of it on her approach, and her smiling all the while because she knew that this was an act of love.

'Oh dear, I'm affronted!' she'd feign on turning the key in the front door. 'What have I reared? What, under God on high, have I reared?'

As I surveyed her happy domain and demeanour I often couldn't help but think that she was masking her true feelings. Sometimes, as she sat in the armchair by the window, she would turn her face towards the street and hold her stare in complete silence, surveying the beaten paths of her dead children returning from football, the baths, the shops, the pictures, the disco, the club, the girlfriend's house. It was easy then to tell her thoughts, and when she turned her face back into the living room, there was pain in its soft lines and contours. How can you lose not one but two of your seven children and not fall apart? What is there to keep you going? Why two from the same family? Parents aren't supposed to bury their children; it's the wrong order of things. For too many families in Derry the wrong order of things had happened. And then, one day, the wrong order of things came to knock at our door in Brookdale Park.

It was November 1987. It was a Saturday. The previous day, Mitchel McLaughlin had given me money for stamps. I'd just finished addressing over a dozen envelopes to the mothers, fathers and siblings of the men and boys shot on Bloody Sunday: Mrs McDaid of Tyrconnell Street, Mrs Kelly of Dunmore Gardens, Mr Wray of Drumcliffe Avenue, Mrs McKinney of Westway, Maura Young from Drumleck Drive, Mrs McKinney of Beechwood Avenue, Olive Gilmour of Blucher Street. I had begun organising the families to claim justice for their dead in the midst of war and chaos. Fulfilling my promise. The annual march was coming up in January. I had just stacked the addressed envelopes neatly by the phone, when it rang. It was my sister.

'Is that you, Tony?' said Karen.

'It is, Karen.'

'Is me ma in the house?' she asked. I could sense the tension in her voice.

'She's up the stairs; ye want her?' I asked.

'Naw. Naw, I don't,' she paused. 'I need to speak to you; can you come up?'

'What's wrong, Karen?' I asked. She was upset. I could hear it in her laboured breathing.

'Jist come up, Tony. It's only me and the wain in.'

'OK. I'll be up shortly,' I said.

'And don't tell me ma.'

I put my coat on and walked the mile or so to our Karen's house in Foyle Springs. It was named after Springtown nearby, where poor Catholics had squatted in Nissen huts abandoned by the Yanks after the Second World War until the last residents were rehoused in 1967. Springtown itself took its name from the Irish: *Baile an Uisce* – townland of the water.

Foyle Springs was a collection of culs-de-sac of pillared houses and red-brick bungalows, mostly built when I was inside. Ballymagroarty also sprang up over the same years, so that the city lurched westward in the direction of the Buncrana Road. In a single generation, the former country road had become a cross-border thoroughfare, with the army checkpoint still ensconced midway.

I was greeted tearfully by my sister, as her daughter, Jennifer, tottered around the sitting room with her doll, *Babóg*. She told me that luck had run out for Patrick Joseph Doherty, our brother, named after me da, aged twenty-five and living in London. Our Karen's words exploded in my ears. I stared silently at the drizzle through her front window, trying to take in the news. Another Derry son was going to die.

Our Patrick had been diagnosed HIV positive by the hospital and had called her from the ward where he was being kept for tests.

'Jesus, Tony, what are we goney do?' sighed Karen, her voice quivering and her eyes moist.

'What did he say, Karen?' I asked, needing to know the full gravity. Her eyes had sunk into their sockets with the new-found worry.

'He said he'll probably die, Tony. He's goney die on us!' she cried into her hands.

I sat totally stunned by the news. The great foreboding of the looming AIDS crisis, chillingly portrayed on government TV adverts, had come to roost with the Doherty family of 15 Brookdale Park. It was two and a half years since I'd been released from prison and life had been good. I was by then studying Irish History, Politics and Society at Magee University, having moved college in 1986 after the RUC raided our digs on Station Road in Portstewart. We were together again as a family. The next generation was appearing. Our Colleen had recently given birth to Paul, son of Decky McGrellis from Carnhill, a 'glass maintenance engineer' (otherwise known as a window cleaner) with McCartneys. Paul was the first baby raised under our roof since Glenn was born in 1971. He was the centre of all attention; his large, round, hazel eyes alert and full of the craic. 'Our wee dote!' me ma called him, thirty times a day.

As I walked home in the rain I couldn't help concluding that our family was blighted. All the evidence was there. Me da's murder, the often stormy and unsettling relationship between me ma and John, here today, gone tomorrow, unable to live together or apart. And now this! Another Patrick Joseph Doherty to an early grave. It's not as if the fear wasn't there already. I had seen it in the faces around the sitting room as the volcano exploded during the AIDS advert, conveying the direst warnings about the disease. If *I* was thinking it, so must everyone else in the room be thinking the same. Patrick was gay and living in London, and AIDS was beginning to take its toll there as it had in New York and Los Angeles.

Are we a family blighted for ever? I asked myself as the rain pelted down. *If so, no one will know until after Christmas.* Karen and I had decided to keep the news from me ma and the rest till then. The only others who would know were Karen's husband, Paddy Concannon from Dunmore Gardens in Creggan, and Stephanie, by then my girlfriend of two years.

I remembered the first time I saw Marc Almond sing the atmospherically gay 'Say Hello, Wave Goodbye' on *Top of the Pops*. It was January 1982, just after I'd been sentenced. I immediately thought of Patrick and wondered if he went to clubs such as the Pink Flamingo? Probably, I quickly concluded. Every time I hear the song I'm reminded of him.

When I went to prison, I knew Patrick couldn't write to me, nor I to him, as this would have brought the attention of the Special Branch in England down on him. Not a good idea when IRA bombs were exploding in London's streets. He did send me the odd postcard, though.

Patrick Joseph Doherty. He had the exact same name as me da and was exactly thirteen months older than me. Karen was exactly thirteen months older than him and our Paul was exactly thirteen months younger than me. Incredible timing. While me ma's love for Patrick was undying, he had put her through the mill from his early teens. He had a tongue on him like a soldier, cursing was his favourite pastime since he was six or seven years old and, in his own words, he didn't really give a fuck. He was thran, single-minded and hardly spent a full day at St Peter's Secondary School in Creggan during his whole five-year stint there. If dobbing school hadn't already been around, he would have invented it and held its patent.

I blame our Patrick for me having a big nose. It was normal enough until that day in Buncrana in July 1971. It happened like this. We loved the bumper cars and couldn't wait, so me, Paul, Patrick, Karen and Lorraine rushed ahead of the posse and waited outside Bertie's Amusements for the rest to come up the road. Me da warned us, 'Now just remember, I'm not made of money, so take it easy in here, OK?' Sparks flashed from the tops of the poles on the metal grid above as the bumper cars trundled by. When it was our turn, me da took me by the hand towards a flashy red car, Paul and Patrick got into theirs and Lorraine and Karen doubled up too. Me da, Patrick and Karen were the drivers, and me, Paul and Lorraine were the passengers. Round we went, overtaking and making faces as we passed.

Near the end, our car got stuck between two others and then there was a crash and I felt myself flying forward and my face striking the chrome bar. When I put my hand up to my nose, blood ran down my fingers and onto my T-shirt. Me da looked round to see that it was our Patrick who'd bumped us, and said, 'What are ye at, ye stupid bein', ye!' and Patrick went red and said, 'I didn't mean it, Daddy.' Me da said, 'Aye, I know ye didn't effin' mean it; look at your brother's busted nose,' as he extracted a handkerchief from his pocket and told me to hold my head back, which I did, through my tears, as the bump was very painful. I staggered towards the exit with my head crooked back and me da guiding me out.

'God, what happened him?' asked me ma when she saw us.

'Aw, that stupid atrocot there slapped right into the back of us,' said me da, pointing at the guilty Patrick, who had tears in his eyes now, 'and busted his nose off the bar.'

When I stretched up to jook in a mirror my nose had swollen up like a fat sausage between my tearful eyes and top lip. It was him all right who'd caused it, but the watery pools of guilt around his own beautiful blue eyes were my vengeance, which I gloated and smirked at for hours afterwards, calling him a yammer. He was lucky me da didn't give him a skelp on the side of the head that hot Sunday in Buncrana.

My nose never did return to its previous dimensions, though, and he was to blame.

***

Patrick came back for a few days to Derry with his Welsh boyfriend, Peter, in June 1985. And, as Peter claimed that he worked in Downing Street in the Thatcher administration, he was given the name of Peter the Spy – but only Peter to his face, of course. His Welshness, Celtic roots or none, curried no favours in Brookdale Park and surrounding rebel estates as he spoke in nothing but the finest of London accents. Margaret Thatcher was Public Enemy Number 1, the most hated figure since Oliver Cromwell had driven our forefathers to Hell or Connaught centuries before. Peter was advised, therefore, in no uncertain terms, to keep his Maggie Thatcher business to himself around these parts in case someone would come to kidnap him or something worse.

Patrick and Peter the Spy looked very alike. Both sported big, black moustaches, as was the gay custom at the time, and wore their hair short and combed to the side. On the Sunday we lounged round the sitting room recovering from a rib-roast dinner, lovingly prepared by me ma and John, who were a perfect match in the kitchen though not in their overall relationship. It was dessert time. Wafers and ice cream – though in Derry we pronounce wafers as 'woofers'.

'What's for dessert, Ma?' asked our Glenn.

Peter the Spy's eyes grew wide as wide as me ma responded with 'ice cream and woofers'.

'Do ye's all want ice cream and woofers?' me ma asked, looking round at me, Glenn, Colleen, John, Patrick and Peter the Spy. We all, apart from Peter the Spy, nodded in response. Ice cream and woofers had been our favourite dessert since Hamilton Street. Peter the Spy didn't nod but simply stared back at her, not knowing what to expect if he consented.

'I've never had a woofa before,' he said, looking at Patrick for guidance.

'Jesus, ye must've had a miserable childhood if ye've never had woofers and ice cream,' said me ma.

'I don't think so,' said Peter the Spy, doubtfully, trying to figure out what a woofer was.

'Ach, sure I'll bring ye in wan anyway,' said me ma, getting to her feet.

Peter the Spy gave a hesitant nod of consent while me ma set about dividing the block of ice cream in the kitchen, laying slices in between the rectangular woofers, before parading back into the sitting room, piece-plates in hand.

'Oh, wafers!' exclaimed Peter the Spy. 'Jesus Christ, I thought you were talking about a bloody dog or something!' as he tucked into his ice cream and woofers.

'And see while ye's are eatin' yer ice cream and woofers, see that shitehawk there,' she said, pointing an accusing finger at Patrick, 'that's the article who got our gas *and* electricity cut off in 1977. He had us robbed blind, so he had.'

The Doherty's gas and electricity crisis stemmed simply from the fact that both services were metered, requiring regular intakes of 5p and 10p coins for gas and 50p coins for electricity. This meant that there was money in the house, albeit secured inside both meters by a locking mechanism that only the gasman or electricity man could open, usually on a monthly basis. The first hint of an impending crisis, though no one caught on, was when we experienced a severe shortage of teaspoons, or wee spoons, as we called them. This mysterious shortage led to us searching down the backs of the sofa and chairs, and stirring our tea with soup spoons.

Had any of us known that a crime had occurred with monetary gain involved, we might also have noticed that Patrick had a ready and steady supply of Embassy Regal, fast taking over from No. 6 which, for some reason, were going out of style. The twenty box, and him flashing the fags around his friends, and sometimes even to me and Paul, should have been a sign that he was being bankrolled somehow. Or meter-rolled, to be more precise, because when the gasman came of a day to empty the meter of its coinage for the Londonderry Gaslight Company, he emptied a boxful of wee spoons on to the white, drop-leaf kitchen table and not a single 5p or 10p coin clinked or clanked. Me ma's face dropped as she realised that what she had been hearing after inserting coins into the meter for the past number of weeks was not the sound of coin on coins, but coin on spoons! Patrick had cut the metal seal and put the wee spoons in the meter box so it would sound as if there were coins in it, rather than just an empty box; he removed the 5p and 10p coins each time they were put in.

'I never worked out how he did the electricity meter, though. Not till this day, do I know!' she said.

'Sure what ye don't know canny hurt ye, Ma,' grinned our Patrick as he bit into his ice cream and woofer sandwich.

'I'll buckin' hurt ye all right, slippy-tit!' me ma shot back with a smile. 'Yer not too big for a skelp across the ear, boy!'

'Tell us how you did it, Patrick,' I asked.

Patrick fell quiet and then said to me ma, 'You remember there was water in the meter box when the electricity man emptied it?'

'I do. He said he'd never seen water leak into one of his boxes before,' she replied.

'Well, I made frozen 50p coins from a plasticine cast. Kept them at the back of the freezer. I didn't know if it would work, and when it did, I was always the one to get the real 50p off you for the meter. Voilà! Fags and sweets galore!'

Me ma could only look and softly shake her head in disbelief.

The ice cream and woofers is one of the funniest memories of our Patrick, I mused as I trudged heavily along the wet footpath on my journey back to Brookdale Park. I even laughed out loud under my hood at the thought of it. In contrast, the most painful memory was hearing him squeal 'the bastards, the fuckin' bastards!' over and over again in our living room in Hamilton Street when me ma broke the news to us that me da had been killed. I can still hear him clearly to this very day as one of my aunts tried to muffle his cries and curses into her chest.

***

Colleen was due to marry in May 1988, and Stephanie and me in September. Patrick came home for both weddings, and even gave Colleen away at the altar. He had lost a bit of weight but still filled his suit well, looking tanned and handsome as they walked down the aisle of St Joseph's Chapel in Galliagh. It seemed as if there was not a bother on him. He had never been a worrier, usually dealing with his life's trepidations with a 'fuck off' or 'fuck all belonging to them'. He laughed and danced and got drunk with the rest of us.

By the time of my wedding, on 24 September in the Long Tower Chapel, his weight loss was a bit more noticeable. However, he was never a well-built man and still looked very healthy, if a wee bit on the thin side. Our guests walked the short distance under the flyover to the Bogside Inn, where we had a fresh salmon buffet upstairs, a wedding band who took twenty minutes to produce a tune after setting up, and a disco. Me ma looked stunning in her red dress and dark perm. She was still only forty-six and was now facing the slow death of her eldest son. But we had all agreed that we had to get on with it and make the best of the time left together, whatever that might be. Me ma wanted him to come back to Derry, but Patrick was adamant that he was surviving well and would remain in London.

Eventually, in March 1990, Patrick called from London to say he was coming home. My mother and John had by then moved to a bungalow at No. 4 Brookdale Park, just up the street from No. 15. We gathered in the living room to welcome him home. Me granny and granda came down too.

Patrick was the only gay in the Quigley household and they loved him all the more for it. However, me granda Connor's hypochondria had developed to such an extent that the sight of the crestfallen Dr Cosgrove plodding down the steps to Mulroy Gardens was almost a daily one, and the shelves were bulging with so many bottles and boxes of potions and pills that it was dangerous to open the cupboard door in fear of an overspill, an explosion even. When he first heard of our Patrick's news that he had AIDS, the most feared disease on the planet, me granda declared: 'Aw, for Jesus' sake, the way I feel the day, he couldn't be as sick as me!'

As Patrick climbed slowly out of the car, silence fell over the gathering at the large window as we looked aghast at this almost skeletal figure, clothes hanging on him, and him shuffle-walking up the garden path.

'Jesus Christ Almighty! Look at the critter!' someone whispered as he came to the front door.

And then: 'Git the stews on! The queer boy's back!' beamed Patrick, his perfect white teeth glistening underneath his black, bushy moustache. This was typical of our Patrick, always ready to dismiss reality for a bit of craic, no matter how bad. What had potentially been the most sombre of occasions was transformed by a single sentence into a party, as the drink came out, more was sent for, and a singsong drifted into the early hours with me ma and our Paul in full flight. Aunts, uncles, in-laws, out-laws and neighbours gathered to drink the health of the blue-eyed boy. Patsy Cline's 'Crazy' boomed around the small bungalow as Patrick demanded that his favourite songs be sung.

'"Two Cigarettes and an Ashtray" now, Mary,' called Patrick to aunt Mary.

'What did I tell ye years ago, Patrick Doherty? It's "Three Cigarettes *in* an Ashtray"!' chided Mary.

'Well, I'm the sick wan, and I only want the two! OK?' demanded Patrick with a broad grin.

'Aw, ye'll never be as sick as your granda Connor! Isn't that right, Daddy?' called aunt Celine across the room.

'Two cigarettes in an ashtray …' crooned Mary, closely followed by aunts Siobhan and Celine. And then the whole house joined in for the chorus.

'Ye know, I'm not afraid to die, Tony,' said Patrick as we regrouped the following afternoon. He was sitting, freshly shaven and showered, in his shiny shell-suit, the colours of which descended in flashes of salmon pink, electric blue and garish green. Me ma and John were in the kitchen preparing a late breakfast. He looked me straight in the eye as he spoke those brave but deadly words. I had no words to give him back. My brain could not compose a suitable response. It was only him and me in the room. I gazed back into his eyes, still bright and blue with the life he had left in him. Nanci Griffith's 'From a Distance' hummed low on the tape deck behind the smoked glass of the music centre stack. She provided some comfort, as did the gentle clatter of pots and pans and the sound of the kettle boiling in the kitchen. My dying brother had just told me that he's not afraid to face his own death, and him not even twenty-nine. And here's me not able to do or say anything.

'The craic was fierce last night,' I said, at last. *Holy fuck,*

what am I saying here? Last night? Last night? My brother's
slowly wasting away and this is all I can say to him!

'A cracker. I coulda sang the whole night,' smiled Patrick.
I let go of the breath I was holding in.

'I think ye did; it must've been four before we left, and we
weren't the last out!'

'Me ma really enjoyed herself; she told me when we got
up. She was buzzin' round the house cleaning up,' he said.

'We'll use the time well that we've left together, Patrick,
not just for me ma's sake,' I said.

'You sayin' that we'll drink and sing till I kick the bucket?'
he asked, smiling.

'More or less. And go to Buncrana to the beach to sober
up.'

'Sounds like a deal to me, though I have to be careful wi'
me medication,' said Patrick with a wry smile. And then,
'Jesus, gwon turn that Nanci Griffith off; she's startin' to do
me head in. Put on the radio for a change.'

'Who turned the tape off?' asked me ma when she came
into the sitting room.

'It was that Tony, Ma,' said Patrick before I got a word in.
'I told him to keep it on!'

'I love Nanci Griffith. Such a beautiful voice,' she said
as she pressed the tape to work again and immediately sang
along to every word of 'Lone Star State of Mind'. Patrick
and I raised our eyes to the heavens. Me ma didn't do
things in half measures. Nanci Griffith was only her latest
fad. And she had a habit of making her fads everyone else's
too, the majority of which were related to her struggle with

her weight. While I was in prison, me ma owned a caravan in Portsalon, County Donegal, and went for endless walks on beaches and country boreens to keep herself fit, often disappearing for ages on her own. When someone told her that skipping would be good for her figure, she bought a skipping rope and practised outside the caravan on the grass in the early mornings. It rained one morning, though, so she took herself inside. At about 6.30 a.m. Glenn, Colleen and me ma's John were woken by a heavy thump. Glenn said it felt like a horse had hit the roof. Then another thump shook the caravan again, and another followed a few seconds later. When Glenn rushed out of the tiny bedroom to investigate the cause of the attack, he discovered me ma standing in her blue leotard, skipping rope in hand, about to launch her five-foot-two, fourteen-stone frame into the air again. Thump! The ornaments shook on their flimsy shelves, and framed pictures trembled on the Beauty-board walls.

'Jesus, Eileen! What in under God are ye at?' cried John, emerging bleary-eyed from their bedroom.

'I'm skippin'! What ye think I'm doin'!' me ma snapped back. Thump! she went again.

'Eileen! The wee caravan'll never hold out to this!' and with that both John and Glenn convulsed with laughter, followed by me ma herself, before returning to bed where they belonged at that time of the morning. That's what was reported to me on a prison visit.

The worst of the fads, though, was probably Uni-Vite, a dieting compound sold in small white tubs from a catalogue dealer. Having dosed herself with it for weeks in the summer of 1985, with no discernible loss of weight, it has to be said, she became a Uni-Vite agent, selling it to friends, her sisters and fellow workers in the shirt factory. Every conversation, whether about cars, sofas, holidays, the IRA, work or gardening, ended with the benefits of the Uni-Vite punchline, driving us all to distraction. Of course, what Uni-Vite really was, was a licence for me ma to eat what she wanted, when she wanted, the Uni-Vite taking care of all the attendant issues associated with an enlarged appetite. She eventually stopped the Uni-Vite in the New Year of 1986 when she realised it wasn't the miracle cure for her weight that she'd convinced herself and others it was. We never ever found out how she explained this to her many customers.

She then progressed to evening primrose oil, which she had even convinced her doctor to provide on prescription. Soon it was stacked up in presses in the kitchen and bathroom, with relatives and friends often leaving the house with a little bottle of the stuff in hand! At one stage, the whole family was taking it on a regular basis, such was the effect her urgings had on us. Even Patrick was on it alongside his own specialised medication. And none of us was even sure what the benefits of evening primrose oil actually were!

By the time Patrick came home she had turned her attention to ginkgo biloba. No matter who came into the house, or no matter the encounter in the street or up the town, ginkgo biloba became the sole focus of her conversation. After a while, we commonly referred to it as 'ginkgo fucking biloba', and our Patrick had to fight her off with the stuff almost every day.

'How are ye keepin' the day, Patrick?' asked our Paul.

'Ginkgo fuckin' biloba!' said Patrick.

'Ye want a cup o' tae?'

'Ginkgo biloba!'

'Are we headin' to the beach later?'

'Ginkgo biloba sandwiches and ginkgo biloba tae!'

Patrick got a new car on account of him being terminally ill. A wee metallic-blue Ford Escort. Me ma drove it, chauffeuring Patrick around, visiting relatives and going for drives to Donegal. On one such occasion they bumped into Maureen and Mickey English, my parents-in-law, in Buncrana Main Street, spending the day together in and out of the shops. On passing a café, Maureen commented on the dirt of the net curtains. She was a very house-proud woman.

'A buckin' disgrace, Patrick! How could ye eat in there and them nets boggin' wi' dirt!' she complained.

'Jesus, Maureen,' Patrick replied, 'ye'd never last a day in London! Nobody cleans their nets. They're either grey wi' dirt or yella from fag smoke. And the dirt on the inside of the windas!'

'Aw dear, Patrick; the dirty hallions!' laughed Maureen at the thought of it, and between them they carried out a survey of all the net curtains on the Main Street, with most receiving a low rating.

'And here!' she barged to Patrick. 'What's this about the Dohertys' doin' their toast on two sides?'

'What are ye on about, Maureen?' asked Patrick, bewildered.

Maureen laughed. 'The first time our Stephanie Mary

was down in your house, ye gave her toast done on the two sides. It was the first thing she told us the next day when we asked for the barrs: "The Dohertys do their toast on two sides, Mammy." It caused a sensation in our living room. We do ours on wan side only, ye see.'

'Sure ye's are nothin' but savages up that Bog! Civilised people toast their toast on two sides, and your Stephanie Mary shouldn't be carryin' stories, anyway!' chided Patrick.

I was quite pleased that Maureen and Patrick had hit it off, as she was the perfect mother-in-law, often I think considering me as one of her own sons; a part replacement for the two that she had lost. 'You only get a lend of them,' she told me ma one day, and me ma said that she was right. I could never fathom how Maureen could apply such simple philosophy to explain the enormity of her loss. Nor could I understand what kept her going, what got her out of bed in the morning, after suffering such a huge personal tragedy. And then she found room in her heart for our Patrick, a gay man dying of AIDS.

'God, but Patrick Doherty's emancipated! God love him but he's totally emancipated!' she said to Stephanie one day. What she meant to say, of course, was *emaciated*, but emancipated really suited Patrick too. He had such free will in his character.

'Tony, you're goney have to do something about that fuckin' Nanci Griffith; me ma's goney drive me round the bend,' said Patrick one day near the end of the summer, suffering too long the effects of me ma's obsession. '"From a Distance" will never be bloody far enough from me! She's at it in the car, and from the car to the house. Wan day she forgot the tape and she turned back to the house for it. I thought I was in for a day without Nanci, but no bloody hope!'

'Where's the tape now, Patrick?' I asked.

'It's in the music centre,' he nodded. Without further ado, I popped open the cassette deck, yanked Nanci out and slid her into my jacket pocket.

'Will we put a bit of music on?' said me ma, coming in from the kitchen.

'Naw, Ma, I've a wile sore head; I need a wee bit of quiet,' said Patrick, rubbing his temples while trying to conceal his grin.

Patrick continued to lose weight over the summer and into September. His shell suits, in garish green, blue and red, hung from his wasted frame. His beautiful black hair was falling out at a rapid rate. He now slept a number of times a day, but wished to do so on the sofa, so as not to miss any barrs, as they say. He still enjoyed a drink, supping several glasses of Guinness a day, as the doctor ordered. He grew weaker as the days shortened with the coming of autumn, but he wasn't for giving up without a fight and always had an excuse for a party.

'I want a Christmas tree and lights up,' he said, one day in October. 'And I want a party, a fucking big Christmas party! And a big fucking turkey rammed to the gills with stuffing! And I want them all now!' he demanded from his position of command on the sofa. He always had a terrible tongue on him. Karen and him had cooked up the idea between them.

Our Glenn, Paul and me were dispatched to the attic for the tree and decorations, and the Christmas party was planned for Saturday night. We were all there: Ma, John, Connor and Sally, Karen, Paul and his wife Fiona, me and Stephanie, Colleen and Decky, and Glenn. Jim Reeves sang his Christmas best on the record player in the sitting room as the Christmas dinner was readied in the early evening: the turkey and ham cooked to perfection, the roasties, sprouts, carrot and parsnip mash and gravy competing for colour and space on the heated plates. Crackers pulled and silly hats on our heads, we ate and drank like nobody's business. Except that Patrick's appetite didn't live up to his expectations as he only picked at his overflowing plate. His lack of appetite didn't put him off his knavery, though.

'Will somebody put Nanci Griffith on?' he grinned across the table towards me.

'Sure me ma lost the cassette tape of her,' I smiled back, trying not to reveal anything.

'I didn't lose anything!' me ma shot back. 'She was in the tape deck and then she was gone. Walked! Wan of yous took her!'

'Jesus, if that woman searched for that hoorin' cassette tape once, she searched for it a hundred times. She must've opened the buckin' tape deck fifty times! She was even rollin' me over and me critically ill on the sofa!' Patrick bawled.

'Was it you, Tony Doherty, that took that tape on me?' demanded me ma across the table.

'Naw, it wasn't me, Ma. I swear!' I replied, trying to keep a straight face.

'It *was* you, ye buckin' article ye!' she accused, raising her voice. 'I loved that tape! You better get it back or you'll dear buy it!'

'Ye'd have more chance of gettin' Shergar back!' shot our Paul. 'But hi, Ma! Know what ye can do? Listen to it "From a Distance",' he chuckled, singing the title and then the whole table joined in.

The bungalow at No. 4 Brookdale Park filled up to breaking point. Every two minutes there was someone else at the door. It was standing room only in the kitchen. Patrick sat up on the sofa, his thin legs protruding from his dressing gown.

'What in under good Jesus is that you're wearin'?' asked Patrick of me aunt Lorraine, who was heavily pregnant with her first child and had arrived in a huge overcoat to protect her from the biting frost.

'Shut you yer buckin' mouth; I'm expectin', ye know!' laughed Lorraine.

Laura Glenn appeared from down the street with her brother, Paul Ford, both reared in Central Drive in Creggan. Paul, a life-long rock'n'roller with Derry band King Rat, brought his guitar, and it wasn't long before the Doherty home resounded to a variety of Beatles' classics as requested by Patrick: 'Lady Madonna', 'Hey Jude', 'Sergeant Pepper', 'Strawberry Fields' and 'Penny Lane'. When it came to 'Let It Be', there wasn't a dry eye in the house. Me ma sat beside Patrick on the sofa, held him, kissed him and caressed the hands of her oldest son. There was a steady stream out to the kitchen and back garden to cry and console each other.

'Hi, Ford, do you know any Nanci Griffith?' asked our Paul, nodding a grin towards me ma and Patrick.

'I'll Nanci Griffith ye!' Patrick replied. 'She nearly drove me mad in me own house!'

'Now, Stephanie for a song!' called me ma.

'Jesus! Here's new light out of an oul bottle!' called Patrick, his voice beginning to weaken. 'What are ye goney sing, Skinny?'

'"Silver Dollar", for you, ye queer fucker ye,' she replied, clearing her throat before giving her stand-up performance:

> Don't you know ...?
> A man without a woman is like a ship without a sail,
> A boat without a rudder or a fish without a tail,
> A man without a woman is like a wreck upon the sand,
> There's only one thing worse in the universe
> That's a woman without a man.
> A woman without a man.
>
> You can throw a silver dollar down upon the ground,
> And it will roll, because it's round.
> A woman never knows what a good man she's got,
> Until he puts her down.

'God bliss us, but I never thought ye had it in ye!' called me ma. 'And every word too!'

'Not exactly the song for a queer man, mind you, but well done, Skinny!' laughed Patrick.

'Right, give us over me gong now for "Triangle"!' he

demanded. The song he wanted was Patsy Cline's 'Tra Le La Le La Triangle'.

The gong, a wee copper ornament with a wooden stick, was ceremoniously passed over and presented to Patrick. Balancing the gong on his knee, he hit it each time they chanted 'Tra la la la,' *ding!* 'Triangle. Tra la la la,' *ding!* 'Triangle,' and, as the song progressed, Patrick delayed his dinging longer and longer, and him grinning like the divil, to the merriment of all, before landing a resounding *ding!* followed by a loud chorus of 'Triangle!'

He deteriorated in the days after the Christmas party and slept for longer periods on the sofa during the daytime. Close family maintained a vigil, ensuring that me ma had enough support. He was far from finished, though, often holding court in his waking hours. Sometimes his voice was steady and strong, while at other times he shone with just a single word or sentence.

The bungalow was just across from where the Duffys used to live. Their father had been killed by the IRA in 1973, accused of being an informer. Patrick was often in their home later in the 1970s, as he was a friend of Kevin, the son. Sitting up on his sofa one afternoon, staring across the street towards the Duffys' former home, he said, swallowing hard between sentences, 'God, but poor Margaret Duffy had a wile hard life. But she was some craic too. She waited for months to get her telephone installed. It must've been 1975. She had us talked black and blue about this phone. She never devalved about it. Never devalved! I was in the house a day or two after it was installed, and didn't it ring.

Loud as bedamned. Mrs Duffy went about her business but didn't answer the call. It rang again and I looked around to see if she would answer. The bloody phone rang out again! A minute later, off it went again; big loud rings echoing around the house.

"'Are ye not goney answer your new phone, Mrs Duffy?" I asked her.

"'Jesus naw, Patrick. Sure I wouldn't touch anything electric!"

'The same year she bought a book of tickets for the Christmas parish draw. The wee boys used to come round the doors wi' them. The first prize, printed on the ticket, was a divan suite, the second prize was £100 and the third was a Christmas hamper. And didn't Mrs Duffy win the first prize, but when the man from the parish council came to the door she told him that she wanted the £100 second prize instead.

"'Jesus, Mrs Duffy, are ye sure?" enquired the man, as the divan suite was worth far more than £100.' Patrick was in stitches laughing at this stage as he drew us toward the punchline.

"'Och, sure what would I be doing with a diving suit at my age!"' and the whole sitting room erupted at the thought of Mrs Duffy in her snorkel and flippers!

'Jesus, there's Charles McEleney outside along wi' his sister!' said Karen all of a sudden.

'What am I like, Karen? What am I like?' asked Patrick. 'Is me hair OK?' he enquired, smoothing it down with the palms of his hands. Charles was an old friend of Patrick and a well-known hairdresser in Derry.

'Aye, yer grand, Patrick. Yer lookin' grand,' said Karen, getting up to open the front door.

Charles and his sister stayed with Patrick in the sitting room while the rest of us retreated to the kitchen to make tea and give them space. They stayed and chit-chatted for around an hour, during which Patrick self-consciously patted his hair flat, only for it to spring back upright. As they were leaving, Patrick insisted on walking them to the door to say goodbye. When they had just left, he caught sight of himself in the hall mirror and was mortified to realise that his remaining fringe was sticking up on his head like a small, black palm tree.

'I thought you said I was lookin' grand! Look at the shape of me! I'm like fuckin' Tich and Quackers!' he roared at Karen.

'Tich and Quackers!' squealed Karen, pointing to his palm tree. 'Tich and fuckin' Quackers!' she repeated in hysterics.

'Aye, Tich and Quackers!' squealed Patrick, rounding his eyes like Quackers the duck.

'Tich and Quackers!' they bawled in unison, causing the rest of us to roll around in fits, with eruptions of giggling and cackling breaking out for the rest of the day.

Gradually, Patrick began sleeping for even longer periods on the sofa. We tried to make life as normal as possible, encouraging me ma and John to get themselves out for walks and drives, or the odd night away. Steph and I stayed overnight several times, sleeping in the spare room. On one such occasion, we awoke in the morning to him standing in the doorway of the bedroom in his shell suit: 'That's me now; I'm away for a jog!' he laughed, moving his knees up and down in slow motion.

When he woke at any time of the day, often too weak to talk much, he would ask whoever was at hand to bring him a glass of water and tell him a story. Stephanie often obliged, usually something insane about her granny Annie and granda James.

'But wait d'ye hear this wan, Patrick,' she said on one such occasion. 'I lived wi' me granny when I was younger. I told her one day that me ma was selling her coffee table to Ruby, a former neighbour of me granny's that she wasn't fussed on and who she referred to as "Humpy Ruby". Ruby now lived on the far side of the Bog. Me ma had no phone, so out came the biro and the notepad and me granny proceeded to scribble a message to her which I was to deliver as a matter of great urgency. "You deliver that note straight to Maureen for me, now, won't ye?" instructed me granny as I left the flat. But didn't I get all mixed in this as I left Dove Gardens and straight I went to Humpy Ruby's house, note in hand!

'The son answered the door. "I've a note for yer mammy," I said before being invited into the sitting room, the fire blazin', the TV on and the place packed. Humpy Ruby's daughter took the note from me as Humpy Ruby couldn't read or write. The daughter was a slow reader herself and addressed each word out loud, individually, before moving to the next.

'"DEAR – MAUREEN. – DON'T – BE – SELLING – YOUR – COFFEE – TABLE – TO – THAT – HUMPY –

WEE – FUCKER – RUBY. – SHE – WOULDN'T – PAY – GOD'S – MOTHER."'

Patrick's chest heaved as he laughed, causing him to wince at the same time. 'Well, Jesus, Patrick, even at that young age I knew I'd messed up big time. I wanted the ground to open up in Humpy Ruby's living room!'

Another day, Karen made a call to her husband, Paddy, who was away working in Canada. Patrick appeared to be in a deep sleep. The phone sat on the matching chair just beside the sofa. Karen became very upset when speaking to Paddy about Patrick's condition and was in floods of tears by the time she hung up. Patrick's eyes shot open: 'Fuck ye, Karen, I thought I was buckin' dead when I heard ye cryin' over the top of me! I didn't realise ye were on the phone!'

'The Maniac Cock!' exclaimed Stephanie, bringing the room to an unaccustomed quiet. 'Wait til yous hear this wan! Me and Tony came in one night to me granny and granda's just before we were married. The TV as usual was up full blast and some poor critter was being strangled on the screen.

'"What is it anyway yous are watchin'?" I asked.

'"The Maniac Cock!" said me granny.

'"What, Granny? What did ye say?" says I, lookin' over at Tony.

'"The Maniac Cock!" she repeated, and her wi' her stockin's round her ankles, sittin' forward on the sofa, all into it!

'Well he looked at me and I looked at him. Both of us fearin' that she mighta lifted the wrong film from the video shop, or somethin'.

'"Aw, Jesus, James, look; he's goney git her! Aw Jesus!" she cried, as her fingers clicked her knitting needles a mile a minute.

'"Dirty big bastard!" puffed me granda on his cigar butt, the smoke clouding over the TV.

'"What did ye say, Granny?" I asked again.

'"The Maniac Cock"! repeated Annie, a bit louder, completely unaware of the image she was unleashin'.

'"Where's the video cover?" I demanded, and me panickin', for wan day she was in Whitey's Video Shop and she took a video up to Whitey and he looks at her and says, "Annie, ye wouldn't be takin' that; sure what would you be doin' wi' a blue movie?" and me granny said, "Have ye no other colour?"

'Anyway, me granny passed me over the cover without looking, still transfixed by the mayhem on the TV and it blarin'.

'"Jesus, Granny, it's *Maniac Cop!*" I bawled, relieved that we hadn't walked in, ye know, on me elderly grandparents holed up watching blue movies.

'"That's what I said," said she, "The Maniac Cock! It's a great show! Isn't it, James?"

'"Great show, The Maniac Cock; a great show," said me granda, as both of them settled in for more gore and senseless mayhem.'

Aunt Lorraine provided tales of my exploits while staying in me granny's house when I was going out with Stephanie.

'One morning, me and him were gettin' ready to go out the door. There were soldiers everywhere and a helicopter flyin' low over the houses. Didn't a wee soldier come to the

door and our Tony went out to open it. I stood listenin' at
the bottom of the stairs, shakin' like a bag of bottles, petrified
they were goin' to raid.

"'Don't give them an excuse to raid!" I warned him, for he
was a wile man.

"'Don't worry about that, Lorraine," says he. And out he
went.

"'Hello, sir," said the wee soldier.

"'What d'ye want?" says Tony, as gruff as bedamned, and I
thought, *Dear Jesus, Tony Doherty, you're goin' to get us raided!*

'And the wee soldier said, "I need to search your back
garden. Can you open the back gate for us?"

'And our Tony said, "Are you a good climber?"

'And the wee soldier said, "Yes, I am."

'And what did our Tony say to him then? "Well, fuck
away off and climb the fence, then!" and slammed the door
in his face. Dear Jesus, I was standing at the foot of the stairs
cursing him. I coulda killed him!'

And so the stories flowed as the late October evenings
grew darker and Patrick became weaker and thinner. Some
days he could hardly rise and needed assistance from me
and our Paul to visit the bathroom. Once on such a visit his
pyjama coat fell open, revealing a skeletal frame, the flesh
pulled in beyond the rib-cage and chest bones.

He fell silent eventually, too pained to use his voice-box,
and could only indicate by single words and gestures. While
knowing that the end was near for him, nearness is merely
relative to your understanding and experience of someone
in the final stages of a terminal illness. For me, and for most

of us, death was still long from us. And then, one afternoon in the first week of November, after Patrick hadn't left the sofa since the previous evening, Doctor Cosgrove told us to expect the worst sooner rather than later and to call all the family to No. 4 Brookdale Park. We lay, heads and thraws, in the two-bed bungalow, on the chairs and on the sitting-room carpet providing company to him as he faced his journey to the other world through the darkest of black nights. He opened his eyes wide from a deep sleep at four in the morning and stared into space. The time had arrived. Dozers shook and steadied themselves and sleepers woke as Patrick's breathing became laboured. Me ma held his hand, caressed his thin, sallow face and whispered mother things into the ear of her departing child. As death came to him he raised both arms into the air like a champion and then let them fall gently on his lap.

Everyone, including the priest, wore something in cerise pink on the day of the funeral on Friday 7 November 1990 as we laid Patrick Joseph Doherty, aged twenty-eight years, to rest with his father, long dead. No finer son. That night, the wake-goers swayed to 'Three Cigarettes in an Ashtray', but the wee copper gong stayed put.

7

Freedom Walk

'I need to thank you for what you did that day,' I said to Paddy Walsh as he stood at the bar with a handsome new pint of stout in front of him.

'Ach, sure anybody woulda done the same, son,' said Paddy, awkward with the praise.

'Don't believe a word. I've seen the photos, Paddy. You're one of the bravest men in Ireland,' I said, meaning every bit of it.

'Would ye believe, when I got home Anna said to me: "What happened that coat o' yours? There's a hole in the collar; ye musta caught it on somethin'."' I hadn't the heart to tell her it was a bullet-hole,' said Paddy, with a shy grin. 'It musta been months and months before I could tell her. Everybody knows now. Even the grandwains.'

'What, were they still firing when ye crawled out?' asked our Paul in amazement.

'A few they fired. They all missed,' he smiled, as he wiped the foam from his upper lip. 'I could feel them whizzin' over me head and thought I was a goner meself.'

He had lost the comb-over wave he had in the photos, succumbing gracefully to a smooth dome. This was the man who had risked his life to bring comfort to me da in his final seconds with an Act of Contrition. We stood in Mailey's Bar, aka The Bluebell, named after Mary Blue's Burn, a stream that runs from the Creggan, under Celtic Park and through the Gasyard on its journey to the River Foyle. This is where me ma and da and granny and granda singsonged and back-to-backed many a night in the 1960s and into the early 1970s. It was handy to both Moore Street and Hamilton Street for the dander home. Brothers Hugh and Liam Mailey gave their patrons lifts in their own cars, especially when the Troubles started.

'These are Paddy Doherty's sons here, Hugh,' said Paddy. The white-haired Hugh stretched a hand out over the bar to shake ours.

'Great to meet ye's, boys!' he said. 'I knew yer uncle Paddy, Paddy Stewart, too. That's where he sat, down there by the fireplace,' he said, nodding towards the shiny, black, cast-iron surround, ornamented with trophies for darts, football and quizzes.

'I was just thankin' this Paddy for what he did for me da,' I said to Hugh.

'And so you should, young Doherty. For if anyone ever deserved a medal for bravery, it was that man there,' said Hugh.

A medal for bravery; now there's a thought! I mused.

As I came close to my father's age when he died, I began to feel more *him* and wondered, more and more often, what kind of man he would have become. When I began appearing on television and in the local newspapers, men his age would stop me in the street and address me as Young

Doherty. 'You're The Skelper's son,' they'd say as we dodged women and prams at the door of Doherty's café. Strangely, all of these encounters happened in William Street. One day it was Dennis Harkin. A week or so later it was Chelsea McBride and then Maxi Gallagher.

It was from a TV film of a crowd in William Street that one day I picked me da out of the marauding and angry rioters, some in their Sunday best, clodding stones and dodging rubber bullets. My heart raced the first time I saw him. I sat watching the six o'clock news and caught sight of him suddenly appearing from the throng near the corner. The TV camera was among the army vehicles and barbed-wire barricade blocking the road just short of the café door. He held his speckled coat up over his mouth from the CS gas, grasping a stone with his throwing arm. The black, unlacquered, Teddy Boy hair and his electric-blue round-neck jersey were unmistakable. He doubled over behind his thick coat at the crack of a rubber bullet, its white rush of smoke further misting the crowd. He disappeared just as suddenly as he'd appeared. I watched to see if he'd come back, but he was gone. He was only minutes away from his death around the corner on Rossville Street.

I often wondered what was in his mind at that moment in William Street. He was a wile man for sure. He hated the Limeys. He was naturally quick and certain with his fists, and on more than one occasion he'd rendered a cocky squaddie horizontal with a blow to the jaw. For a man of five foot four in his stocking soles, he had the heart of a lion, the power of an ox and the temper of a shrew. While studying Irish I was enthralled to find out that the word *sceilp* meant 'a clout' or 'a swipe'. This has translated into 'a skelp' in Northern Irish English, as in 'a skelp on the ear', which is still a common threat in these parts. 'Skelper' would therefore mean a thumper, more or less. Did The Skelper think of his six children at home as he scrambled, head down, at the sound of the first sharp crack of a rifle? Did he go searching for me ma and granda, or was it by that stage a petrified dash for an escape route through the flats as the single shots increased to automatic fire, echoing in that cauldron of glass and concrete? It was hard to imagine him petrified. I had never seen him scared in my life.

He spent his last minutes probably dodging projectiles from rioters too far behind the lines and shrinking himself down to avoid rubber bullets from the front. Seamus Heaney wrote about the futility of rebels, mown down 'shaking scythes at cannon' in the heat of a one-sided battle. My father pelted fist-sized stones at armoured cars, then retreated into the *bearna baol* (dangerous gap), out of which they carried him prostrate, shoulder-high, facing the skies, to an ambulance on Rossville Street. Straight to the morgue. He stood up for what he believed in. He paid with his life. I am proud of him.

Was it the opening of his grave to accommodate his son, or was it the sight of men me da's age, white or greying in their only suits, punching the air outside the courthouse in London some months later that put big notions into my head? *Go ndéana Dia trócaire orthu* carved on the Celtic cross was now definitely plural in the claiming of two Patrick Josephs. Me ma had whispered, 'Let go, Patrick. Let go, son,' into his ear as he veered between worlds on that dark November morning. It was one of the bravest things I've ever witnessed. I sat near her on the floor and heard everything. Her words will never leave me. A mother encouraging her eldest son to succumb to his early death. To free himself of the pain of a modern wasting disease. And he did let go. He freed himself. But when the heavy clay was excavated from my father's grave, did it release something else into the air for us all to breathe in? Life springing from death? Is that how it happened?

***

In March the following year, a free man walked, with disbelieving eyes, through the cordon of airport police. Johnny Walker, sentenced to life imprisonment for his part in the Birmingham pub bombings in England, was coming back from the dead zone of over a decade and a half in prison. And him now declared an innocent man after all. He was lucky they'd stopped using the gallows, otherwise he and his five friends would have dangled for sure. His eyes, round as saucers, took it all in. All this freedom. All this wide-openness. Remember, there are no horizons in a prison cell. Only in your imagination and in your mind's eye. Getting an aeroplane the day after getting out after all that time would be akin to rocketing to the moon for your birthday. It's astronomical; beyond belief. It's a parallel universe.

He looked old. Not elderly, but old. He was an old man coming home, blazer in hand and the sleeves of his good shirt rolled up his muscular forearms. Old and fit with the stride of a twenty-year-old. He was bald on top but pure white and tidy at the sides, his white sideburns shaved neat, and his face was of the healthiest pink. He stood embarrassed for the cameras as they snapped and flashed. The deal was that there would be no questions and no statement. He was here to go home to his wife and wains in Carnhill Estate.

'Tony here, Johnny!' I called out over the clicking cameras and manoeuvrings of the press. 'We're here to look after you,' I smiled, referring to Pat, Paddy and Jim, all ex-prisoners, who had travelled up from Derry. We knew the score. Nothing to see past the cell or the length of the yard for thousands of days and then, suddenly, new horizons the following morning stretching out far beyond. It's very hard to take it in all at once.

'Young Doherty!' he called across, glad of the familiarity amid the sea of strange faces.

'Just give us the nod when you're ready,' I said, giving him the thumbs up.

His accent was mostly Derry but with more than a speckle of prison Cockney. Had he been in jail in the States he would've been labelled a Derry Yank on his return. Nothing worse than a Derry Yank! You don't notice your accent changing in prison, though, but prisons have accents that affect your own wording and rhythm of speech. When I walked to freedom in 1985, when Johnny Walker was in his eleventh year, I was speaking with a Belfast accent. Even my Irish was Belfast!

On the road home from the airport, RTÉ Radio na Gaeltachta played a medley of joyous songs including 'Óró, Sé do Bheatha Bhaile!' ('Oh, welcome home!'), which Pat,

Paddy and I sang out loud as we knew all the verses from prison recitals. It was 1991. A huge chink had appeared in Britain's monolithic suit of armour. What we had known since the 1970s to be true was now *confirmed* as true: the English police and the judiciary had set these men up as being responsible for the IRA bombings in Birmingham, which had killed twenty-one innocent civilians and maimed dozens more. But the unimaginable had now actually happened. Instead of dying in prison as the police had expected, here they were proclaiming their innocence and casting insults upon the court behind them as their long nightmare drew to a close with the new dawn. And all broadcast by the BBC.

It was no act of genius on my part, or anyone else's, to relate old, innocent prisoners on their freedom walk to the fourteen dead of Bloody Sunday, accused in their final hours between mass, Sunday dinner and their execution, of offences that they did not commit. Half of them were on a wanted list, said the Para commander, and many of them had fired weapons and had been handling explosives, said the English Lord Chief Justice, Lord Widgery, less than three months later in his official report to the British parliament. In spite of his report, supposedly designed to restore confidence among the people in the institutions of the British state, there were very few facts known about this dreadful event. What was clear, though, was that each of the executioners had a letter in place of their name. It was Soldier F, more than likely, who had done the deed on my father, who, after throwing his stone, had bolted up Chamberlain Street and into the courtyard of the Rossville Flats just as the Paras swung their

Pigs and Saracens into the same place and dismounted to exact revenge on the people of Free Derry.

In the late 1980s I had made a number of attempts to get the fourteen families together ahead of the annual march at the end of January. The Sinn Féin headquarters in an old, turn-of-the-century terraced house in the Bogside's Cable Street, with huge mushrooms sprouting from the dampness in the walls, was our meeting place, but not all the families were Sinn Féin supporters, so not all of them showed up. The parents of the young men killed were all old by then, and usually accompanied by a son or daughter to keep them right. Almost twenty years on, the mantle was passing from one generation to the next without any clear expectation or notion except the need to be there to remember, and not to forget.

The year before our Patrick died, a number of us had set up the Bloody Sunday Initiative (BSI) to plan and organise a series of events to mark the twentieth anniversary, in 1992, of Derry's massacre, under the banner *One World–One Struggle*. I had just graduated from Magee University and was looking for something to do with my knowledge and free time. I found it very strange at first, naming an organisation with Bloody Sunday in the title. While I thought something more inspiring would have been better, anything less than the obvious would always have to be explained.

I soon got used to it. We set up an office at No. 1 Westend Park, a large, early twentieth-century townhouse at the top of the Bogside and the foot of the New Road to Creggan. We had the whole of the first floor to ourselves, including one large, rectangular drawing room with a bay window giving a panoramic view of the Bogside, Derry Walls, the city centre and the river meandering towards Lough Foyle. The Rossville Flats had been demolished in 1989, radically altering the townscape. There was also a commanding view across Laburnum Terrace and Bull Park in the direction of the imposing and impressive St Eugene's Cathedral, the construction of which began in 1851 as Ireland convulsed in the wake of the Great Hunger that brought many of our ancestors to Derry from Donegal and north County Derry, where the numbers of poor farmers and labourers of the rural hinterland had been decimated.

There was a large table of faux-leather in the centre of the drawing room, with benches and shelving around the edges, making it perfect for both meetings and working. The huge house was like a freezer in the winter and a sweathouse in the summer. It had a large wooden and glass front porch, accessed by a number of steep steps. In its heyday, there was a tennis court just below the porch, now long gone, smothered under bramble, weeds, reeds and rough grasses right out to the bottom on the New Road. No. 1 Westend Park was the former home of none other than Mayor Glover, a former unionist mayor of the corrupt Londonderry Corporation in the early 1960s. Taking the office was a sure sign that we meant business, and taking Mayor Glover's former residence was a sure sign that the tide of justice was turning.

No. 1 Westend Park had been a nucleus of progressive cultural activity since the early 1980s. My wife, Stephanie, worked there from 1985 with Derry Film & Video, making

Mother Ireland and *Hush-a-Bye-Baby* in the late 1980s under the tutelage of Margo Harkin and Anne Crilly. That company had folded, though, by the time the BSI took up residence. Camerawork Darkrooms was located on the top floor of the four-storey building, and had been established to record Derry's history in stills.

Robin Percival, whom I first encountered as a hippy in the Brandywell in the early 1970s, and who had since taken up permanent residence in Derry, was a founding member of the BSI and first penned the purpose and value of the organisation, part of which included a Bogside Interpretive Centre, which felt hugely tangential and way beyond reach for the time. There were bombs going off and people being shot and killed in Derry and all over the North. Who in their right mind would come here in their spare time to visit an interpretive centre? Despite having lived in Derry for two decades, Robin spoke with a crisp north of England accent. A bearded, bespectacled, public-school-educated Quaker from Widnes, he had travelled extensively in Europe, Asia and the United States in the 1960s. Widnes' claim to fame, he told us, apart from rugby, was that Paul Simon wrote 'Homeward Bound' as he sat on a bench in Widnes railway station while waiting for a train.

One of the stalwarts of the civil rights movement, Éamonn McCann, joined our loose but independent group of free-thinkers, who wanted to focus international attention on what the British state had done in our city and beyond since 1969, shifting the blame for all the violence onto anyone but themselves. Another of the team, Paul O'Connor, had left Derry in 1972 for the States and then went on to West Germany. He was a fluent German speaker and able to deal directly with the German media. He had been brought up in Westend Park, so knew all the neighbours well, including John Hume in No. 5. Martin Finucane, the younger brother of the Belfast solicitor Pat Finucane, who was killed in February 1989 by loyalists in the pay of the state, joined us too, and, with me, they became the core of the new organisation, working five days a week. The crew-cut Martin, nicknamed 'Fucked-Up Stories' by his family because of his inability to convey a tale without deviating to something completely irrelevant or trivial, was a thinner version of his executed older brother.

Other members were Helen Harris, from Cobh in County Cork, who came to Derry straight from university and joined us, as did Margaret Makowski, whose family was rooted in Derry, but who came here from the USA, where she and her sisters were born. Finally, there was Tony Gillespie, affectionately known as Father Tony because he was an ex-priest. Tony did not have good health and so helped out only occasionally. He was a great storyteller, though, often regaling the office with tales of his life as a missionary in Guam, or at the seminary in the Basque Country.

Most of the members were politically active or interested in one way or another, and we agreed that Bloody Sunday had been successfully labelled by the British as a firefight between the British Army and the IRA, or at least sufficient doubt had been cast, a clouding of the facts, so as to excuse the actions of the Paras. A little-known fact about the aftermath of Bloody Sunday was the depth of the belief within the British Army, passed down from one regiment to another, that the dead of Bloody Sunday actually belonged to the IRA. I remember me ma would say, on hearing that a new regiment had come into Ebrington Barracks, 'We'll expect a raid in the morning, then', and we would be sent hoovering, cleaning and polishing so that the soldiers wouldn't think we came from a dirty home. Which we didn't. And, sure enough, within a day or two, the army jeeps would squeal to a halt outside our house in the early hours to pay their first unwelcome visit to an 'IRA family'. It was the same for many of the Bloody Sunday families, I am told.

One of the first things we in the BSI had to do was to re-establish the dead as real people with real lives and coming from good families. The twentieth anniversary was the perfect opportunity to do this. It was agreed that we would produce a book, and that Éamonn, given his grasp of words as a journalist, would write it.

Derry was about to look in on itself to find inspiration and truth. For the first time since 1972, Derry was about to bring the dead back to life by telling their stories in simple, everyday terms. I was tasked with the door-knocking. It was felt best to knock rather than call on the phone. I met every one of the heads of the fourteen families in their homes in Creggan, Shantallow, Bogside and the scattered outskirts of the city. My task was to clear the way for two local women, Bridie Hannigan and Maureen Shiels, to carry out recorded interviews, to be transcribed and edited for publication as the core of the book.

When the book, *Bloody Sunday in Derry: What Really Happened?*, was launched in the Bookworm Community Bookshop, Bishop Street, in January 1992, it was the first time that many of the families had been in the one place at the same time since 1972. From the conversations which took place in Bookworm that day, it was obvious that no one, my own mother included, could provide any clear recollection of the journey they had gone through, or any details of the Widgery Inquiry, set up in haste the day after the killings by 10 Downing Street, and located thirty miles up the coast in Coleraine. Very few could even name the solicitor acting on their behalf or knew how he came to be appointed.

All the dead were working-class, from among the second-class citizenry of a place at constant war for over twenty years. When I went to prison in 1981, I was shocked to find that Bloody Sunday had been the catalyst that drove many of my fellow inmates into the IRA. Not just in Derry, but all around. It was a turning point. A point of no return. There would be no going back to the days of enforced second-class citizenship.

No one had ever suggested to the families that there would be power in numbers, in unity, until they came through the door of Bookworm on that Saturday afternoon. They gathered along the shelved walls, at the till and around the display tables where wine was being served, and heard descriptions of their fathers, sons and brothers as they themselves had known them. Good men. Strong boys. Great boxers. Creggan charmers. Hard workers. Proud fathers. Loyal brothers. Nifty dressers. Brilliant dancers. Mass-goers. Surrounded by a variety of radical books on anarchism, Marx, Cuba, Nicaragua and any other decent left-wing cause, we took pride that we had come this far after all these years. Our loved ones were innocent and hadn't deserved to die on the cold streets of the Bogside. Moreover, they didn't deserve the lies that had been spread about them, and the cruel assertion that there would have been no deaths had the Civil Rights Association not decided to break the law by holding an illegal procession, even though their cause had been the liberty of others.

As a measure of the contrast between Derry and Dublin in 1992, when the same book was launched several days later in Buswells Hotel beside Leinster House, only a small gathering of journalists and political activists attended. One TD showed up – Tony Gregory, a left-winger from north inner-city Dublin. He knew Éamonn McCann personally. Because of the prolonged conflict in the North, twenty-year-old human rights abuses appeared to matter little as the endless body count continued to rise, often spilling across the border into the South.

During the anniversary, the BSI office became the conduit for the national, British and international press to gain access to the families and other contacts in Derry. They would almost always ask the question: Was your son/your husband in the IRA? Sections of the British press seemed obsessed with the idea of bodies of IRA men being spirited out of the Bogside and secretly buried across the border. The reply to that was that Derry was such a close-knit community, with everyone knowing everybody else's business, that it would simply be impossible for someone to disappear in that way.

And, no, he wasn't in the IRA. It was also well known that the press over the years had been given photographs and other personal effects of the dead, only for them never to be returned, to disappear for ever. We were determined that families would be treated with the respect they deserved but had seldom received.

The BSI took charge of all aspects of the anniversary, including involvement in a conference on the theme of *One World–One Struggle* with Denis Goldberg of the African National Congress (ANC), who had been imprisoned with Nelson Mandela in 1961. Securing the support of the ANC was a major coup as it placed the events of Bloody Sunday in the popular imagination alongside the Sharpeville Massacre in South Africa in 1960 by the forces of apartheid. We were no longer going to allow our cause to be boxed in or explained away by others to maintain the British status quo. We also determined that the march of Sunday 26 January 1992 was not going to be boxed into the Bogside, as the original march had been, having being blocked on its way by the British Army on William Street. We were taking it to the Guildhall Square. Around 20,000 people agreed with us on that bright, freezing-cold afternoon, the weather uncannily similar to the Sunday twenty years before when the most dreadful news had filtered along the icy road from the Bogside to Hamilton Street. We sang 'We Shall Overcome!' as we marched up William Street and into the city centre.

We had finally made it! Not just to the Guildhall Square, but also to the idea that we had reached another point of no return and had enough fight in us to take our cause further. Through the winter and into spring the BSI office in Westend Park was a hive of activity as we sought to capitalise on what we had already done. Families called in to voice their appreciation, well-wishers sent flowers and small gifts, and a number of sizeable donations were made.

'Good Morning, Westend Park!' big Martin Finucane would announce, Robin Williams-like, each morning as he mounted, often boogieing, the broad flight of squeaking stairs to the kitchen with his bag of buns. During February 1992, exactly three years since his brother Pat had been shot dead in front of his wife and children, we planned the formative stages of what would become a long and arduous campaign to set the record straight about Bloody Sunday. While Martin and I could commit full-time to the project, Paul O'Connor had been giving us his time on his day off from Bookworm, where he worked, and brought a deep knowledge of political campaigning to the group that he'd learned in the trade unions and among the left in Freiburg.

It's hard to escape or ignore your history in the Bogside, both communal and personal. Even with the flats gone, it's still easy to trace everything that's happened since 1969. Some days I'd pass the busy T-junction of William Street and Chamberlain Street several times, where me da was last captured on moving film before being caught on still film in the seconds before he died. Sometimes I can look at the stills, suppressing my emotions, and at other times I simply have to look away. My mother gave me his clothes when I moved into 25 Lower Nassau Street, a terraced row in Rosemount, with Stephanie in 1989. They were in the same thick plastic bag in which they had been returned to 15 Hamilton Street after the Widgery Inquiry concluded. There is a small notch in his leather belt where the bullet had clipped it when entering his body.

Pilot's Row is a community centre erected on the site of the old Bogside street where the river pilots who guided boats and ships up the river in the nineteenth century used to be housed. It is a nondescript, modern, red-brick building erected in 1976 by the City Council and the Western Education Board, but on Bloody Sunday this was the open ground through which the Paras sped in the direction of their prey. It was here, several weeks after celebrating the success of *One World–One Struggle*, that we convened a public meeting, chaired by Éamonn McCann and addressed by a nervous Johnny Walker, to announce the formal setting up of the Bloody Sunday Justice Campaign.

John Kelly, brother of seventeen-year-old Michael Kelly, shot dead on Rossville Street near Pilot's Row, was asked to read the three objectives of the campaign, prepared by Robin Percival, which were: repudiation of the Widgery Report; the formal acknowledgement of the innocence of all the those killed or wounded; and the bringing to justice of those responsible for the murders and attempted murders. His words echoed off the bare brick walls before settling in our minds. Prosecutions? Hardly a single member of the self-described security forces had been prosecuted successfully since 1969. And at that very moment, someone said, there was a joint RUC and army patrol stopping cars right outside as if to emphasise who was in charge!

A tall man with jet-black hair stood up from the crowd of fifty or so in attendance. He must have been six foot four, wore a dark gaberdine coat and looked like a Special Branch man. 'I'm Harry Devenny. Me da was Sammy Devenny, who was beaten to a pulp in our house in William Street by the RUC in 1969, and as ye know, he died shortly after. I'd just like to say that I'm really glad that I was home from Manchester to attend this meeting. It's about time the people of Derry stood up to be counted again and not let our city, our families be criminalised. Anything I can do over in Manchester, give me a shout!' A huge cheer went up around the sports hall. The Devennys were a large and popular family, and many of them still lived around the Bogside.

Seán Semple, dark and moustachioed, also brought up in the Bogside, suggested that, with Derry City Council being a majority nationalist body, the campaign should seek formal recognition and funding from it. Soon after, John Kelly was appointed as chair, I was appointed public relations officer (PRO), and Gerry Duddy, brother of seventeen-year-old Jackie Duddy, shot dead in Chamberlain Street, agreed to accept the position of finance officer. Jim 'Hawks' Collins, a Camerawork photographer and dab hand at design, agreed to produce a suitable symbol to characterise the campaign and created an intricately drawn dove in Celtic style with an oak-leaf in one wing. It was perfect!

The campaign members began to meet regularly every Tuesday evening around the large table in Westend Park. Brothers, sisters, sons and daughters, as well as a few nieces filed in at 7 p.m. On the first evening the large room couldn't accommodate the numbers, so several had to stand listening on the landing. Geraldine Doherty, niece of Gerald Donaghey, the youngest killed on Bloody Sunday, at sixteen, volunteered to take notes. Micky McKinney, eldest brother of Willie McKinney, another of those killed that day, took charge of organising a public petition. It quickly became clear, though, that John Kelly's role of chairing would be the most difficult.

John had little experience of chairing meetings, and to say that there were different levels of organisational and political awareness among the expanded group of families would be to grossly understate the facts. While John was at pains to emphasise that everyone must be heard, no matter what they had to say, most people ended up saying exactly what they wanted, sometimes all at the same time, sometimes in the room and sometimes outside on the landing. Chaos often ensued, compounded by the dense fog of cigarette smoke that layered the air across the room, people lighting up and flashing their Embassy Regal around like nobody's business.

The cry of 'Through the chair! Through the chair!' occasionally brought the disorderly proceedings to a temporary halt, only to resume once more as soon as they could draw a breath.

Me ma! Me ma was the worst for saying just what she wanted. If it wasn't trying to come up with the best formula of numbers for the Free State Lottery to make money for the campaign, she would suggest contacting whoever had appeared on *The Late Late Show* the previous Friday night! When she suggested we write to the controversial Judge

Pickles, our Paul laughed so hard he nearly wet himself and had to take to the street to get the hysteria out of his system. Me ma was mortified and had great difficulty maintaining her dignity as his loud chortling was still audible in the room. He couldn't help himself. She chewed the bake off him on the way home.

George Downey, John Kelly's brother-in-law, came a close second to me ma. George was a tall man with white hair and matching moustache, who said 'fuck' every fifth or sixth word. There was a greater preponderance of 'fucks' if he got excited, and he would often lose the run of himself in 'fucks' as he tried to explain his point. He had large, round, Nooky-Bear eyes, which made his face naturally funny, even when he was trying to be serious. One Tuesday evening, he felt he had to remind the gathering of the time a group of Native Americans had smoked the peace pipe and beat their drums around the Bloody Sunday monument. Which was fine until he proceeded to place his hand over his mouth, going 'Ow, wo, wo, wo! Ow, wo, wo, wo! Fuckin' powerful, John! Fuckin' powerful! Ow, wo, wo, wo!'

The monument theme continued on another evening when he suggested that we should get sculptures of each of the heads of the deceased placed on low-level plinths around its base. Baldy McKinney, youngest brother of Willie McKinney, almost collapsed off his chair, followed closely by our Paul and Glenn. The meeting broke up in chaos as George demanded the right to be heard, his Nooky-Bear eyes blinking hugely with self-pity as he turned to John, who could hardly conceal his own hilarity.

'John! Fuck!' exclaimed George. 'John, I thought, ah, we fuckin' agreed that, ah, everybody had the right to fuckin' speak and, ah, make fuckin' suggestions here.'

John, sitting next to me along the bench, steeling himself, lifted his face out of his hands and said, 'George, you're right, so ye are. Ye have the right to speak. But can we not ah, not ah,' before rubbing the laughter out of his cheeks, 'can we not talk about this next week?'

'What do *you* think, Tony?' asked George, turning to me, sitting right behind him, blinking his Nooky-Bear eyes, brows deeply furrowing in my direction. Our Paul again had to leave the packed room and we could hear his loud horse laughs as he retreated to the kitchen, closing the door behind him.

'I agree wi' John, George,' I said, trying to keep my face straight and not allow any of my words to rush out or escape as a giggle. George was looking right into my eyes.

I'm hammered here if I show him I'm goin' to laugh! I thought to meself. It was difficult to even *think* the words in case I leaked a titter or allowed my mouth to curl up in a smile leading to a bellow of laughter. George was a *big* man, a bouncer, and, word had it, could fair handle himself.

'Sure, we'll put it on the agenda for next week,' I eventually mustered. 'Is that OK, George?'

'Fuckin' OK wi' me, Tony,' he smiled back. 'I'll be here next week and every fuckin' Tuesday after that too!' John had to call a halt to the meeting. There was no point in proceeding. Our Paul drove us along Laburnum Terrace, and, as he was laughing that hard at the wheel, tears streaming down his cheeks, I had to steer the motor towards the kerb in case we crashed. We sat in fits of laughter for ten minutes, unable to go any further, while children playing on the footpad kept their distance from the car, fearing we were all mad.

George, despite his initial and highly comedic interventions, proved to be a long stayer and loyal volunteer for the campaign. And, of course, he brightened up many an uneventful affair with his effing and blinding.

Among the more serious endeavours we undertook in the first few months of the campaign was a conscious effort to establish our bona fides, independent from party politics. As PRO, I therefore wrote, on our new headed paper, and in no particular order, to Cardinal Cahal Daly, Primate of All Ireland, to An Taoiseach Charles Haughey, and to the president of Ireland, Mary Robinson, among other notables. I also wrote to Derry City Council, asking to be heard before the full council. Because our local MP and member of the European Parliament John Hume lived up the street, he would call into the office, or we would sometimes bump into him in McGlinchey's shop on the corner of Elmwood Road. On one such occasion he told us he was going to write to John Major, the British prime minister, on our behalf.

The embossed reply letters started to trickle in. It was usually John or me who read them aloud, often to a quiet and sullen gathering. The good cardinal, Charlie Haughey and Mary Robinson all felt in their own peculiar ways that they could not provide us with their support and that there was no purpose to be served by meeting up over a cup of tea. There were many practising Catholics around the room, some of whom described Cardinal Daly as a 'cold man', aloof and uninterested in the travails of the common people. Haughey was viewed by everyone outside Fianna Fáil as a shyster, a gombeen, only interested in ripping off the system for his own grubby ends. While history proved these descriptions to be correct, the greatest disappointment was, however, reserved for Mary Robinson, President of the Irish Republic, who had assumed office in no small measure because of her interest in human rights and civil liberties, both at home and abroad. We had our work cut out for us in Ireland, let alone abroad. The major difference this time around, compared to 1972, was that we were working together, united and determined to be treated as nothing less than first-class citizens.

The Catholic bishop of Derry, Edward Daly, who had been so central to the events of Bloody Sunday and had become a close friend of the Duddy family, was more forthcoming in his support. However, while understanding why the third demand had been included, that of prosecutions, he stressed that it would be off-putting for many people. It was around this time that I began to think of Soldier F again and what I would do with him, given the choice. He had been with me since my early teenage years, just as soon as I could comprehend from the Widgery Report that he, in all probability, shot my father. At one stage, I felt I could have killed him, or any of his comrades for that matter. However, lately I had been revisiting my father's words, spoken on a sunny July morning in 1971 as I considered revenge after the killing of my classmate Damien Harkin, under an army truck, when we were both eight years old, that 'hatred eats at your own heart'. I know that to be true now. When I decided to stop hating Soldier F I felt liberated from the shackles of the past. I reasoned that I wasn't looking for justice *against* him, but *for* the memory of my father and the other men and boys who died that day. Soldier F as an individual meant nothing to me.

John Kelly and I became the chief spokespeople, often being interviewed on BBC Foyle and other broadcast outlets. I lived near Radio Foyle, so it was handier for me to simply walk to the studio. On one such occasion, around June 1992, as I was taking part in a pre-recorded interview with a young journalist who had the accent of a south Dublin smart alec, he put it to me that would it not be better if people like us simply moved on with our lives rather than raking up the past, or words to that effect. Going through him for a short-cut, I did everything short of question his parentage, and left the studio in a rage.

That just happened to be the day they came for me. As it was a sunny morning, I decided to finish work on a coal bunker that Brian McCool, my old friend and neighbour from the Brandywell, had built for us. Several weeks earlier, as I was leaving the house, I ran right into a joint RUC and army patrol. We had a large, black mongrel by the name of Pesski, who despised RUC and British Army uniforms but was otherwise friendly. He became frantic, barking and baring his teeth at them until Stephanie came out and dragged him into the house by the collar. A tall RUC man walked back to my front door and called out for all to hear, 'Dutchie Doherty lives at No. 25 Lower Nassau Street!' For our personal security, we had managed to conceal our address from them since moving in in 1989, using our respective addresses of Brookdale Park and Cable Street when stopped by them down the town. This game was now up. What we expected shortly was an early morning raid.

Pesski was a smart dog with a variety of barks. One was for the postman, whom he'd follow woofing from the bottom of the street as he popped the post into the letterboxes up one side before going down the other side. Pesski stayed with him the whole time. He had a bark for old John Bradley, who lived alone next door in No. 23, as he staggered up the street half-jarred from the Phoenix Bar on the corner. Another bark was for Willie Edgar, me granny and granda's old neighbour from Central Drive, who now lived in the Glen and walked his three greyhounds down our street twice a day. We could often tell who was in the street simply by the tone of his bark. He was known throughout the Rosemount and Glen areas as Pesski Doherty.

The rear of our terraced home had a back return, with a thin strip of concrete rising to a double step towards the back gate. We had removed the inner wall between our two downstairs rooms to make one large living room. The front street was therefore visible from the back yard, and vice versa. I had stripped down to the waist in the heat of the yard, manoeuvring the heavy wooden lid in place over the coal bunker, when I heard Pesski barking ferociously in the front street. It was his British Army and RUC bark! I dodged slightly out of view from the front window in case any of them would be nosying through. When I jooked around the corner of the wall there was no one there, but the barking continued unabated. Just then, Sheila, a neighbour from across the street, came into view on the opposite footpad. The barking got worse. A shiver went up my spine.

Brian McCool had left his block-hammer in the shed along with his trowel and spirit level. Still bare-chested, block-hammer in hand, I approached the back door. Sheila could see me through the front window and had a strange, fretful look about her. She held her hand up for me to stop, but I couldn't. I could hear Pesski still barking and snapping as I went in the back door, through the sitting room and into the hallway towards the windowed vestibule door. The front door was open wide, but there was no sign of the dog. Sheila had moved up level to the front door and began gesturing to me again with her hand to stay put. I couldn't stop. I opened the vestibule door and walked into the sunny street. Pesski, his raven coat standing on end from mane to tail, had two young men pinned against the front wall of John and Rosemary Harkin's house next door. Each wore a bomber jacket zipped up to the neck. One had a short, mousy crew cut while the other, taller one had a blond skinhead. I had come face-to-face with my would-be assassins. Their pistols were surely concealed under their jackets. And they were terrified of my mongrel dog!

I knew instinctively that I had to exert complete control as any sign of weakness would probably result in me, and our dog, being mown down in the street. The block-hammer rose in my hand till the narrow, chipping-edge rested on the sweaty temple of young Mousey, who stood closest to me. Pesski, still frantically asserting his dominance over the situation, growled and snarled rabidly as if he were a wolf.

'You feel that?' I asked, pressing the hammer against his temple while keeping an eye on the taller one. 'Now, here's what I want you to do. You hear me OK?' Mousey nodded and blondie the skinhead nodded in tandem.

'Now, I want the two of ye's to turn around. Come you out this way, youngfla,' I commanded, hooking the hammer round his wing-nut ear. 'Now, start walkin', and if one of you turns round again, I'm goin' to sink this here block-hammer into your fuckin' skull. You hear me?' The two of them nodded, walking calmly towards the top of the street while Pesski barked by my side like a hound possessed by the divil himself. When they disappeared out of view around the corner, I ran back again through the house and climbed the back wall. Peeking over the top I saw two BMWs, a black and a red, take off down Florence Street. I jumped down into the back alley and ran into Florence Street in time to see the two cars turn into the traffic at Park Avenue and out of view.

If Sheila hadn't come out to see what Pesski had been barking at, I could well have been shot down in my back yard and Pesski shot in the front street. She had seen their faces. She bore witness. Had they known she was from a well-known republican family from the Top of the Hill, though, they might well have shot her first, then the dog and then me. When I went back through the house, Sheila was still rooted to the footpad outside our front door. Apart from her, the street was deserted, which was good. I sat down on the windowsill, the block-hammer still beside me. 'Sheila,' I said, slowly and purposefully, 'we know what we saw here, but I want you to promise me that you'll tell nobody nothing. Not Stephanie or any of the neighbours. I don't want this ever to get back to Stephanie or she'll be demented with worry. She's already lost two brothers. She won't be fit for this. We'll end up moving out.'

Sheila didn't need to be asked twice. She said nothing. I said nothing. Pesski sauntered back across the street to lie in the shade, out of the hot afternoon sun. His work was done. When Stephanie came back later, the coal bunker was almost finished. She even took a photo of me putting the final touches to it! I acted as if nothing had happened. Given the hostility towards and from the RUC, I never reported this event to them and went back to Westend the following day, keeping it quiet for fear of Stephanie finding out. But our Pesski Doherty was the hero of the day!

***

Despite initial setbacks, the campaign had an enlivening effect on the families meeting each Tuesday night, agreeing smoke-breaks, forging respect, appearing in press photos and travelling to meetings and gatherings the length of Ireland and Britain. We were together and, at last, after all the years of nothingness, of suffering silently at home, many having taken their heartache to the grave, we were laying down a formidable challenge to the state. There was no going back.

We even had the temerity to protest at the gates of Áras

an Uachtaráin, the official residence of the President of Ireland, in the Phoenix Park, Dublin, with our campaign banner.

'Did ye kill any children, today?' a man snarled out his car window at us, before taking off again at speed. A garda car appeared with two burly gardaí, equalling Robin in height but dwarfing Baldy McKinney, our Paul and me.

'What's the craic now, lads? What did the President do on yous boys?' enquired one, removing his cap.

'We're here because she's refused to meet with us. We are families of the dead on Bloody Sunday,' I replied.

'Is that so, now? Well, don't be hanging around here all day. What time are ye's leaving at?' he asked.

'After lunchtime, probably,' said I.

Less than an hour after they left, another, unmarked, car approached and sat fifty yards away. The two faces inside stared coldly at us and muttered from the corners of their mouths.

'That's the Taskies!' said Baldy. 'Ye'd spot them a mile away, so ye would.' Taskies were the Armed Garda Anti-Terrorist Task Force, much despised in the border region, especially by northerners on the run. 'They'll be tanked up with Uzis, I bet ye,' he whispered. A few moments later, the pair got out and walked around their car with their Israeli Uzi machine-pistols over their shoulders for us to see. They kept their distance, though, and waited.

Shortly afterwards, when we decided it was time to leave, they followed us out of the Phoenix Park through the city's streets until we were on the main road back to Derry.

Our very own armed escort followed us the whole way to Monaghan before turning back!

***

In December 1992, as we were making preparations for the 1993 January commemoration, I stood in contemplation by the tall bay window observing a funeral procession slowly making its way across Laburnum Terrace from the cathedral. Suddenly, two grey vans pulled to a halt outside Westend Park. The rear doors swung open and, to my horror, masked and armed men jumped out, sprinting up the steps, roaring like demons. I turned to those in the room and said, 'There's boys wi' guns comin' into the building! Doesn't look good,' I added. 'In other words, you may prepare to meet your maker.' Simultaneously, the sound of breaking glass downstairs snapped everyone to attention. We froze in fear.

'Get down! Get down! Get fuckin' down on the ground!' they yelled to Geraldine in the office downstairs. The breaking of glass and wooden panels continued underneath us for what seemed like ages. No one in the room spoke. Then we heard footsteps rushing the stairs. The campaign office door swung open and the masked men bounded into the room, screaming, 'Get down on the floor! On your fuckin' knees! On your fuckin' knees! Hands on top of your heads! Get your hands on top of your fuckin' heads!'

In all, it was probably no more than twenty seconds from witnessing the masked figures rushing the steps to us being forced onto the floor. At the time though, it felt much longer, like a slow film-reel. For a few seconds, as we knelt upright, backs straight, facing the walls of the room, I believed we were about to be executed. We were lined up for it, like the black and white footage from the Second World War of Nazis shooting Jews in the back of the head. Then, it suddenly dawned on me that they all held Heckler & Koch 9mm machine guns, by then standard issue for the RUC.

They continued to rampage throughout the rest of the house, breaking down doors and smashing windows. They soon found that it was empty of people apart from those they'd already discovered. Furniture tumbled over on the floor above and objects thudded and smashed loudly off walls. The armed RUC men stood behind us pointing their machine guns at our heads.

'Name?' screamed one. 'What's your fuckin' name?'

'Paul O'Connor,' said Paul calmly.

'What the fuck are you doin' here?' screamed the cop.

'Working,' replied Paul. 'This is the office of the Bloody Sunday Justice Campaign,' he added.

'Fuck your mouth up! I didn't ask you that!'

'Name!' the same one yelled.

'Martin Finucane.'

'Martin what?' screamed the cop.

'Martin Finucane,' Martin repeated. 'You're standin' on me legs! Get off me legs!'

'Shut your fuckin' mouth! What the fuck are you doin' here?'

'Working! Now, get off me legs!' replied Martin.

'And you! Who the fuck are you?' he demanded, poking

the back of Hawks' head with the muzzle of his machine gun.

'James Collins. Stop pokin' me!' he replied.

'You, fuck up, Collins!' screamed the cop into his ear. 'What's your address?'

'Cable Street,' Hawks replied.

'Date of birth!' the cop demanded.

'Over twenty-one,' replied Hawks, becoming braver by the second. I was shaking, though, with a blend of natural fear and of being forced to kneel in an upright position. I could sense that the others were struggling too. The sound of tables and cupboards being shoved around, above and below, reverberated on the hard floors, while other objects, files and the like, were being emptied out on the stairwells.

'What's your fuckin' date of birth, I asked you!' screamed the cop right into his ear.

'I said over twenty-one,' Hawks replied. The cop hesitated and then moved on to me.

'Name?' he snapped, no longer shouting. Even in these few short and terrifying minutes we had all sized the situation up. While they were firmly in control, they also realised by the various reactions of their prisoners, well accustomed to regular street harassment and armed intimidation, that we weren't going to fold in submission in front of them. Neither, however, were we going to entice the butt of a machine gun across the skull, which it would have been unwise to rule out.

'Anthony Doherty,' I replied as calmly as I could.

'Address!' he commanded.

'4 Brookdale Park.'

He hesitated. 'You sure that's not 25 Lower Nassau Street?'

'No. 4 Brookdale Park,' I repeated.

'Date of birth!' he snapped.

'Over twenty-one,' I said.

'We'll fuckin' *over twenty-one* you when we get you to Castlereagh!' he hollered into my ear.

We remained kneeling in an upright position, getting a sharp poke in the back if we tried to relax downwards onto our calves. The wrecking and marauding continued to resound throughout the four storeys. The cops were still screaming at Geraldine, who was clearly in some distress on her own downstairs, and whose cries carried along the stairwells. They showed her no mercy or compassion. More vehicles pulled up on the road outside, some with sirens blaring, with much coming and going. The office floor trembled with the heavy footsteps of a number of unknown visitors keen to discover who the captives were. After around an hour, the noise stopped and Westend Park fell to a deathly silence. The cops spoke only in whispers on the landing, quietly sifting through documents and taking coded messages from their radios. We remained kneeling, facing the white walls, hands above our heads, under constant observation.

The mid-December darkness started to fall. The single bare bulb cast a harsh light, framing our shadows darkly on the bright white walls. My lower back nipped in pain. Each of us shuffled uneasily from side to side, trying to lessen the hurt. We waited. I guessed we would be arrested. They could hardly cause all this drama and then drive back to their barracks empty-handed. Whatever their original intentions, they would need to return with a number of live bodies. This was no ordinary raid. They were no ordinary raiding party. Time passed. It became completely dark outside.

Then, over a ten-minute period, we were taken out one by one to the landing, dressed in white forensic suits complete with hood, hands tied tightly behind our backs with white plastic straps, and taken outside by two cops to waiting cars. A crowd had gathered, the street was taped off as a crime scene and bright lights illuminated the house. I was placed, kneeling again, in the footwell behind the front passenger seat and told to put my head down while the car took off. Around two hours later, we landed in what I assumed to be Castlereagh Holding Centre, but it turned out to be Gough Barracks in Armagh. During the five days they held us, the detectives made little serious attempt to interrogate us. In fact, it was exceedingly boring, the tedium broken only by practising my limited Spanish in the evenings through the door with Paul, who was going steady with a woman from Almeria.

'Hey, Dutchie, *qué tal*?' called Paul.

'*Muy bien, muy bien. Y tú; qué tal*?' I replied.

'*Estoy sentado aquí*! [I am sitting here]' sang Paul out the door. It was the only line I recognised, but it must have confused the hell out of the jailers! The following day, the CID remarked to me about speaking in Spanish, enquiring if we were in league with ETA, the Basque separatists!

The RUC had raided all our houses while we were in

Gough Barracks. It was the first time our home in Lower Nassau Street had been searched. Our arrests and the raid on the campaign office only served to reinforce the determination of the families, though. It appeared to me that resolute, peaceful campaigning was viewed as more of a threat by the state than armed insurrection. Armed loyalists had never come to my door to execute me.

***

The Bloody Sunday Initiative became a casualty of sorts in the aftermath of the Bloody Sunday Justice Campaign becoming established, as we now had two groups with Bloody Sunday in the title. Over lunch one day in the Pilot's Row centre, I suggested that we rename the BSI in memory of Pat Finucane. The Pat Finucane Centre (PFC) came into being shortly afterwards, enabling broader human rights casework and campaigning to flourish. The PFC has gone on to become one of the most successful, grass-roots human rights groups in Europe, diligently probing, questioning, and eventually proving, the state's role in colluding with loyalist groups over almost four decades.

The families remaining steadfastly together was half of the battle for the Justice Campaign. We made the rest up as we went along! John Hume arranged for the families to deliver 40,000 signatures to Downing Street. Old friends of ours, MPs Tony Benn and Jeremy Corbyn, showed up too. At last, we were getting some recognition. No longer were we going to be ignored. On top of that, the war that had taken so many lives, caused so much suffering and sent thousands of people to prison, was clearly coming to an end. John Hume was talking to Gerry Adams, and the Irish government became more animated in its moves towards peace. Expectation of a breakthrough was in the air. Marching in January on the anniversary became much more popular and more focused on furthering the demands of the campaign. When the IRA ceasefire eventually came in September 1994, it changed the landscape, the language and the mood. Suddenly, the eyes of the world rested on Ireland and the end of one of the planet's longest-running conflicts.

One afternoon, while waiting in the black taxi queue in William Street, I felt a tap on the shoulder. 'Hello, I'm Don Mullan. We met when I brought students up to Westend Park some time ago,' said the dark-haired man.

'Hello, Don. Jesus, you're not goney believe this, but I've just been reading the statement you gave to the Widgery Inquiry in 1972!' I said.

'God, I'd forgotten I made one! Where did you get it?' he asked.

'The family of Johnny and Bridget Bond left in loads of them a few weeks ago in two shopping bags,' I replied. 'They'd been lyin' under their stairs for years. There's hundreds of them. All typed up and some of them signed.'

Don's eyes widened to take in the news. 'I'm in Derry for a few days, can I call in this week and take a jook? I'd be really interested in reading through my statement,' he said.

'Not a bother, Don. Sure take a run up when you're ready,' I said as I climbed into the taxi.

Little did I realise that this chance encounter would set in motion a series of incredible events with huge ramifications. Those words, so carefully typed by young activists, teachers and office-workers in the days following the massacre, which had lain untouched under the Bond family's stairs in Creggan, among old shoes and paint tins, for more than two decades, were about to come back to life. The truth has a habit of showing up again, one way or another.

Peter Madden, the senior partner in Madden & Finucane Solicitors, Belfast, had employed a young Derry woman, Patricia Coyle, to work directly for the Bloody Sunday families to uncover any new evidence and pursue all relevant angles to an approach to the European Court of Human Rights. We had made useful contacts among the civil liberties fraternity in Belfast, Dublin and London. Jane Winter, a soft-spoken Englishwoman, also became involved, offering whatever support she could in terms of research.

One day, I received a telephone call from Patricia.

'Hello, Tony,' she said. 'I don't want to alarm you, but Jane Winter has found something in the Public Record Office at Kew [in south-west London]. It looks really interesting, but I wouldn't feel right discussing it over the phone.'

'So, where are you now?' I asked.

'I'm in Belfast. I've shown it to Peter and he wants you and John to see it right away. I'm coming down to Derry tonight. You about around seven?' she enquired.

'I am; I'll call John and we'll see you at Westend Park at seven o'clock.'

What Jane had found at the Public Record Office was the

typed minute of a meeting held the day after Bloody Sunday. The occasion was the setting up of the Widgery Inquiry and in attendance were the British prime minister, Ted Heath, Lord Widgery, then Lord Chief Justice of England, and Lord Chancellor Hailsham. In the memo, Mr Heath advises Lord Widgery that 'we are in Northern Ireland fighting not only a military war but a propaganda war'. John and I couldn't believe our eyes as we scanned the faxed copy of the memo. It was the most significant piece of evidence to come to light in almost twenty-five years, proving that the political establishment had secretly colluded with the head of the legal establishment about state murder in Derry. A propaganda war indeed! This was exactly what we needed to throw back in the face of the doubting British media. Things were heating up.

One day Don Mullan returned to Westend Park. He had read not only his own statement, but also almost all of the other several hundred civilian witness statements that Widgery had completely ignored.

'There's somethin' big in this, ye know. This material has never been published at all. It's dynamite! As well as that, many of the witnesses describe shooting from the Derry Walls. I could talk to a publisher I know who might be interested in making a book out of this.'

Not only did Don know a publisher who agreed to publish his resulting seminal book, *Eyewitness Bloody Sunday*, to critical acclaim, he also had close relations with officials in the Irish government and promised to set up a meeting with them. So began a series of engagements with the Irish government at a level we could hardly have contemplated previously. We were determined that what had commonly become known as the Peace Process wasn't going to leave us out of the equation in the event of a political settlement. We argued that the truth about Bloody Sunday should be viewed, not just as a massive boost for peace, but as an essential precursor to a lasting political settlement. In short, there could be no lasting peace without justice. We repeated this mantra with Sinn Féin, the Social Democratic and Labour Party (SDLP) and the Irish government until it was well understood.

I was mostly a jeans man. By 1995 I had one good pair of dark trousers, but no decent jacket to go with them. Stephanie and I weren't bringing much money home as she was now studying. Several days before I was due to address the new Forum for Peace and Reconciliation in Dublin, she returned home with a cool blazer she'd bought in a charity shop for £3. This jacket, with borrowed brogues, became my standard outfit in meeting a series of taoisigh, tanáistí, foreign affairs ministers, MPs and party leaders over the next few years.

'I seen ye on the RTÉ news again last night,' said Stephanie's granda James one evening as we sat in her ma and da's in Cable Street. We were down for our tea.

'Aye, aren't you lucky?' I replied as he salted his plate.

'Ye never take that buckin' coat off ye,' he grinned.

'That's me lucky coat. Sure don't I look the part?'

Maureen stood with her back to the fireplace with her windowed view up Cable Street, while Mickey sat on the armchair by the window facing the other direction. On the opposite side of the street Johnny Boy McMenamin had his brindle greyhound with him and one of the tall Gilmour sisters was walking past him, mini-skirted and long-legged.

'God, but that's a fine shape of a wee bitch there, James,' said Mickey. 'Look at the legs on her.'

James continued salting his dinner.

'That there, Mickey English, is only a wee girl! Ye wanny be ashamed of yerself!' complained Maureen.

Mickey, who only ever had eyes for greyhounds, looked at Maureen with confusion on his brow. 'What are ye on about, Maureen?' he asked.

'You talking about that young girl Gilmour like that! I never heard the likes of it in all my born days!'

'He's talking about Johnny Boy's wee brindle bitch, Ma!' squealed Stephanie's sister, Michelle, from the sofa.

The whole sitting room erupted in fits of giggling while Maureen stood with her redner and her in kinks of laughter too.

'I'm affronted for ye, Ma!' called Stephanie, through her tears.

Once we had everyone we needed to support our cause, including the Irish government, we were in the land of opportunity. An Taoiseach, John Bruton, instructed senior government officials to compile a comprehensive dossier of all evidence, old, unused and new, for submission to the British government at an opportune time. This included a series of investigative features broadcast by *Channel 4 News* in Britain uncovering crucial new material. On one memorable occasion in Dublin, our minibus-full of relatives was given a garda escort through the city centre, complete with motorbike outriders stopping traffic at junctions to allow us through. Some contrast to our armed escort *out* of Dublin in 1992!

In October 1996 Steph and I became parents. Our son was named Rossa Pádraig Ó Dochartaigh: Rossa after Jeremiah O'Donovan Rossa, the famous Fenian rebel rumoured to be connected to Steph's father, Mickey; Pádraig after his granda Paddy; and Ó Dochartaigh instead of Doherty, reinstating our ancient Irish surname. The following January, I carried him proudly in my arms into St Mary's Chapel, where a special anniversary mass was held each year. Strangely, we ended up sitting in almost the exact spot the Dohertys and Quigleys occupied on that dull, stormy day in February 1972 when we buried my father. I now had this man's wee boy in my arms as he gazed around him in wonderment at the candles, the deep shadows and the sea of strange faces.

***

In 1997 the stars aligned in the campaign for justice. In January, 40,000 people marched from the Creggan shops to the Guildhall Square. It was the largest demonstration ever in Derry. Don's book was released to major acclaim and became a huge topic in the media. Tony Blair was elected in May, the first Labour prime minister since the 1970s, and, in June, Bertie Ahern was elected An Taoiseach in Dublin.

In October I stood at the top of Brooke Park on a cold, sunny day giving a TV interview to the BBC, when the reporter suddenly said to me: 'Tony, I want you to speak straight to camera and appeal to former soldiers to come forward to admit what they and others did on Bloody Sunday.' Here I was, a former IRA volunteer and ex-prisoner, appealing to British soldiers on British national television to come forward and admit their wrongdoing! That moment, almost five years since the beginning of the campaign, was when I fully realised that we would overcome. Their game was up. It was only a matter of time before the house of cards collapsed.

I had been in constant personal touch with Martin McGuinness, while John and Mickey kept in contact with John Hume, as the parties attempted to broker a peace deal involving Ireland, Britain, Europe and the United States. Martin went out of his way to assure us that he had kept Bloody Sunday on the agenda of every meeting with both the Irish and British governments. Sometimes he'd call us, having just come out of Downing Street or Ivy House in Dublin. He would also call into my work on the Lecky Road, where I was now co-ordinating the redevelopment of the old Gasyard site. It was my first paid job, transforming the decommissioned site into a community-owned venue for health, culture and education purposes, designed to allow the community to find a better way forward after decades of armed conflict and government neglect.

'There's our Martin comin'!' announced his sister Geraldine one day, as he passed the window on the ramp up to the office. Geraldine was the financial administrator.

'Are you in to see me?' she laughed as she rose to hug him. They were a very close family.

'Well, I've seen ye now!' he smiled. 'But I'm really here to see this man,' he said, looking in my direction.

'Blair's considering an apology,' he told me that sunny day, as we dandered around the Gasyard, now a green field. Martin loved walking.

'Me and John have talked about this,' I replied. 'It was leaked to the papers too. Their resolve is weakening by the day. An apology is fine, and the proper thing to do, but it can only come once the full truth of what they did has been established.'

'That would be my view as well,' he confirmed. 'I felt obliged to pass on what Blair had told me. The whole thing needs to be overturned.'

'What are the chances of Blair going for a second inquiry?' I asked him.

'In my view, if anybody can do it, it's Blair,' Martin replied. 'But he's pushin' against a solid block at the Home Office. The international bit makes it even worse for him.'

'Britain's on the ropes and their reputation is sufferin' car-crash after car-crash,' I laughed. 'They haven't had it as bad since the Black and Tans!'

'But what do we do if he just appoints another English law lord?' he mused. 'Sure nobody's goin' to go for that!'

'It needs to be international, otherwise no one will really be expected to go for it. There's more than one way to skin a cat,' I smiled, as we continued our stroll around the site. 'They love being the mother of parliaments and having all these English-speaking countries and their judicial systems modelled on their own. Not all of the British Commonwealth judicial systems are near as bad as the British one.'

In the days leading up to the end of January 1998 there was much speculation that Blair was going to make a special announcement about Bloody Sunday. Our contacts in the Dublin government had told us that Blair took their completed dossier home over the Christmas break. Word had leaked back that Blair was overwhelmed by the sheer weight of material and felt he needed to break new ground to create a renewed momentum for peace.

Martin asked to meet John Kelly and me at John's house in Beechwood Avenue.

'This is to go no further than this room,' he said, with a wide and playful grin. 'Blair is going to announce an International Inquiry in the House of Commons this Thursday into the events of Bloody Sunday!'

Even though we had kept a sure and steady course on this matter for a long time, it was still difficult to take in. We stood speechless in his front room as Margaret, John's wife, came in.

'God, but ye would think ye's had seen a ghost or somethin'!' she said, looking at the shock on our faces.

The phone rang at home at noon that Thursday. I was expecting to receive a call from British Secretary of State Mo Mowlam. But it wasn't her, it was me ma!

'What's the craic? Any barrs?' she asked.

'Nothin' that I heard,' I lied.

'They're on about it all morning on the TV. It looks like they're goin' to announce a new inquiry,' she said, pausing, waiting for me to respond.

'Is that right? What news was it on?' I asked, pretending I knew nothing. Me ma was the last person on this earth I would tell. It would be with me aunt Anna in Canada and Laura Glenn down the street as soon as I put the phone down!

'See you, ye atrocot ye! Ye know fine rightly! Sure what are we meeting about later this afternoon for, then?' she accused in a light-hearted way.

'I dunno, Ma. Sure nobody tells me nothin',' I laughed. 'We'll just have to wait and see. I'm waiting on a call, Ma. I really need to go.'

'OK. I knew ye wouldn't tell me anything, anyway. I was only calling to tell you that I'm proud of you, Tony. And your daddy would be proud of ye too.' I felt a lump rise in my throat and had to cough into my fist.

'Thanks, Ma. Sure I'll see ye at three, then.'

Within seconds, the phone rang again. Me ma would often call right away if she forgot something.

'Ma, I said I'm wait–'

'Hello, Mo Mowlam here,' said the Secretary of State. 'Can I speak to Mr Tony Doherty, please?'

'Speaking. I'm sorry, I thought you were my mother,' I said.

'Yes. Well, I've been told to call you to formally let you know on behalf of Her Majesty's Government that the prime minister is going to announce a new inquiry into the events of Bloody Sunday under Lord Saville of Newdigate, and that there will be two other senior judges appointed from Commonwealth countries.'

It was truly surreal. I, and many others, had lived the previous twenty-eight years with the loss of a father, a son or a brother. Now, we were making history from the history that made us!

'I have been strongly advised that there are indeed grounds for such a further inquiry,' Tony Blair told the House of Commons later that afternoon. 'We believe that the weight of material now available is such that these events require re-examination. We believe that the only course which will lead to there being public confidence in the results of any further investigation is for a full-scale judicial inquiry into Bloody Sunday to be set up.'

The headline in the *Derry Journal* the next morning, Friday 30 January, exactly twenty-eight years after, ran 'THE BEGINNING OF THE END!' And, with a colour picture of our press conference in the Guildhall right across the top, it truly felt like it.

***

Mitchel McLaughlin has a habit of passing his wisdom on to others. Not just on matters of peace. I remember him telling me in the 1980s that, to keep himself abreast of developments in Derry, he checked the planning notices in the local papers on a regular basis. I took his advice and would casually read through the list every Tuesday in the *Derry Journal*. It was a very proud moment for me to read the planning notice for the reconstruction and landscaping of the Gasyard site on Lecky Road. I knew it had been due to be published. However, on opening the paper to jook through the same section on another Tuesday morning, in 2004, the following jumped off the page:

> Demolition Notice: Northern Ireland Housing Executive hereby gives notice of its intention to demolish 3 number flats at Nos 55, 56 & 57 Glenfada Park, Bogside, Londonderry.

My eyes nearly popped out of their sockets! There were two large bullet-holes in the wall of these flats; the only two still visible in the Bogside from Bloody Sunday. They had been fired from hip-height by a Para as men and women fled in terror away from the killing ground at Rossville Street. Jim Wray had been shot in this fusillade, only to be finished off on the ground as he lay wounded. While I initially became angry at the very idea of this government sub-department seeking to get rid of part of our history, my thoughts soon turned to the opportunity that it presented. Within twenty-four hours, John Kelly, Éamonn McCann and I were sitting at the desk of the local manager of the housing executive making the case, not just for preservation of the Glenfada Park flats, but for them to be given over in trust for historical purposes. There was no resistance across the table. Some fifteen or more years after the Bogside Interpretive Centre had been first suggested, the Museum of Free Derry was born!

***

The sense of anticipation was palpable. The public gallery was packed full of nervous family members who had been coming to London for several months to hear evidence from soldiers and other witnesses too afraid to come to Derry's

Guildhall in peacetime, where the bulk of evidence was heard. Soldier F sat in the witness box at the Bloody Sunday Inquiry in Westminster Hall. On seeing his face for the first time, I felt nothing at all towards him. Mind-numbness is the only way I can describe it.

Éilís MacDermott, our dark-haired and diminutive barrister, stood away from her desk as she prepared to ask him the first question.

'Mr F, I represent the widow of Paddy Doherty. You know who that is, don't you?' she began.

Silence followed.

'Do you know who Paddy Doherty was, Mr F?' she continued.

More silence.

'Paddy Doherty was killed by a single shot from an SLR rifle from a range of less than fifty yards on Bloody Sunday. Do you remember that day?'

'I do,' replied Soldier F, almost inaudibly.

'Oh, you do? Well, what do you remember about it?' asked Éilís.

More silence followed.

'I don't recall,' he said weakly.

'You left a widow with six young children. Paddy Doherty's widow is sitting behind me in the public gallery. Do you wish to look at her?' she said, turning round to face us. Everyone else on the floor of the Bloody Sunday Inquiry turned towards us as well. My mother trembled beside me. I grasped her hand and held it tight.

'Well, do you wish to look at Mrs Doherty?' she repeated.

'Ungh,' said Soldier F.

'Could you repeat that, Mr F? I didn't hear you right.'

More silence. Éilís let it draw out for full effect.

'Mr F, have you ever heard of a Texas Star shot?' she asked, her voice booming across the room.

'Why do you ask?' he enquired.

'Well, have you or haven't you heard of a Texas Star shot? You're a soldier aren't you; a marksman even? You must be very familiar with shooting and hunting terminology,' she said.

Silence followed.

'Are you not going to answer my question, Mr F?' she pursued.

'I don't know what you're getting at,' said Soldier F.

'Do you hunt, Mr F?' she continued.

'Yes, I've hunted,' he replied.

'Then, you must know what a Texas Star shot is, mustn't you?' Éilís continued.

Another long silence. Silences are massive in legal cross-examinations. These were totally gaping.

'You don't want to tell us what a Texas Star shot is, do you?' she stated, more than asked.

'Ungh,' said Soldier F again.

'Indeed,' she said. 'Well, if you're not going to tell the Inquiry what a Texas Star shot is, maybe I can help out,' she said, before pausing. 'It's a sitting target, from close range, isn't it, Mr F?'

Silence ensued. Soldier F stared blankly back at her.

'How far was Paddy Doherty away from you when you

took him into your sights?' she continued. 'Thirty, forty, fifty yards? No great challenge for you, was it, Mr F?'

'I don't recall,' said Soldier F weakly.

'You saw him crawling on his hands and knees, didn't you, Mr F?'

'Ahm, I don't recall.'

'You aimed at the centre of the target and you fired, Mr F. Isn't that right?'

'I don't recall,' he repeated.

'You don't recall,' Éilís repeated. 'Indeed.'

Don Mullan counted the number of times Soldier F said that he couldn't recall or remember during his two days in the witness box. He reached a total of 500.

⁎⁎

The June sun reflected brightly from the wee greenhouse in the back garden where the herbs and young tomato plants were growing well and healthy. I meandered along the path in the early morning, poking up the odd weed on the vegetable beds while listening to the chorus from the robins, blue tits, thrushes and wrens as they hopped in and out of the hawthorn hedges, studded cerise and white. It was Wednesday 15 June 2010. This was the day. The day of all days. The day that would have defied anyone's imagination in 1972, or even 1992. My second son, Oscar, had brought home a letter from his Gaelscoil the previous afternoon, informing us that the whole school was getting a half-day on account of the Saville Inquiry. I had been on Radio

Foyle, inviting the people of Derry to descend on Guildhall Square for this occasion. It was a day, not just for nationalist Derry, but for all, including unionists. There would be no flags and no banners except for the banner of the Bloody Sunday Justice Campaign, now well-seasoned.

Stephanie joined me in the garden and we sat in silence on the edge of a raised bed, holding hands.

'This is what the £3 jacket has brought us!' I joked.

'And me da's borrowed brogues!' she laughed.

As I drove across the Craigavon Bridge from the Waterside where we now lived, the faltering voice of Hugh McMonagle came on Radio Foyle right after the nine o'clock news. I felt a lump in my throat as he described what he had done, along with Father Daly and others, as they tried to get the dying Jackie Duddy to safety all those years ago.

'I'm an oul man now, but I'll never forget it to the day I die,' said Hugh. I found myself welling up as this courageous man, now in his late sixties, described his deeds. I had to switch the radio off as I wouldn't be worth tuppence by the time I got across to Rossville Street, where we'd planned to gather. I had the whole day ahead of me and couldn't afford to begin it red-eyed! *Conceivably, this could be the greatest day in the history of the city*, I thought. *It could also be a disaster.* No one really knew for sure what shape or form it could end in. Lord Saville could say anything! David Cameron, the British prime minister, could easily come down on the side of his army, taking us back to square one.

Éilís sat in the main hall of the Guildhall waiting to tell us the truth. The Guildhall was made the property of the

British parliament for a forty-eight-hour period, so that the Saville Report could be conveyed directly to the families and other interested notables shortly after it was delivered to Westminster.

'Saville has said that Soldier F shot your father dead and that he did so without either fear or panic. Do you realise what that means, Tony?'

'That he was shot in cold blood; that he was murdered,' I replied.

'Well, he says everything but the word "murdered",' she pointed out. 'He has said practically the same thing about all the deceased and wounded. That they were all shot by soldiers in circumstances where there was no fear or panic.'

'And Gerald Donaghey?' I asked, looking across the floor at his sister, Mary, and her daughter, Geraldine. Two representatives from all the families were there, gathered around their solicitors, getting the details right.

'He said he probably had nail-bombs on him when he was shot,' she said, shaking her head in dissent. 'He was still killed by a soldier who shot him without either fear or panic. He too was shot in cold blood.'

Large screens had been erected inside and outside the Guildhall. Thousands had gathered in the square outside and, word had it, were backed up right across to Waterloo Square and William Street. At 3 p.m. exactly, David Cameron appeared on the screen and spoke these words:

The Secretary of State for Northern Ireland is publishing the report of the Saville Inquiry – the tribunal set up by the previous government to investigate the tragic events of 30 January 1972, a day more commonly known as Bloody Sunday.

Mr Speaker, I am deeply patriotic. I never want to believe anything bad about our country. I never want to call into question the behaviour of our soldiers and our army, who I believe to be the finest in the world. And I have seen for myself the very difficult and dangerous circumstances in which we ask our soldiers to serve.

But the conclusions of this report are absolutely clear. There is no doubt, there is nothing equivocal, there are no ambiguities. What happened on Bloody Sunday was both unjustified and unjustifiable. It was wrong.

A hearty cheer went up from the inside of the Guildhall, outdone only by the huge roar from the square. Many of the staunchest campaigners wept with joy as they hugged one another in disbelief. It was truly a sight to behold! David Cameron continued:

I know that some people wonder whether, nearly forty years on from an event, a prime minister needs to issue an apology. For someone of my generation, Bloody Sunday and the early 1970s are something we feel we have learnt about rather than lived through.

But what happened should never, ever have happened. The families of those who died should not have had to live with the pain and the hurt of that day and with a lifetime of loss. Some members of our armed forces acted wrongly.

> The government is ultimately responsible for the conduct of the armed forces and for that, on behalf of the government, indeed, on behalf of our country, I am deeply sorry.

The ancient hall echoed to the elated cries and expressions of relief from long-suffering brothers, sisters, sons and daughters that at last the truth was out and that the British had apologised. Cheering voices rose over the pleasant clamour inside as the crowd outside waited for us to emerge. Derry had come out in the warm summer heat. As we emerged from the Guildhall onto the platform, the crowd went wild with delight. Many were openly weeping and were in a state of disbelief, as if to say, *Is this really happening? Has the British government really apologised after all these years?*

The families crowded onto the platform, preparing to take their turns at the microphone. I basked in the hot sun and thought of Paddy Walsh, now sadly deceased, and hoped that his wife, Anna, and daughters were among the crowd. I also thought of me granda Connor and granny Sally, also deceased, and the brief but insightful chat we'd had in the days after my release from prison. Memories came too of Eddie O'Donnell, my teenage friend who had died at sweet sixteen. As I came forward to the microphone, I winked at my old friend Conor Murphy, now an MP, below in the crowd next to Martin McGuinness. Conor winked back with a broad smile.

It was agreed that I would speak on behalf of the families in the immediate aftermath of the Saville Report and David Cameron's statement to parliament. The battlements of the Derry Walls straight ahead of me overflowed with the world's press. I had never felt prouder in my entire life. The delight on the faces in the crowd was infectious. I caught sight of Minty Thompson and of Stephanie in the crowd, waving and cheering. I thought of their two families, who had incurred devastating losses since 1971, when the British Army had shot dead Minty's mother in front of their house in Creggan. *This is their day, too!* I thought.

The sun shone warmly on our faces. I stood proudly beside the brothers and sisters and sons and daughters of the fourteen men who had been shot dead thirty-eight years before. I thought again of Paddy Walsh and his huge act of bravery as my father lay dying in front of him. I thought of our Patrick, whose cursing and blinding accompanied the news that my father had been killed as we gathered around my mother in our living room in Hamilton Street. *He would've loved to be here on such a glorious day*. And Maureen. Maureen English, also deceased, for she was such a loving and proud woman. It was Maureen who first told me that me ma and da were the most glamorous couple in Derry in the late 1950s; 'him suited and booted and her in her taffeta,' she said. *This is your day! This is your day, too!* I said to myself, as I began my address. *And this is for you, Daddy!*

Unjustified and unjustifiable. Those are the words we have been waiting to hear since 30 January 1972.

The victims of Bloody Sunday have been vindicated and the Parachute Regiment has been disgraced. Their medals of honour have to be removed. Widgery's great lie has been laid bare. The truth has been brought home at last.

It can now be proclaimed to the world that the dead and the wounded of Bloody Sunday, civil rights marchers, were innocent one and all, gunned down in their own streets by soldiers who had been given to believe they could kill with perfect impunity. The Parachute Regiment are the front-line assassins for Britain's political and military elite. The report of the Saville Tribunal confirms this. It was the Paras' mission in Derry to massacre people they thought of as enemies of the state. They will have known that murder is what was expected of them when they erupted onto our streets.

Bloody Sunday wounded Derry very, very badly. We may hope that from today we can begin to bind up those wounds. But we recognise, too, that the issues arising from the Report go wider and deeper than Derry's concerns. When the state kills its citizens it is in the interests of all that those responsible be held to account. It is not just Derry, or one section of the people of Derry, it is democracy itself which needs to know what happened here on 30 January 1972. The British people need to know. The Irish people need to know. The world now knows.

Our campaign in the first instance was for justice for our loved ones. But we didn't fight only for ourselves. We have tried to stand in the place of others who have suffered the same grief and the same grievous wrong at the hands of unaccountable power and who may never win any official inquiry, who may never have their truth told. We are mindful of the victims of the Ballymurphy massacre by men of the Parachute Regiment in August 1971, of the families of the two men murdered by the Paras on the Shankill Road in September 1972. And of all families bereaved by the paratroopers and other state forces over the course of this bloody conflict. And of all who have died here, from whatever background, at whomever's hand.

Bloody Sunday was the price the Bogside paid for Free Derry. So it is, always and everywhere. Just as the civil rights movement of forty years ago was part of something huge happening all over the world, so the repression that came upon us was the same as is suffered by ordinary people everywhere who dare to stand up against injustice. Sharpeville. Grozny. Tiananmen Square. Darfur. Fallujah. Gaza. Let our truth stand as their truth too.

Bloody Sunday was a great injustice. But the fight for truth and justice has also been an inspiration to us and to the people of Derry. It has deepened our sense of who we are and made us more aware that we are also citizens of the world. Nobody who struggles for justice will be a stranger here. Nobody who dies in the struggle for justice will be forgotten here. Thank you, Derry.

A representative of every bereaved family spoke from the podium, proudly declaring the innocence of their loved ones. John Kelly and Jean Hegarty, sister of Kevin McElhinney, tore up a copy of the hated Widgery Report and scattered the powder-blue and white strips into the approving crowd. The pride we felt was immense. We had at last achieved the impossible. We had lifted Derry's darkest cloud. We had made history of the history that made us. We had overcome.

Sometime later, after an interview with a TV crew on Derry's walls, I looked down onto the Guildhall Square below and saw me ma in conversation with Conor Murphy as they sat together on one of the smooth stone blocks placed around the square. She looked very happy as they chatted, gently airing her sandalled toes in the warm breeze. *This is where it all started*, I thought. *This is the very place that my father first set eyes on his future bride and mother of his children.*

For it was here, one Saturday afternoon in the autumn of 1959, as the green buses deposited shoppers and posers below the row of cannons, that Eileen Quigley first roved by Patsy Doherty, a Teddy Boy, and his mucker, Johnny McFadden, he too a Teddy Boy, and Patsy says to Johnny, 'D'ye see that girl Quigley over there with the ponytail and the tanned feet?'

Johnny looked across and nodded.

'I'm goin' to marry her,' he smiled.

'You're buckin' nuts, Doherty,' Johnny McFadden replied, shaking his head.

But nineteen-year-old Patsy Doherty in his blue-suede shoes never took his eyes off the gorgeous Eileen Quigley, aged seventeen, as she click-clacked in her high heels across the square with her friends, unaware of the years of happiness and then sudden tragedy that lay in store for them both.

I suddenly realised that I had been waiting for this moment to arrive since I was nine. As I turned to face the cameras again, I never felt more proud that he was my father and that she was my mother.

POSTSCRIPT

You never know in these parts if you're ahead of history or behind it. During the editing of this book, the final part of my trilogy of memoir, three events occurred that brought the distant past right into the present day.

The first was in March 2019. The Public Prosecution Service announced to expectant families in the City Hotel in Derry that charges of murder were to be brought against Soldier F in relation to the killings of Willie McKinney and Jim Wray on Bloody Sunday. He also announced that Soldier F would face additional charges of the attempted murder of Patrick O'Donnell, Joe Mahon, Joe Friel and Michael Quinn. But there would be no murder charge for the killing of my father and the rest of those killed that day. In my adult years I've become philosophical about charging Soldier F and his comrades in arms, while those higher up the chain of command remain aloof and in comfortable retirement. However, it is a different story when the state informs you that there is insufficient evidence to secure a successful conviction despite the fact that it was a public execution in the full glare of the media.

The second event was several weeks later. Lyra McKee, young, gay, talented and highly optimistic, was shot dead in the name of Irish freedom. The chances are that her killer wasn't even born when the IRA declared for peace in 1994.

Any guerrilla organisation needs to be spectacular, even in its own terms, every now and again to prove its worth, its effectiveness and to keep it in the news. But the only spectacular thing her killers have done is become singularly unspectacular, with blunder following blunder. It truly is time to stop. The young people of Derry deserve a better future.

The third happened shortly after Lyra's murder. It was announced that a former British soldier was to be charged with the murder of fifteen-year-old Daniel Hegarty, killed in July 1972 during Operation Motorman. Operation Motorman was conceived to crush Free Derry and was the largest British Army operation since the Suez Crisis of 1956. They sent in Centurion tanks to quell the people of Moore Street, Hamilton Street and Central Drive.

You cannot go far in Derry without walking into your own history. I was born on the same street where Lyra was killed and just two streets from where Daniel was killed. Susan McKay, Lyra's friend, said that she didn't die for Irish freedom, she was Irish freedom. I wish I had said that, as it perfectly describes the way she led her life, fought for others and believed in a better way, just as our mothers and fathers taught us to do.

I didn't know Lyra McKee, but I do know that when she came to Derry she fell in love with the city and made it her home. The following passage, which I read out loud in the Guildhall Square in June 2010, could have been written for her: 'Nobody who struggles for justice will be a stranger here. Nobody who dies in the struggle for justice will be forgotten here.'

GLOSSARY

Argackil	prisoners' word for Largactil, an anti-psychotic drug
atrocot	rascal
barrs	local news, tittle-tattle
Beauty-board	wood-effect sheet panelling
black enamel bastard	common expression of hatred of the RUC, usually only 'black bastard', but 'enamel' was often added to strengthen the effect
Bru	Bureau – Derry's unemployment exchange
cack	faeces
cat	bad or terrible
catch yerself on	wise up!
chew the bake off someone	chastise someone severely
craic	news; also fun/enjoyment
crims	short for criminals, i.e. non-political prisoners
dander	walk/meander
deadner	a chancer; an unreliable person
devalve	to shut up; as in *she wouldn't devalve*, she wouldn't stop talking

do a line (with)	go steady with a girl/boyfriend
dobbing	truancy, avoiding school
Fleadh Cheoil	an Irish music festival/ competition
flicks	the hair, usually long, is curled upwards at the ends
footpad	footpath
Gaelscoil	Irish-speaking school
go through someone for a shortcut	speak sharply and angrily to someone
gombeen	shady wheeler-dealer
grandwain	grandchild
gulder	utter a loud shout, typically in anger
gwon	go on
half batch	a half bottle (of alcohol)
hallion	worthless person – usually female, but can be used for males
heads and thraws	lying head to toe
Henry Halls	crude rhyming slang indicating courage, or lack of it
hoaching	smell of, or stink
hoor	whore
jook	a quick look
lose the run of	get carried away
mucker	mate, friend; from Irish – *mo chara* – my friend

OC	Officer Commanding
odds	spare change
on the threes	on landing or floor No. 3 of prison
palladic	stupid drunk
PDF	Prisoners Dependants Fund – support network for republican prisoners
ploughtered	plodded
praties	potatoes; from Irish *prátaí*
red fish	smoked fish
redner	a red face/embarrassment
reel	fool
rift	belch/burp
scéal	news
screw	prison officer
shyster	someone who is disreputable or unscrupulous
Sixer	a large, six-wheeled army vehicle
skelp	clout, swipe, smack, e.g. on the ear
slippy-tit	someone too clever for their own good
snorkel jacket	a style of parka jacket with an elongated hood
Stradreagh	Derry mental hospital
taken offsides	removed from the scene
take the hand	make fun of

tanáistí	deputy prime ministers
taoisigh	prime ministers
TD	Teachta Dála, a member of Dáil Éireann, the lower house of the Irish Parliament
the craic was ninety	we were having a ball
the day	today
the marra	tomorrow
the night	tonight
thran	stubborn
tilled	ajar, half open
wains	children
Walter/a bit of a Walter	from Walter Mitty, a teller of tall tales or a liar
wans	ones (as in 'Derry wans' – people from Derry)
wile	wild, meaning terrible, or very
yammer	someone who's always crying or complaining
youngfla	young man (young fella)